Robert C. Suggs · Burgl Lichtenstein

Manuiota'a · Journal of a Voyage to the Marquesas Islands

Published by Pa'eke Press
Boise, Idaho
Translation and copyright by Robert C.Suggs
Library of Congress Control Number 2001093169
ISBN 1-887747-38-9
Printed in Canada

Robert C. Suggs · Burgl Lichtenstein

Manuiota'a

Journal of a Voyage to the Marquesas Islands

2001

Pa'eke Press

Boise, Idaho

Table of Contents

Dedication

This book is dedicated to the Marquesan stone sculptor, Manuiota'a, who lived about 300 years ago on the island of Hiva Oa, in what we now call the Marquesas Islands of French Polynesia. In this remote archipelago, 3850 km straight south of Hawai'i and 6000 km from the coast of Peru. Manuiota'a was one of the most famous sculptors of his time. Right up to the present day, the most unusual and impressive stone sculptures of the ancient Marquesas bear witness to his great creativity. (Note: Marquesan letters are pronounced exactly like Spanish or Italian; the apostrophes indicate slight hesitations between sounds, just like the break in the English exclamation „Oh-oh.")

His story begins in Puama'u Valley on the island of Hiva Oa. This deep fruitful valley was the home of several tribes, including the Na'iki tribe. The Na'iki were a proud and warlike people, feared by other tribes in Puama'u and the adjacent valleys of Hiva Oa. They were not only warriors, however, for among the Na'iki were many woodcarvers, tattoo masters, stone sculptors, and other artists and craftsmen. But there were no sculptors who knew their craft better than Manuiota'a. We know a number of his best works but we don't know much about him personally, except that he had a wife who was a female priestess, a *ta'ua*. She bore the fascinating name of Butterfly Priestess.

As befits his era, we suppose that he was a tall, muscular man of considerable strength, which had been acquired through long days in the stone quarry where he wielded basalt adzes to produce his works from the sacred soft red tuff known to the Marquesans as *ke'etu*. His brown skin was certainly covered from head to foot with blue-black designs from the bone needles of the tattoo masters. This was a sign of prestige and wealth among the Marquesans, and Manuiota'a must have been one of the most prestigious and wealthiest of the Na'iki, because he could afford to employ the best tattoo masters with the many pigs he received as payment for his sculptures.

On the stone platforms and paved terraces in the deathly still Na'iki holy-of-holies, the temple of Te I'i Pona, stood many of Manuiota'a's works: *tiki* figures, representing various gods, and massive stone heads which he carved to commemorate important human sacrifices. The times in which Manuiota'a lived were characterized by great violence, as well as a great lust for life, so there is no need to wonder why his art also had its bloody side. This art was an expression of the culture that gave it birth, and Manuiota'a stood in the middle of that culture.

All evidence indicates that Manuiota'a was also an artistic trailblazer, not holding to the rigid rules of the accepted Marquesan artistic canon, but striking out in new directions. He wanted to add a touch of realism into an art style that had already lost nearly all its life. When his beloved wife, Butterfly Priestess, died in childbirth, he created a unique statue in her memory, showing her as best he could, as she lay writhing in her death agony. This sculpture expressed his own great pain, but served another purpose as well, because Butterfly Priestess was soon deified by the Na'iki tribe and came to be worshipped on the platform of the Te I'i Pona temple.

One of Manuiota'a's most famous sculptures was a huge stone head, a "victim head," or *'upoko he'aka* in Marquesan. This work differed from other heads of the same type, not only in its great size but in the extent of facial tattooing and other gruesomely realistic details. It obviously represented the head of a very important victim who had been captured and eaten by the Na'iki. This head reposed for many years on the terraces of Te I'i Pona.

There came a time when the Na'iki warriors pushed their victim hunting a bit too far, and killed an important chief from a neighboring tribe. In revenge, the other tribes rose up against the Na'iki, and drove them from the beautiful valley of Puama'u.

The refugees fled to almost every island in the archipelago. Manuiota'a also fled, leaving his masterworks behind. More than a hundred years later, Karl von den Steinen, the ethnographer from the Berlin Ethnographic Museum, appeared in Puama'u and visited the temple. When he left Puama'u, Manuiota'a's great stone head went with him. Von den Steinen gave this head the sculptor's name, because the name of the actual victim already had been long forgotten by even the best Marquesan informants at the time of the German's 1896 visit.

Since that day, Manuiota'a has stood in the Berlin Ethnographic Museum, far from the green quiet valley of Puama'u. A stranger in a strange land, he is lonely and not infrequently mocked by visiting schoolchildren. It's there that we met him. The head done by Manuiota'a impressed us more than any other *tiki* figure we had seen. Manuiota'a has motivated us to write this book about his homeland, the Marquesans of today, their culture, their past, and their future. We'd like to build a bridge with him back to his homeland, a homeland which has also become a part of us. We'd like to take him back to Puama'u where he once had his proper place in the shade of huge breadfruit trees, surrounded by the red and green leaves of the sacred *ti* plant (*Cordyline terminalis*).

And so we salute him in his native tongue:

E Manuiota'a, tuhuka ha'atiki, tuhuka have, tuhuka ma'ama, te e ite'oko e! Ka'oha atu ma'ua ia 'oe me te mata'eina'a Na'iki. A 'oho te i'i, a'e matou a e tuha'e ia 'oe!

Oh Manuiota'a, sculptor, talented master, brilliant master of great skill! Together, we greet you and your Na'iki tribe. Have courage, we will not forget you.

9

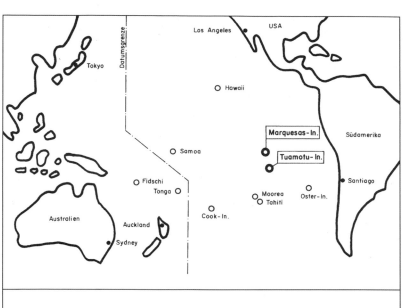

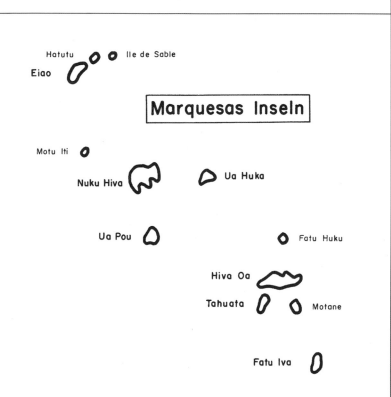

Hatutu ○ ○ Ile de Sable
Eiao

Marquesas Inseln

Motu Iti

Nuku Hiva   Ua Huka

Ua Pou   ○ Fatu Huku

Hiva Oa
Tahuata   Motane

Fatu Iva

Introduction

by

Robert C. Suggs, Ph.D.

In April 1956, standing unsteadily on the pitching and rolling deck of the aged, over-loaded copra schooner "Vaitere" (built in 1910), I saw my first Marquesas Island. It was Fatu Iva, the southernmost, and according to some, the most uncivilized of the entire Marquesas Archipelago. I was an archeologist from the American Museum of Natural History in New York, and my mission was to conduct the first stratigraphic archeological excavations in these islands.

At the time, the Marquesas could only be reached from Tahiti by schooners that collected copra (dried coconut meat) from the islands and brought basic consumer goods in return. The voyage from Tahiti was certainly no five-star luxury cruise. The 113-foot, solid wood *Vaitere* didn't even have an elevator, an orchestra, or a boutique. I was one of the 20 or so passengers who lounged around on the deck and the deck house, sleeping everywhere with blankets, pillows, and sleeping mats spread among chickens, coconuts, heaps of taro root, and assorted cargo. There were only four bunks, all infested with copra bugs, and these presented a challenge even to insect-hardened Polynesians. For the majority of the passengers and crew, the sea was the latrine. For those with a bit of modesty, like me, there was a tiny "WC" which also served as the "shower:" you simply filled up a small chamber pot and poured it over your head.

Despite the somewhat Spartan accommodations, we ate very well, with the captain, at the ship's only table (which at night also became a bed). Captain Mimi was a taciturn man who always wore a mysterious smile. Similarly sparing of information was the "Super-Cargo" (cargo master) Leontiev, a White Russian who talked a lot, wanted to know everything, but revealed very little. The absolute opposite was the gregarious engineer, Bonassieur, who joined our "first class" table (the other passengers brought their own food or shared the crew's less exciting fare). Our tasty and ample meals were prepared on a wood fire in the forward deck-house of this battered and coconut oil-soaked ship, but no one seemed to worry about the fire hazard. In high seas, a wooden framework was fastened over the table into which our dishes could all be safely wedged to prevent them from landing in our laps. Water was available, but no one seemed terribly interested. The standard drink was French wine, known as *Pinard* or *Gros Rouge*. This was not especially effective against sea sickness, but gave a striking purple hue to one's teeth after a few applications.

On the deck, among the freight, animals, passengers, and busy crew, I stared fascinated at the island we were slowly approaching. Fatu Iva thrust itself abruptly out of the sea, a haphazard heap of dark green mountains and serrated ridges, constantly emerging and disappearing in the morning rain clouds. The entire island was enclosed by high, almost vertical black-brown cliffs, against which the waves broke unceasingly.

This cliff wall was interrupted by a small bay, toward which our bowsprit was now pointed by the helmsman, who was steering with his naked feet. A squadron of dolphins accompanied us as we slid into the bay. At the edge of the steep-sided valley, behind the beach, I saw small houses over which hovered clouds of smoke from cooking fires. This was O'omoa Valley, one of the two currently inhabited valleys on Fatu Iva. At the time, the name was of little interest to me; my first priority was to take a shower, or at least hop into the river for a bath.

Looking at the towering peaks and green valley walls, I was also forcibly struck by the atmosphere of timeless mystery, tinged with brooding sadness, which emanated from this beautiful island. This atmosphere seemed to reach out and envelope me. From among the jagged peaks and dark green valleys of Fatu Iva something was calling out to me, saying: "Come on, stay with us! There's much here to explore; enough for your entire life. We want to talk to you, and teach you, if you have ears to listen." And I began to listen.

The whaleboat, propelled by six hefty sailors, took us to shore. When the children along the street greeted me with their shy: "*Ka'oha nui!*" I heard for the first time the strange sound of Marquesan. At that time, I never dreamed that in not too many months, Marquesan would become my favorite foreign language. And then came the biggest surprise: I was invited to shower at the house of Willy Grellet, a Knight of the French Legion of Honor and chief of the valley. Willy was a descendant of a hardy Swiss colonist who came to the Marquesas in the late 19th century. Finally, the long awaited shower!

It doesn't happen very often that one meets a Knight of the Legion of Honor (especially on an island known for its supposed lack of civilization), and it's even less often that such a highly honored person invites you to take a shower; the invitation was certainly not declined!

And it was in this tiny settlement, standing under the cold-water shower, that something very important happened to me: I was infected; infected with the "Marquesas Virus," a virus for which there is no known cure; a virus whose main symptom is a fascination with all that is Marquesan and a burning desire to return as often as possible. In the course of the many months I subsequently spent among the Marquesans, my ties with this archipelago and its people grew ever stronger and more pervasive. We worked, laughed, cried, celebrated, loved, and dreamed together, at home with families, on sites deep in the bush, on the beaches, and in the cool mountains. I got to know the Marquesans well, although to really understand them is a life-long task. Now, more than 40 years and many trips later, these islands and their people have become an inseparable part of me.

Under the Marquesas' magic spell, I became a member of a very special group of people from all over the world, people who were also bewitched by these islands and cherished memories of them for their entire lives. Among this group there are Russians, such as Vice Admiral Ivan Fedorovich von Kruzenstern, the natural scientist Tilesius von Tilenau, and Count Fedor Tolstoy. These gentlemen visited Nuku Hiva in 1804 on a globe-circling Russian Navy expedition and left detailed observations of Marquesan culture. Tilesius gave us the oldest engravings of Marquesan tattooing, beautiful engravings which stand as a benchmark for all studies of that fascinating art. Count Tolstoy was so enthralled by this Marquesan tattooing that he had himself tattooed right on the deck of the "Nadezhda," to the later enjoyment and often embarrassment of the ladies at the St. Petersburg Court.

Another admirer of the Marquesas and their inhabitants was the small and combative Capt. David Porter, USN. During the War of 1812, he interrupted a highly successful commerce-raiding cruise against British shipping to call at Nuku Hiva and refit his ships. Caught in local tribal power politics, Capt. Porter was forced to go to war against the fierce Taipi tribe, but he still esteemed the Marquesans as the most reliable and bravest inhabitants of the entire Pacific.

In the mid-1800s, the French occupying forces arrived, bringing many well-educated people to the islands. Among these were the missionary Fr. Mathias Gracia, who reported quite sympathetically his observations of Marquesan culture in a series of letters. He was joined by M. Max Radiguet, Adjutant to French Admiral Du Petit-Thouars. We are indebted to Radiguet for his outstanding memoir, *The Last Savages*, which describes the turbulent initial years of the occupation. At the same time, a simple able-bodied Yankee seaman named Herman Melville arrived on

14

Nuku Hiva. Melville stayed for 6 weeks and found in Taipi valley, and in a Taipi girl, the inspiration for his first novel, *Typee*. This book, although explicitly a "romance," is an inseparable part of the standard literature on the Marquesas and is available in translation in all western languages. Later in the 19th century, Robert Louis Stevenson also was struck by the magic of this remote and beautiful archipelago and described the islands in his memoirs, entitled *In the South Seas*.

The best chronicle of the late 19th century was written by the indefatigable Fr. Gérard Chaulet, the beloved "Petero Mihi" (Peter the Missionary) of the Marquesans. Fr. Chaulet saw and recorded nearly everything that happened during his amazing half-century in the Marquesas. His exhaustive chronicles are found today in the mission archives and in the Vatican Library in Rome. He was joined in the late 19th century by Fr. Simeon Delmas, who also wrote extensively on the Marquesas. In 1896, the German psychiatrist/ethnologist, Dr. Karl von den Steinen, arrived in the islands for an exhausting six months stay. His specialty was the Tropical Forest Indians of Brazil, but he wrote the best book ever written on Marquesan traditional culture. Although he never returned, von den Steinen remained devoted to the Marquesas for the rest of his life, publishing the final volume of his master work 30 years later. In the 20th century, more anthropologists came, among them the husband-wife team of Edward and Willowdean Handy, as well as more writers, such as Jack London and Alain Gerbault.

A special mention should be made of Mgr. Hervé-Marie Le Cléac'h, former Bishop of the Marquesas. As a result of his innumerable works of unparalleled kindness, and his expertise in their language and culture, the Monsignor is regarded as a living saint by modern Marquesans. He raised the Marquesan language to a new level of importance, translating the Bible and the Missal into Marquesan. Even in his 85th year, in retirement, he works tirelessly for the good of the flock that was once entrusted to him, currently energetically translating the Latin Prayer book into Marquesan. There is no better authority on the collective Marquesan mentality and soul; he not only knows them as no other has known them, but has helped them to rediscover their true nature, which somehow seemed to have been lost among the deep silent valleys and cloud-shrouded peaks of their rugged islands.

The present book was written by two of those fortunate people who have been incurably infected with the Marquesas Virus. I've already described how I was bewitched by these islands 45 years ago. Burgl Lichtenstein experienced the spell that the Marquesas can cast in 1997 and since then we have shared the addiction or the love of these islands (the Marquesans call it *Ka'oha i te henua* = longing for the homeland). Burgl and I met in October 1997, on the *Aranui*, the freighter that has long since replaced the schooners of my day. We began a correspondence and met again in 1997 on the *Aranui* with other German friends, for yet another voyage.

During our correspondence, Burgl impressed me with excerpts from her *Cruise Journal*. These were loaded with lyrical, humorous, and ironic observations of the islands, their population, the ship's crew and passengers, and the magnificent tropical environment. I suggested that we write a book together. I had already written several books about the Marquesas but this book was to be something different. I would handle the scientific side of the trip and Burgl would take care of the very important other aspects of the book, e. g., scenery, people, and feelings. In two trips on the *Aranui*, she has seen and understood more than many Westerners who have spent years in the islands. Hers is not the understanding of an academic, but a very special emotional understanding or sensitivity that one cannot acquire through academic training, but may certainly lose! Burgl understands her fellow man intuitively. She can write and understand written Marquesan and when she's not feeling too shy, she can also speak it.

Our book is a travel book. It contains some history, geology, ethnography, and archeology, but is certainly not a dry academic treatise or a multidisciplinary university text. We describe our present-day cruise through the islands, and at the same time experience a voyage into the past, a voyage that extends back in geological time 6 million years and includes one of the greatest wonders of the ancient world: the discovery and settlement of these far-flung unknown islands by ancient Polynesian voyagers from Indonesia and Melanesia.

But we won't limit ourselves to these events. We'll also describe some of the early European seafarers of the Age of Discovery, naval operations of both World Wars that touched these islands, and nuclear weapons testing as well. Our focus is on the Marquesas and Marquesans, but we'll also be scrutinizing the tourists who visit the archipelago every year, and the very colorful *Aranui* crew.

It's our intention to try to get on the same wave length with the spirit of the Marquesas, that mythical but yet very real power that has captivated us and so many others. We'll explore the mysteries of these Islands, mysteries that will not let us go, which lie behind the black basalt cliffs, hidden in the ruin-strewn valleys and beneath the beach dunes. To adequately describe all this, we'll be using a vocabulary reflecting the full range of human emotions; sadness and happiness, pleasure and pain, falsehood and truth, friendship and hatred, lust and love.

The story that we'll finally tell is like *pu'u*, the strong traditional Polynesian cord braided out of many strands of coconut fiber. And like the *pu'u* which was endlessly braided by the men in the old Polynesian households, we hope our book will also weave everything together and will always stand as a tribute to these islands.

We'll be traveling on the sea, like the ancient Marquesans, but we won't be using their giant double canoes. Instead we'll be aboard the *Aranui's*, which is the present day life-line of the archipelago, connecting the Marquesas with Tahiti. Since the book will follow the *Aranui*'s itinerary, the *Aranui* is the main thread of our *pu'u*, our coconut fiber cord. But she is joined by other main strands, including key personalities, data from the sciences, and the all-important human qualities of understanding and emotional sensitivity.

The *Aranui* slid down the ways in Flensburg, West Germany, about 30 years ago and first plowed the seas as the *Bishop of Bremen*. She was later acquired by the Compagnie Polynésienne de Transport Maritime (CPTM) of Tahiti and rechristened as the *Aranui*. With her overall length of 107 meters, and her stable seakeeping qualities, she meets all the requirements for intensive scheduled service between the Marquesas and Tahiti. Rebuilt as a passenger-freighter, the *Aranui* offers accommodations for about 100 passengers and 2000 tons of freight. In addition to comfortable, air-conditioned state rooms, a C-Deck with dormitory accommodations was added for those more daring passengers who want to experience "adventure freighter" life. A salon for bridge games and conversation, a small library, a boutique for the "necessities," a bar, and a pool and sundeck complete the amenities. The cuisine and the wines deserve an "outstanding" rating and the dress is strictly informal: T-shirts and shorts! In the evenings, the talented crewmembers congregate in the bar as the inspired "*Aranui* Band" to provide musical entertainment.

The entire cruise lasts 16 days; after leaving Tahiti, the *Aranui* calls first at Takapoto, a Tuamotu atoll, and sometimes at another atoll, Apataki. Then follow calls at the inhabited islands of the Marquesas: Ua Pou, Nuku Hiva, Hiva Oa, Tahuata, Fatu Iva, and Ua Huka. On the return run from the Marquesas, the ship calls at dazzlingly beautiful Rangiroa, another Tuamotu atoll. Throughout the cruise, daily calls at new islands and new harbors give passengers the opportunity to watch plenty of spectacular cargo-handling operations, and to take part in a full schedule of planned activities ashore including dance exhibitions, opportunities to sample Marquesan foods, mountain hikes and motor tours, handicraft exhibits, swimming, beach and mountain picnics, and visits to archeological sites and museums. There's no time for boredom on the *Aranui*!

The *Aranui* is the life-line of the Marquesas. Despite air transport improvements, the inhabitants of these remote islands depend on freighters for their necessities as well as their luxury goods. And so, in *Aranui's* roomy hold, construction materials find themselves stacked in close association with containers and pallets of food and other supplies, snappy motor boats, luxury trucks, canoes, (and once even a helicopter!), not to mention crates of beer and wine, two very important commodities in the Marquesas. Sometimes even a double bed sneaks in! On deck there's usually a full load of aviation fuel drums for thirsty transport aircraft of Air Tahiti. In exchange for these supplies, the ship takes on cargoes of citrus fruit of all kinds, *noni* fruit (a current medicinal fad), copra, wild goat, and often handicrafts. These represent the main sources of revenue for the Marquesans.

Forty years ago, it was impossible to visit the entire archipelago with the old copra schooners. You only got to see places where there was copra to pick up, or significant amounts of goods to deliver, and only the tight-lipped captain and the supercargo knew where the copra was. The competition between the smaller trading companies was so fierce that all commerce took place under security restrictions approaching those found in the most sensitive military or intelligence service operations. Every evening at the "captain's table" the captain and supercargo listened to Radio Tahiti's record request hour, during which records were played and personal messages were broadcast for listeners all over French Polynesia. Some of the supposedly personal messages were, in fact, coded messages for our two officers. For example: "Greetings to Papa Te Ui'a from the family in Hatiheu," might actually be a prearranged code, meaning that our ship had to hurry to pick up a load of copra in O'omoa Bay in Fatu Iva before the competition got there. Watching the knowing looks exchanged by our skipper and cargo master, I could always tell which messages were coded transmissions for them, but never knew what the messages actually meant.

Today everything is changed: copra is not very important anymore, and a relatively fixed itinerary can be established, so that passengers will know what islands and bays they'll be visiting. We'll be following this itinerary, not only because it recalls the voyages of discovery of the ancient Polynesians, but because the unique ambiance of the *Aranui*, with its carefully selected, colorful crew members, makes this trip an unforgettable experience.

We'll get to know enchanting atolls, their white sand beaches shaded by towering coconut palms, ringing turquoise lagoons filled with colorful sea life. Overhead, frigate bird messengers of the ancient gods will be hovering in lazy circles. Breath-taking vistas of land, sea, light, and cloud will captivate us, such as the jagged stone "needles" of Ua Pou which rise abruptly out of the morning sea mist. The island of Nuku Hiva, a remnant of a huge volcanic cone, with its jumble of knife-edge ridges, grim cliffs, and deep yawning valleys, will reveal itself in every nuance of green, rising 1300 meters above the sea. Giant mantas will lazily circle our ship and dolphins will provide excitement at many points along our course, while mysteriously remote, wide-eyed *tiki* keep watch over mossy ruins of ancient temples, house platforms, and tribal ceremonial centers. And on one such center we'll see a performance of the traditional *maha'u* "pig chant" dance, one of the few remaining vestiges of a brilliant but now almost extinct culture. We'll also visit the last resting places of two well-known Europeans; Paul Gauguin and Jacques

Brel, both of whom ended their days on these remote islands. We'll also get to know the only negative aspect of the Marquesas: the irritating bite of the tiny *nono* fly, which is happily only found on Nuku Hiva and Ua Pou. Those who do not take the few necessary precautions against this little critter will find themselves doing a lot of scratching!

Are you ready to sail with us on this voyage of discovery? Wonderful! Cast off the bow and stern lines! Port astern slow; starboard ahead slow! Off we go; into the fascinating world of the South Seas to explore the secrets of the Marquesas, our paradise.

Boise, Idaho
2001

Pape'ete: boarding the *Aranui*

Bob picks me up in a tiny taxi; wedged among luggage, we flit through the tortuous, noisy streets of "downtown" Pape'ete, snaking our way between the numerous 4x4 trucks that many Tahitians consider to be the "In" thing, and dodging the colorfully-garbed pedestrians who appear on the streets from every direction.

The faces of these pedestrians are fascinating. To those who are perceptive, they reveal the entire history of French Polynesia. There's every kind of racial mixture, Polynesians of every shade, numerous Chinese and Vietnamese who play significant roles here; the French "masters" appearing as officials, businessmen, and military, and now and then even Korean and Japanese fishermen.

The Tahitian girls with their lovely dark eyes are quite easy to look at, as are the elegant Far Eastern beauties and Eurasians But there's another type of Tahitian "girl," the *raerae*, or transvestite. Frequently encountered in downtown Pape'ete, they belong to the street scene there, and have become a common sight throughout French Polynesia. Their feminine style and appearance would be perfect, if it weren't for the wide almost square feet they often force into high-heeled shoes, ultimately betraying their true gender. Naturally, there also the tourists, easily identifiable by their somewhat dazed looks and their clothing, especially when they try to dress like locals. The men are usually decked out in brand-new Aloha shirts and pandanus leaf hats, the women in their newly-purchased but improperly-worn *pareu*, or wrap-around skirts. *Pareu* are simple to don but often make quite a different impression on bystanders than the purchasers desire.

We head for the Motu Uta docks where the *Aranui* is tied up. The young driver knows the way through the maze of streets, thank God! Tahitian traffic has it's own peculiar rules, which will forever remain an enigma to foreigners. The town consists of a complex network of one-way streets complemented by a series of recently-installed traffic circles. For foreigners, these circles pose no problems, but for Tahitian drivers, they are both a novelty and a challenge. They don't reduce traffic jams; they produce them! The important question of precedence is settled in practice by the testosterone level of the driver. To drive into a Tahitian traffic circle, blend in with the flow, and come out where you want to without an accident, demands great decisiveness and a significant dose of courage.

Pape'ete, having grown to 70,000 inhabitants, is constantly changing its appearance. Today, modern multistory concrete buildings dominate this waterfront town which is slowly creeping up the mountainside and into the side-valleys. There are boutiques, art galleries, and wonderful French restaurants and even *pizzerie*! *Coutouriers* and "fitness centers" are all well-attended. Modernization has cost the town its old charm, although some of the buildings from much earlier times are still preserved. The cavernous noisy market stubbornly seems to defy all reforms, remaining the special attraction that it always has been. All the products of the South Seas are offered under its corrugated tin roof: the counters are groaning under heaps of mangos, papayas, bananas, lemons and limes, breadfruit, coconuts, aromatic and exceptionally tasty pineapples from Mo'ore'a, ginger, taro roots, and the entire harvest of the sea, as well as handicrafts of all types. Colorful cloth, woven hats, and a sea of flowers dazzle the eyes in a riot of color, while the air is heavy with the scent of *tiare* gardenias.

Although Tahiti considers itself to be the center of Polynesian culture, the more interesting aspects of its culture have been expropriated from all the islands of French Polynesia, especially the Marquesas. These traits have been mixed, in odd ways, with elements from all over the world, in a kind of Polynesian "New Age" blend. The traditional Tahitian culture has degenerated so far that one activist has been tattooed with the ancient Egyptian "Eye of Horus." To many people of this type, such a hodgpodge of symbols poses no problem (*aita peapea* in Tahitian, an often-heard phrase). After all, don't all these symbols mean the same thing, in the end? Well, not only: "No," but "Hell, no! There's no relationship at all!"

Forty years ago, Pape'ete was a sleepy village of mostly one-story frame buildings on the shore of a quiet bay. The name Pape'ete means "Water basket" and derives from the originally gentle curve of this bay shore. Back then, a flying-boat came every two weeks and occasionally a freighter arrived to tie up at the small dock. Colorful sailboats and yachts of every description adorned the rest of the shore line.

In the middle of the bay lay a tiny gem of a tropical island with white sand and coco palms. This was the Quarantine Island, where the seaman-novelist Herman Melville spent some time in the mid 19th century. This dream of an island is recalled in Melville's novel *Omoo*. It also was used during World War II as an internment camp for both Free French and Petainist sypathizers, who alternated residency as the governments in France periodically alternated, as they are still wont to do.

Forty years ago, bikes were the preferred mode of personal transportation, and for long-distance commuters, there were the famous "Trucks," with their roofed-over flat beds and wooden benches. These carried people, chickens, pigs, fish, and every conceivable kind of material, including messages, back and forth between the most remote parts of the island and Pape'ete.

Back in those days, Pape'ete emitted a kind of happy, unashamed, and completely natural air of decadence. In the "downtown" of that era there were a number of *boîtes du soir*, the most famous of which was Quinn's, well known for its good music and its hordes of unattached women, many of whom would put on "theatrical" performances. One in particular used to display an ability to make her stomach muscles ripple in a most amazing fashion. Another attraction was the Unisex lavatory, a little room opening onto the dance floor with only a bit of *pareu* cloth draping the door. Around the room ran a narrow trench, which permitted customers to answer Nature's calls. Couples desiring to use the facility didn't even have to let go of each other's hands. Quinn's was the place where you could find a girl (or two or three), for the night, and where the hefty Tahitian son of Paul Gauguin came to sweep out the trash in the morning.

Tahiti also was probably one of the few places in the world where hotel desk clerks were so understanding. When you called the desk for breakfast, the question was always: "Breakfast? For how many?"

Not far from Quinn's on the dock was the tiny Club Zizou, so small that on the miniature dance floor you were constantly in danger of getting burned by cigarettes held in the hands of other dancers. Zizou is still there, but it has lost its atmosphere as well as its bamboo walls, tables, and chairs, and has been submerged in the midst of neon-bedecked "clubs," in which the indiscriminate visitor can find love of any variety he or she wants, along with a startlingly wide selection of interesting sexually-transmitted diseases.

In less than 50 years, Pape'ete has undergone a radical transformation, not only in its own internal self-image but in its outward appearance. And these changes have not always been for the better. The lovely little Quarantine Island has totally disappeared, now buried beneath sprawling ugly Motu Uta, an artificial peninsula which was built out from the northern shore of the harbor, sealing off the northern reef pass and engulfing the little dream island. Is this progress? The Motu Uta piers are jammed with freighters, container ships, fishing boats, and naval units. The flying boats come no more, their place in the lagoon having been taken by a 3,000 meter runway, on which jumbos of Air New Zealand, Air France, AOM, Hawaiian Air, and Air Tahiti Nui disgorge crowds of passengers almost daily. The old buildings in the waterfront area have also disappeared, victims of a roaring fire about 30 years ago. Quinn's vanished in this conflagration and with it went a lot of Tahiti's odd charm. Was this an accident or arson? There are plenty of rumors. In any event, the buildings were all replaced by neat, new concrete structures, including a shopping center with an escalator!

Our little car carries us past the navy base and over the bridge to Motu Uta. On the right is the dark sea wall, on the left are the docks for local ships such as the *Aranui*. Arriving at our destination, the driver slickly maneuvers our car around trucks, forklifts, containers, snack wagons, freight pallets, and very busy sailors and longshoremen.

And there she is, just as she was when we left her two years ago, and just as we remember her! A bit older, showing a bit more wear from her hectic operational tempo, but still the old reliable *Aranui*, already a living legend. We climb up the ladder and are delighted to be aboard once more, for 15 fantastic days.

Bob has to meet the old friends of many decades ago, but the first greeting is from Capt. Taputu, a fellow who so amazed me on the first trip. At that time, I thought it was a deckhand who was waving to me from the bridge. In his shorts and T-shirt, he stood in sharp and happy contrast to all the other skippers of dream boats and cruise ships I had ever seen, which made him especially congenial to me. He has lost neither his hearty laugh nor his modesty. Théodor, the first mate, instantly recognizes me; his pat on the shoulder shrinks into seconds the seemingly endless two years that I've waited for this voyage.

We discover Hu'uveu Teikitekahioho, the ship's stout Marquesan "supercargo" (freight purser), and Bob's closest Marquesan friend. In 1956–58, he was among the most reliable members of Bob's excavation team on Nuku Hiva. Since then, they've never lost contact and their friendship has only grown deeper. Today, Hu'uveu, known to the crew and passengers by his French name, "Casimir," is the "gray eminence" of the *Aranui*, a model of trustworthiness. He's always in the first whale boat ashore to keep a very close eye on all operations and personally handle all financial affairs. He's also the last back aboard, with his mysterious black attaché case. He beams at me: *"Bonjour Madame, comment-allez vous?"* (Good day Madame how are you?). What more can I say than: *"Ohhh, c'est mervielleux! Je suis si content de me retrouver ici!"* (Ohhh, it's marvelous, I'm so happy to be back here!). And that's the truth!

The Marquesans, so it's said, are complex, proud, and sensitive people. They're also people of few words. After a long, painful history of deception at the hands of Europeans, they've learned to mistrust Whites. Once a Marquesan comes to trust a European, however, with that trust comes a friendship for life.

And that's in fact true! The initial reserve melts and there's an even greater joy when friends recognize each other. There are bear-hugs, endless pats on the back, traditional French-style pecks on the cheeks and both parties have more questions to ask than can possibly be answered. Iakopo, a giant sailor, winds his way through the crowd, his white teeth glistening in a broad smile. "Robert, ehhhhhhh, Roberrrrrrt!" Bob almost goes to his knees from the powerful handshake, only to be happily embraced. Iakopo comes from the north coast of Nuku Hiva. Bob lived there for a long time, and got to know the family well.

"Ça va, Robert?" (How's it going, Robert?) and here's Josephine too, the demanding chief of the house-keeping force. A smile spreads across her broad face and she hugs him to her heart. She throws me a quick questioning look. I tell her: "No problem, Madame Josephine; everything's the way it always was. You can still mother him all you want!"

A bit stressed from all the hullabaloo, I'm really happy when I get my cabin key. "You have cabin 101, one flight up and the second door on the left." It looks like I've really lucked out; with two windows, a sofa, a chair and table, a big bed and two closets, there's plenty of room to set myself up quite comfortably. There's also a place for my big luxury Samsonite suitcase. In black lacquer, this is a Rolls-Royce among suitcases, as my friend Kathrin maintains. I love this suitcase, not only because it cost me $ 48 in overweight charges in Santiago de Chile, but because everybody thinks I'm a bit nutty to lug this monster around. On the *Aranui*, people travel in a practical, utilitarian, non-deluxe fashion.

Neither practical nor deluxe, however, except possibly for an entomologist specializing in cockroaches, are the little brown beetles that busily scurry around my baggage. They are an inseparable part of the Polynesian scene, but to tell the truth, I really don't care much for them, and so I leave this animal shelter a bit faster than I'd planned and seek the fresh air on deck. There, the feelings that were initially thrown a bit off-kilter in the cabin return to normal. Pape'ete lies spread before me in the golden evening light, a light that brings the dark green, overgrown slopes and ridges so close and envelopes everything in such an intense glow that there's no more room to think of cockroaches and their hunting grounds.

With the certainty of sleepwalkers, making full use of every square meter, the tough tattooed Marquesan and Tahitian sailors load the ship. Every maneuver is carried out with a minimum of verbal communication; the crane operators don't miss their targets by a millimeter. And they're all there again, all the sailors from the first trip in 1997: there are Brutus, Big Bull, Terrier, Gecko, Mr. Gloom, Steve, and all the rest to whom we gave nick-names. Their real names: Kohu, Teiki, Ta'utu, or Tima'u, are just as mysterious.

More passengers come on deck to enjoy the spectacle. Among them is Margitta, my friend from the last trip. We had so much fun together that we decided to come again. We take a deep breath and fall in each other's arms: we did it! Yoyo's welcoming *aperitif* still tastes just as good and heightens the pleasure and exuberance of the moment, which also proves infectious to the bystanders. That Yoyo recognizes me immediately proves that you can leave a lasting impression with a bar bill that lists 35 Schweppes Tonic Waters!

Over lentil soup, veal, french fries, and salad (the good wine hasn't changed either!), we make our first contacts at the table. Our tablemates are a very friendly French couple: he's a fidgety, somewhat nervous gentleman and she's the soul of pure friendliness. I call them Mr. Bean and Little Bean. Everyone dives into the delicious food set before us. Who knows? It may be the last meal for a while: once the *Aranui* leaves the calm waters of Pape'ete harbor and hits the Pacific rollers, appetites may not be so great.

This concern is soon removed, because the captain had to push the departure ahead until the next day. The repair of a malfunctioning crane took more time than expected and the big backhoe awaiting transport to the Marquesas couldn't be loaded. The ship sinks into a cozy slumber. There's an "all clear" for the plastic seasick bags that have been thoughtfully provided. And I make an agreement with my active little roommates: if they let me sleep in peace, they needn't fear anything from me. But did we really understand each other?

Departing Pape'ete

My wish was granted: my little brown friends spent the night elsewhere.

Around 0700, the dining room is opened, and by 0830 the breakfast buffet fruit, rolls, croissants, cheeses, Muslix, and assorted breakfast cereals has already been pretty well plundered. Was it the Seniors, a resolutely voracious group of elderly American women, with a couple of totally subservient elderly men? Self-centered, the Seniors have scarfed up their chow and occupied the best places on deck as the rest of the passengers drifted in to breakfast. The Seniors solemnly inform us, however, that they are not tourists, but actually "serious students."

The sailors have been at work since about 0500. The dock, up till now jammed with all kinds of cargo, is visibly emptying as the cavernous holds of the ship fill up. Containers, pallets, crates, building materials, autos, all vanish into these dark catacombs. Beside the hatches on deck stand the orange drums of jet fuel for Air Tahiti aircraft which operate between the Marquesas and Tahiti. But at the end of the day, the problem backhoe stands there on the dock, alone and defiant.

Curious people on the dock, the passengers on deck, everyone is now held spellbound, focusing on the effort to load this huge hunk of machinery. Planks, chains, rubber tires, poles, all kinds of lifting tackle are put to use and teams are racing here and there. After a while, the monster rises slowly, high above the dock, swings doubtfully back and forth a bit over the hatch, tips a bit to one side and rights itself again. Then, with a resounding thump and a tremor that runs through the ship, the backhoe finally comes to rest, very precisely on the center line of the hatch. The applause and cheers are well deserved. Look at the crew, they're jubilant!

The man we named: "Brutus, King of the Nubians," our crane operator, is the hero of the day. With his leopard cloth around his tattooed and shaved skull, a Harley Davidson T-shirt, and his tight bermuda shorts, no one could be more photogenic. With the *grandezza* of an Italian tenor, he wipes his face with a white towel and accepts the standing ovation as though he were on stage in La Scala.

But the *Aranui* sinks a bit deeper in the water and a neighbor comments: "In a storm, we'll go straight to the bottom with this load! Without a bang or a whimper!" This doesn't build confidence. Could he be right?

No, he's dead wrong, as I'm quickly informed. The Polynesians have learned to rely on their intuitions in the course of thousands of years of navigation. They know how to load a canoe or a ship and have an intuitive grasp of the physics involved, the handling qualities of the ship, and the sea itself. All the *Aranui's* officers are fully licensed and have many years experience, far more than most of their western counterparts. The crew of the *Aranui* are also a specially formed elite. They undergo a thorough selection examination in which they're put to various severe tests, including tests of strength, before they win the right to a berth aboard this ship. The CPTM administration consistently makes the highest demands on its crew. The security of the passengers and cargo must be assured; this is the first commandment for the CPTM sailors. With this assurance, you can ride out the most severe storm in confidence, provided of course that you can control your personal reactions to rough weather!

The engines begin to rumble: we swing slowly away from the pier and steer out of the harbor, shaping a course to the northeast. The slopes of Orohena are clothed in dark impenetrable green, and the narrow, deep valleys carved in those slopes provide tantalizing glimpses into the mysterious interior of Tahiti.

After Matavai Bay, we pass Point Venus. On this point, in 1769, Capt. Cook built a fortified astronomical observatory to observe the transit of the planet Venus across the sun. It was hoped these observations would make it possible to measure the distance between the earth and the sun. Cook's astronomer, Charles Green, installed two telescopes, an astronomical quadrant, an astronomical clock, and a big bronze sextant to make his observations. This part of Cook's voyage wasn't productive, however, since poor visibility made it impossible to measure the exact time of the transit of the planet. Further, Mr. Green died on the voyage home and his notes proved to be sadly indecipherable.

Cook wasn't the only visitor here, however: Captain William Blight, dubbed "Breadfruit Billy" by his not-so-admiring Royal Navy comrades, gathered his cargo of breadfruit tree shoots at Point Venus before loading them aboard the "Bounty." The precious shoots were planted in small containers and scrupulously watered so that they would withstand the rigors of the long trip from Tahiti to the Caribbean. The British saw in the breadfruit a cheap food for slaves on their plantations, and it seemed that the trees would thrive in the Caribbean climate.

Today, a lighthouse marks Point Venus. It stands, somewhat obscured, in a grove of trees between modern houses and the lagoon. We cruise on and the entire east coast of Tahiti is gradually revealed to us, all the way south to Tahiti Iti, the smaller volcanic cone that marks the southern end of Tahiti and is connected with Tahiti Nui by a narrow isthmus. We're out on the open sea now, a stiff breeze coming over the bow, and the *Aranui* plows bravely through the waves, shuddering and creaking a bit under the impact of wind and seas. The deck clears out surprisingly quickly, and my tummy also seems to be heading for that rather indefinite state that fits the category of the first signs of seasickness. Bob's pills help to prevent anything worse from developing. But Margitta disappears into her bunk with sick sacks.

With a 10-hour departure delay, it's going to be impossible to reach the Tuamotu islands today. This is a real pity, because the

unexpected stop at Apataki on my first cruise provided an un-
foreseen and most unusual experience. Wearing our life jackets,
we climbed down into the whaleboats for the first time. The
well-muscled arms of Marquesan sailors lifted us into and out of
the boats, helping those of us who a were a bit tense to regain
our composure.

At the bow of our boat, like a rock pinnacle in the midst of
surf, stood a giant of a man. My eyes were drawn to his impressive silhouette. His shaven tattooed skull, his massive build, and
his tattooed arms radiated great strength and forced me to make
a comparison. But with whom? While we were rattling around
Apataki in the soft enchanting afterglow, my thoughts went back
to the book *Quo Vadis* in which a faithful protector (today we'd
call him a bodyguard), saved the life of a king's daughter, using
his brute strength to break the neck of a wild bull in the Roman
Coliseum. This must have so deeply impressed me when I was a
young girl, that it pops into my mind again, here and now. What
was the name of this powerful giant protector? Ursus? Brutus?
Brutus was one of Caesars murderers, but to tell the truth Brutus
fits this man better.

The entire population of Apataki, a small village with boxy
little houses and a church, was right along with us and accompanied us to the school. Along the way, an older woman stroked
me suddenly on the cheek and I embraced her spontaneously.
Two people who had never before seen each other!

Bedecked with flower garlands (*hei* in Marquesan), we listen
to a foot-stamping musical presentation interrupted by the powerful voice of the mayor who gives a brief welcoming speech.
Cool coconut water is refreshing and quite tasty, and on the way
back to the dock, the elderly lady whom I'd previously embraced
surprises me with a shell necklace which she lovingly places
around my neck. It's a gesture of farewell, just as the *hei* signifies
"welcome." Deeply touched, I thank her profusely and stare after her into the darkness until she disappears from view. This

gift, born out of the spontaneous feelings of two human beings, holds a very firm place in my memories, and is with me on this cruise. I hope to meet with the kindly old soul again, but it's not to be.

The clouds hang low, the wind blows strong and steady, and even the hard cases have vacated the deck. But this evening, life goes bravely on in the bar, the reception area and the salon. We wander about a bit and visit Hu'uveu in the little office where he's already busy with his seemingly endless monumental book-keeping tasks. He's still glad to see us and although my "Ka'oha nui" is a bit uncertain, it's understood. Thanks to my language instruction, it's soon possible to understand some spoken Marquesan.

The first meetings take place in the salon over coffee and tea. These are conducted by Heidi and Sylvie, our two hostesses, in English, French, and German. The coming day is discussed in minute detail and many useful hints are given out.

The rest of the evening we spend in the salon and hear the sad story of another passenger for whom a visit to the Marquesas had been a life-long dream. He was a big bear of a fellow, a warm hearted Frenchman, gifted with a great sense of subtle humor, and he joined Bob every evening at dinner. The closer the ship came to the Marquesas, the more excited he became, and on the evening before the arrival at Ua Pou he was espe-cially happy, conversing with great animation and wit to the entire table, infecting all with his enthusiasm. But he took his leave early, going off to first check on his companion, who wasn't feel-ing well, and then to hit the bunk early so that he wouldn't miss the island of Ua Pou when it poked its peaks above the horizon.

In the morning, it was clear from the mood of the ship's per-sonnel that something was definitely amiss. As it turned out, the gentleman whose happy anticipation had been so infectious had died of a heart attack during the night, a hundred miles or so short of his dream islands. Respecting the wishes of the family, as well as Marquesan law, he was buried in his beloved islands. In Taioha'e valley on Nuku Hiva, encircled by jagged mountain ridges, he found his final resting place, in the company of Marquesans, sailors, soldiers, missionaries and wanderers, whose paths all ended here.

On course for Takapoto and the Tuamotu Archipelago

The suns rays penetrate my window bringing hopes for a good day. It's 0600 and I've got to get some fresh air. Last night we talked about morning exercises on deck. The wind blows unabated, however, and karate and ju-jutsu lessons on deck are more of a struggle for balance than a learning experience. The lessons quickly end, and we disturb the Seniors as they mount their morning assault on the breakfast buffet. Unashamedly, we break through their formation and take good helpings of tasty avocados, sweet papayas, and aromatic pineapple.

Across from us sits an older woman with a red bandana, a Swiss, if I hear her accent correctly. She admits it, but says she's lived for a long time in New York and asks: "Are we going to speak German or English at this table?" She then goes on in German and enthuses about folk-dancing in New York and Bümplitz. Interestingly enough, Bob, the non-dancer, takes a bit of criticism from her because he doesn't know a certain Mr. Dudley, an apparently renowned New York folk dancer.

We leave Frau Helvetia and look for a comfortable place, sheltered from the wind, until it's time to attend the requisite lifeboat drill. There's plenty of laughter at the drill; the life vest strap that passes between the legs isn't really popular with anyone, and leads to a lot of interesting comments and facial expressions. And so the day rolls uneventfully along, with lots of good talk and interesting observations of some of our more conspicuous fellow passengers. In early afternoon, a row of thin, ragged green stripes peeks above the horizon: we've reached the western islands of the Tuamotu archipelago, a chain of low coral atolls.

The Tuamotus

The islands of the Tuamotu archipelago extend over a thousand miles in a northwest-southeast direction, between Tahiti and the Marquesas. The archipelago covers a surface area larger than that of Europe, but most of that expanse is empty water. The actual land area in this vast archipelago amounts to only 880 square kilometers.

The more than 78 palm-covered islands of gleaming white coral sand and turquoise lagoons rise barely above sea level; they seem to accord well with everyone's notion of an earthly paradise. Behind this charming romantic exterior, however, lurks a hard reality. The meeting of the Southern Equatorial stream with the Humboldt Current produces turbulence, constantly changing currents and winds, and often violent storms in these islands.

These low-lying islands, with their often scarcely noticeable coral reefs can be just as dangerous as the weather. Innumerable ships have battered themselves to bits on these reefs or simply disappeared without a trace. Even today, shipwrecks bear testimony to man's often hopeless struggles against these forces of nature, so it's quite fitting that the Tuamotus bear the name of "Dangerous Islands." Are they a paradise or a hazard? To answer this question, we're going to have to take a little detour into the geology and culture of these islands.

Beneath the Eastern Pacific lies a huge tectonic plate, the so-called Pacific Plate. This monstrous piece of basalt is moving slowly northwest at the rate of about 15 centimeters per year, propelled by lava spewing out of the submarine Mid-Pacific Ridge, which runs roughly north–south, between the Marquesas and the coast of South America. Beneath the plate, in the earth's mantel, "hot spots" have formed. Between 6 million and 100 million years ago, molten lava forced its way upwards from the earth's core through these hot spots and burst through the Pacific Plate, spewing forth upon the sea bottom. The flows first formed deep sea mounts, but more lava flowing from below forced many of these mountains to ultimately rise above the sea-level, producing the foundations of not only the Tuamotus, but the Marquesas and Society

Islands as well. After the pressure from the earth's interior relaxed a bit, many of the islands slowly sank again beneath the sea. Over millennia, the sinking volcanic cones accumulated coatings of countless generations of coral polyps; hordes of these tiny creatures covered the sides and tops of basalt sea mounts. Finally, the volcanic cones were completely submerged, but encircling their tips stood necklaces of coral reefs which became today's atolls. Over hundreds of thousands of years, these reefs became covered with fine sand produced by dead coral organisms. Clouds of migratory birds carried in seeds and these barren coral reefs became green atolls. Today, the Tuamotus are the remains of a sunken volcanic landscape.

The islands of Makate'a and Mata'iva are exceptional cases: they sank beneath the waves and were then forced upward again by pressures from deep within the earth. They offered sea birds nesting places for hundreds of millennia. The sea birds left behind great deposits of guano (dried bird droppings), which once played a significant role in the economy of French Polynesia. Guano was sold for use as fertilizer or for the production of explosives. In contrast to Makate'a, which now seems fixed in the "Up" position, the little atoll of Mata'iva is still going up and down. Its lagoon is filled with deep deposits of shiny golden stone which formed from guano that had been subjected to pressure and chemical changes during periods of submergence. At this time, Mata'iva has once again sunk a bit, so that you have to dive to get at the guano deposits in the lagoon. In 1996, a European company wanted to once more begin commercial mining operations there, but the inhabitants refused. They were correct to do so, because they wanted to preserve their beautiful little world and what remained of their ancient culture. Whether they were successful in the long run remains unclear.

As a result of their geological history, the Tuamotu islands aren't very people-friendly. The only source of fresh water is the rain, which is collected in cisterns, and provides the necessary life-giving liquid. Without water, the sand can't transform itself into the fertile soil needed to grow Polynesian tree and root crops. Only pandanus and coconut palms do well in coral sand, while breadfruit and taro could only be raised with great difficulty. These marginal conditions exerted great pressures on the prehistoric and present inhabitants of the Tuamotus, and did not exactly lead them to be overly friendly to strangers who might consume scarce food and water.

In sharpest contrast to the rather depressed Tuamotu land flora, the lagoons offer outstanding crystal-clear diving areas, with an enormous variety of colorful sea life. Armies of fish of the most diverse forms and colors rule life on the reef sides. Not infrequently one also encounters lurking reef sharks as well hammer heads, tigers, and other types. The lagoon bottoms are covered with molluscs of all sorts, among them the Tridacna clam, with its protruding colorul zig-zag mantels. This shellfish was a staple of the ancient Tuamotu diet. Forty years ago, the undersea wonderlands of the Tuamotus, such as Fakarava, were Eldorados for divers and snorklers, but this has changed in many places.

Naturally, these low islands are totally defenseless against the cyclones and tidal waves which have often left their trails of devastation through this part of the Pacific. In the 19th century, there were at least three devastating cyclones. Those of the 20th century—1903, 1906, and 1946 —were strong enough to inflict many casualties and leave many of the island settlements in ruins.

Today, only about 40 of the islands are seasonally inhabited. Another 20 are permanently inhabited; these are the islands upon which tourism, copra, or the black pearl industry are established. The prehistoric population of the Tuamotus was originally much larger, however, and distributed across many more islands than today. It's uncertain exactly when these atolls were settled and whence the settlers came, but it's generally believed that they were settled early and from two directions: the eastern atolls were settled from the Marquesas and the western atolls from Tahiti. Most of the settlers were probably refugees from intertribal warfare on the "high" volcanic islands. For these unfortunates, fleeing to a remote island was the only viable survival option. Many of these islands were only of interest to prehistoric Polynesians because of their fish, shellfish, or birds. It's quite certain, for example, that the Marquesans frequently visited the Tuamotus to collect mother of pearl and other highly *sought-after shellfish not found in their homeland. In the course of time, Takapoto, Rangiroa, Fakarava, Raroia, Napuka, and Ana'a came to support larger populations, and today they are still among the most heavily populated of the Tuamotu islands.*

On course for Takapoto, we glide past more new and tempting atolls. Strings of islets, some of which support only a half- dozen palms, surround turquoise lagoons; they beckon to us across the white surf breaking against the outer reef walls.

But we cannot and will not forget that not all the islands in this archipelago are so attractive. Far to the south are two islands which are only blackened dead radioactive wastelands, devoid of palms and pandanus trees. They will continue to be wastelands for tens of thousands of years. These are the islands of Mururoa and Fangata'ufa, heedlessly sacrificed for nuclear weapons testing by French politicians and the military, against the wills of the people of France and the world.

During the Cold War, the Grand Nation needed it's "Force de Frappe," it's own nuclear strike force. After leaving NATO, there was no way for France to draw on American nuclear weapons know-how, and for some inexplicable reason, the US wasn't about to give such information to France anyway. France thus built its own very capable research and development capability, and after the loss of its Algerian test site, tested an arsenal of weapons on the atolls of Mururoa and Fangata'ufa. De Gaulle announced this grotesque adventure with high-flown words in 1963. His ambition to create a place for France among the nuclear powers of the world set in motion a direct assault on the health of the Pacific peoples.

Between 1966 and 1996, France detonated more than 160 atomic, thermonuclear, and neutron bombs on and beneath these two islands. In 1995, when Jacques Chirac announced a new series of tests, France was caught in a violent crossfire of criticism because of the obvious environmental threat posed by these tests. The nations likely to receive the fallout from these tests escalated their protests in a most threatening fashion. In Pape'ete, rioters burned and looted; in Australia, a French consulate was torched, a Greenpeace activist was murdered by French counterintelligence, and there were many tense standoffs between the "Greenpeace Warrior" and the French Navy.

Regardless of all this, the two atolls today are lifeless, ruined pieces of real estate, covered by heat-glazed coral sand or layers of asphalt, which are supposed to prevent the leakage of radioactivity into the environment. Beneath the surface, however, radioactive pollution seeps into the sea, permanently destroying and deforming sea life. France can't be absolved of this insanity, but it's also necessary to recall that all the nuclear powers — the US, the UK, Russia, China, India, Israel, and Pakistan — have done the same thing. With the efforts of various nations to confirm their own Great Powers status, this slow genocide continues, and the Planet Earth will be exposed to arbitrary destruction.

Gradually the throbbing of the engines abates, and about 500 meters off Takapoto the *Aranui* comes to a dead stop. An anchor is useless in these waters, because it would never reach the bottom and so the ship "keeps station," using bow-thrusters and screws.

We descend for the first time into the whale boats. Lancelot, a stylish American gentlelady with page-boy hairdo, champagne roll-neck shirt, a pearl necklace and crocodile purse, joins somewhat reluctantly in the procession with her partner, who's also the absolute embodiment of a fashion magazine cover. They both appear to be on the wrong ship. One of them has already expressed concern that there's no "lift" aboard, while the other has found fault because the maids don't fill her water bottle for her before she goes ashore. It seems a bit odd to hear two Brooklynites using terms such as "lift" for elevator, but then one must use various ways to impress one's fellow passengers. Lancelot tries a little Italian to further impress us, but when Bob responds in fluent Italian, she retreats, claiming that she doesn't speak the language.

Sometimes fearfully, sometimes with devil-may-care ostentation, our fellow passengers negotiate the ladder with us, then the sailors grab us and deposit us safely in the whaleboat. There's no way for anyone to avoid their grasp. Hu'uveu and his black attaché case are also there, ready to take care of business ashore.

Because there's no pass into the lagoon at Takapoto, freight and passengers have to be carried across the outer reef in whaleboats. Naturally, this type of arrival is rather unusual and one feels a bit cramped in the unwieldy life jackets. Clenched fists and fearful faces signal the level of tension created by the prospects of such a landing. But there's no reason for concern: the waves are moderate, the famous 7th wave as well, and our sailors have no problem steering the boat with its nervous human cargo over the reef and to the jetty. Strong brown hands grip us firmly, and before we know it, we're standing on the shore with dry feet. Only Marquesan sailors can make this kind of perfect landing.

When Bob first visited Takapoto in 1956, he says that the sailors made short work of his arrival. A huge grinning sailor grabbed him under the elbows, lifted him high as though he were a flyweight, and despite his protests, gently deposited him in a jiffy on the dry beach, to the great enjoyment of all onlookers.

"Watch out for the jetty stairs, they're slippery!" was the warning that we also got today, while on the way ashore. It wasn't the attraction of the forbidden, but the desire to get a good photo which tempted me to venture onto the dangerous area. And it happened, just as it had to happen: I promptly slipped and landed quite hard on the slick algae carpet. It wasn't only the embarrassment of the fall, but it was even more humiliating to do this in front of the whaleboat crew, who just stood there shaking their heads in disapproval. Hell's bells! (and a lot of other words, too) why did that have to happen? Gratefully, I grab for the outstretched arms of a helpful gentleman and just pray that he's got enough traction and strength to hold us both up. What a grotesque performance that would be, tumbling over each other, to disappear into the tidal shallows! But he stands firm, as I'd hoped. Subdued, I fall in line with the rest of the passengers and meekly accept a beautiful flower wreath that the pretty young girls and musicians are presenting to all the visitors.

We can select from two possibilities to reach the swimming and picnic spot: either we can hike around the lagoon, or we take a boat across the lagoon, directly to the beach. We're already familiar with the route of march, and beside sweat and thirst, it has really nothing much to offer, and so we opt for the boat trip.

Margitta now takes over leadership of our little group. Does she really know the way to the boat? A bit skeptical, we follow her along the wide coral sand street, which is lined with corrugated-roof houses. The church, the post office, and several rainwater cisterns all hide behind pandanus trees, whose green foliage sharply contrasts with the blue sky. The village seems otherwise devoid of life, with the exception of a few scrawny dogs lounging around. Today's *Aranui* day, so all the inhabitants are on the beach!

We wander to the original boat-landing, but soon find out that it has been moved since our last visit. Just as a precaution, we ask directions of an elderly lady who's sitting in front of her house. But whether the question is put in French, Tahitian, or Marquesan, she points us in every direction under the sun, and we know as much as we did before we asked. Rivers of sweat are flowing freely. Thanks to a glimpse of the characteristic hat of "Captain Cook," a 74-year old world traveler from the *Aranui*, we finally find the boat landing. Loaded down with a complete set of snorkeling gear, a German woman joins us, sweating profusely under the heavy burden. "Why did you lug all that gear with you?" asks her husband, who's also soaked with sweat. "Well, last evening, someone said to bring it with us ... !"

The boat trip lasts about 10 minutes, and this time, there's a shout of enthusiasm as we go out into the lagoon. Changing from hunter's green and turquoise, into deep cobalt blue, the lagoon unfolds before us, surrounded by gleaming white sands. A thick palm forest, its tree-tops straining into the azure skies, contributes the much-desired shade. Who could ever turn away from such a spectacle?

Sixty tourists, all dying for a swim, throw themselves into the crystal clear water and no one's really willing to leave. Margitta splashes about near me sighing: "Isn't this great? Isn't this great? I never want to got home!" Dagmar twirls and twists, swimming pirouettes; the American women shriek, and the French are singing. We only leave the water out of necessity: the black pearl culture demonstration is about to begin!

"Big business" on Takapoto is no longer copra, but the culture of these black pearls. Forty years ago, such pearls were completely unknown and even when natural pearls were found in mother of pearl oysters, they really had little perceived value. Then, in addition to copra, the big business was diving for pearl shell, with its gleaming rainbow-colored inner surface of mother of pearl. It was a dangerous business, because these shells were found often in depths of 40 meters, and the most modern diving equipment consisted of crude homemade goggles of brass and window-glass. Given these primitive conditions, many men died, attacked by sharks or barracuda, or became crippled from cumulative oxygen deprivation. The return for all this effort and risk was about a dollar for a kilo of pearlshell. Later, modern scuba gear was introduced, but diving remained a very dangerous business, because divers weren't taught how to use the new equipment. Bob's foreman in the Marquesas lost his son and son-in-law during one two-week period in 1956: no one had told them about decompression requirements!

Today, black pearls are the major source of income for Takapoto and many other atolls of the Tuamotu archipelago. But this industry has brought many problems with it. The special pearl oysters needed to produce these pearls brought with them a virus which has seriously impacted the ecosystem, causing sea life to die off or to flee to other waters. The underwater world of Takapoto was once known for its profuse and colorful sea life, but many areas of the lagoon are now as good as dead and coral is dying off. But does this bother those who have made a big business out of the pearls being sold at horrendous prices? It's the Japanese who really control this business and the Polynesians only work for them. When there are no more black pearls, or when the limited market for these rather peculiar items is glutted, who's going to worry about the Polynesians, and who will accept responsibility for the dead fauna of the lagoons?

The disappointed snorklers confirm that there's no sea life in this part of the lagoon, except for the unlovely sea cucumbers lying about in the shallows. Their words certainly support what we've written above on the environmental impact of this industry. It's therefore understandable that the demonstration of black pearl culture isn't especially interesting to us. We prefer to lie around on the sand, and let our South Seas fantasies carry us far away. We're also quite grateful for the feelings of contentment that this afternoon has given us. A short walk into the palm grove is interrupted in a most surprising fashion. We stumble over Mr. Bean, crawling through the undergrowth, once more ardently pursuing his photography hobby. Little Bean's "Hi" sounds a bit bored.

Time is running out. The majority of the passengers have been standing around with their life jackets for about half an hour, ready to be returned to the ship. But a misunderstanding must have crept into the time schedule. We're a bit concerned, but calm down when we find that Capt. Taputu, a member of a distinguished family of Tuamotu mariners, is still ashore, playing the ukulele with the musicians. As long as he's still ashore, the *Aranui* is not going to leave without us!

Finally everyone is loaded onto the ever-present jeeps and off we go, in an admittedly somewhat uncomfortable fashion, around the atoll to the beach and the waiting whaleboats.

An eventful day comes to a very pleasant and peaceful end, as the long next leg of the voyage to the Marquesas begins, a leg that will last 42 hours.

Onward to the Marquesas

Since leaving the shelter of the Tuamotus we're on the open sea, with the winds and swells coming from the southeast. Undeterred, the *Aranui* pitches through the night, besting the waves and swells in her own specially reliable fashion. Those who are accustomed to this motion are cozily rocked in their sleep. Others, however, may suffer a bit from the motion, which is the only way that we can explain the almost empty breakfast buffet at 0800.

Thick clouds race across the sky and rain showers alternate with brief periods of sunshine. The sea has lost its normal aquamarine color and is now slate-gray. A comfortable sojourn on deck is clearly out of the question. We gather on the lee side, where the wind is least noticeable. In the hectic daily routine, how often we hope to find time to talk with each other, to philosophize, to exchange thoughts and experiences and become better acquainted. Perhaps for this reason, more passengers join us, listening to Bob as he talks from his wealth of experience in these islands. They ask him all kind of questions, about *tiki*, about his digs, and about the origins of the Marquesas and the Marquesans.

Several haven't heard about tectonic plates and their movements, a theory that was first advanced as "continental drift" in 1914 by the German scientist Alfred Wegener. Up until 40 years ago, this theory was considered heresy by many US geologists, but it has finally won full recognition today as a result of an enormous amount of geological research, much of it done in the depths of the sea.

All scientific support aside, Dr. Wegener's theory was simply unacceptable to the smart Thai girl with cornflower blue eyes (thanks to contact lenses). As a self-appointed clairvoyant and specialist in auras, the occult, and other esoterica, she *knew* that the Marquesas had risen out of the ocean as a result of mudslides. But whence came the mud slides? Does mud slide upwards from under the sea? Totally at a loss for answers to those questions, she remained unmoved in her faith in gravity-defying mud.

With broad grins, we also recall the French pseudo-ethnologist who saw an ancient astronomical observatory behind every ruin, every randomly arranged group of stones, every hole in a knife-edge ridge or every oddly-shaped peak. In response to the question as to exactly which stars might have been observed with the help of these supposed installations, he reacted with irritation: "Please! Such questions are totally irrelevant! These observation points are highly significant in their own right!"

As expert navigators, possibly the best of their era, the Marquesans ranged over the eastern Pacific from Hawai'i to Easter Island, and probably reached the Americas. Their knowledge about the risings and settings of stars and constellations and the practical use of these celestial bodies for navigation must have been extraordinary. This knowledge of the heavens was also reflected in their lunar calendar which assisted them in designating the months and the seasons for planting and voyaging. We know that Marquesans identified and named a large number of stars and constellations, but with only a few exceptions, the missionaries who recorded these names did not associate them with any of the known heavenly bodies, recording them merely as "star name" or "constellation," and so they'll remain unknown to us for all time. There are archeological sites which may in fact have been used for observatories, but without knowledge of the ancient Marquesans' sky, we can make no astronomical interpretations of these ruins and natural geological formations.

It's a fact of life: on every cruise, there are always the self-appointed experts who feel constrained to instruct others, even if it's about upward-flowing mudslides.

For the handicrafts enthusiasts among the passengers, the hat-weaving session in the bar offers a welcome diversion. This session is under the sponsorship of Josephine, chief of the female housekeeping staff, who's missed her calling as a teacher. She likes nothing better than to instruct others, and does it quite well, too. Participants produce palm leaf hats, which are found everywhere in the islands, woven in various fanciful shapes. These hats usually cost about $10 dollars, although the Polynesians can make them in about 5 minutes with one hand tied behind their backs. From this point of view, the instruction is definitely worth the effort because the hats provide good protection against the surprisingly strong tropical sun that quickly burns the sensitive skins of European or American visitors. Several passengers have already learned this painful lesson on Takapoto.

After the substantial midday meal, with its customary wine, siesta time comes quite naturally. Because the wind has abated somewhat, the deck chairs are fully occupied, some people snoozing while others are reading, or immersed in intense discussions.

My threesome decides to get an introduction into the basic rules of the Marquesan language and we've got a very distinguished teacher.

Marquesan belongs to the Austronesian language family. At the time of the European's arrival in the Pacific, Austronesian languages comprised the most widely-distributed language family on the face of the earth. Austronesian languages were spoken from Madagascar to Easter Island, and from New Zealand to Hawai'i, as well as in Malaysia, Indonesia, Melanesia, and the Philippines, the north coast of New Guinea, the islands in central Taiwan, and in scattered spots along the coast of Viet Nam. In about 4700 BC, however, Austronesian languages were also spoken on the China mainland. Today one can hear them only on Taiwan. The aboriginal (non-ethnic Chinese) inhabitants of Taiwan, dwelling around Moon Lake in the central mountains, for example, still speak Austronesian languages. Additional small pockets of Austronesian speakers, such as the Cham, who inhabit the coast of Viet Nam, while some of the "Montagnard" mountain tribes also speak languages of this family.

Marquesan itself is most closely related to the languages of Hawai'i, Mangareva, and Easter Island. It shares with these languages a fairy simple grammar. The language is spoken with a very distinctive intonation. It's quite melodic and flowing, but sounds much more powerful than other Eastern Polynesian languages. There is no grammatical gender, nouns don't change endings depending on case, and verbs don't change for person or number. Pronouns, on the other hand, are a bit complicated: All three persons have forms which distinguish singular, dual, and plural. There are also separate forms for the "inclusive we" which includes the person addressed, as well as "exclusive we" which excludes the person addressed. The typical word order normally follows a simple verb-subject-object pattern. Tenses are indicated by particles that stand before the sentence ("sentence markers"), and a few affixes, which are easy to learn.

The rich vocabulary is full of nuances and interesting areas of concentration. For example, there are many words for lying, cheating, treachery, and other negative human traits such as laziness, mistrust, anger, aggression, and several shades of jealousy.

We diligently jot down the most common sentences and phrases, and are quite curious to see whether we'll be understood tomorrow when we go ashore for the first time in the Marquesas.

With the last rare rays of sunshine of this rather gloomy day, we leave our comfortable spot and head for a cup of coffee in the salon where by chance we meet Nancy, a very sympathetic and delicate American who's also making the trip for the second time. We exchange thoughts, favorite episodes, and fondest memories from these trips, and it looks like we have another case of the "Marquesan Virus!" The record for the number of voyages logged, however, belongs to a young Swiss girl who's made seven trips aboard the *Aranui*. But this tenacity owed more to the presence of a good-looking sailor, who led her to the altar.

The Marquesas

Among all the archipelagos of French Polynesia—the Australs, the Gambiers, the Societys, and the Tuamotus—the Marquesas are the fartherest removed from any continent:

in the east, they are over 6000 km from Peru.
in the northeast, they are 4800 km from the Gulf of California
in the south, they are 450 km from the atolls of Pukapuka and Napuka,
in the southwest, they are 1400 km from Tahiti
in the southeast, 3000 km from Easter Island
and in the north, 3850 km from Hawai'i.

The group consists of a 350 km chain of 14 volcanic islands and rocks, jutting abruptly above the empty wastes of the East Pacific. The archipelago is divided into a southeastern group, consisting of the inhabited islands of Fatu Iva, Tahuata, and Hiva Oa, and a northeastern group, consisting of the inhabited islands of Nuku Hiva, Ua Pou, and Ua Huka. All of these islands are volcanic and have arisen from the depths of the ocean; their foundations extend 4000 m. beneath the surface. Their geological ages range between 1.25 million years for most of the southern group and 7 million years for the northern group. The constantly recurring signs of volcanic activity in these islands indicate that the Polynesian volcano goddess, Pele, is not yet sleeping too soundly. Pele is a Hawaiian goddess, but she's also known in the Marquesas and in parts of Indonesia. Pele shows her presence in the Marquesas by active gas vents and mineral springs, but there's also a small reef up by the uninhabited island of Eiao which has shown some upward movement within living memory, as Pele stirs in her slumber.

With it's position between 9 and 11 degrees south latitude, the Marquesas archipelago is the closest of all French Polynesian groups to the Equator. The cold Humboldt Current, originating in the Antarctic and flowing up the west coast of South America, turns west below the equator and flows in the direction of the Marquesas. This is at least partially the reason why no fringing coral reefs have formed around the islands. When there is coral, it's always near the relatively few beaches or on tiny inshore reefs in a few of the harbors. The sea around these islands was once teeming with fish, whales, and other types of marine mammals. The whales were hunted down in the 19th century and once the modern fishing fleets of Japan, Russia, Korea, and China discovered this area, they seriously reduced the number of fish species, often fishing illegally, a practice continuing to this day.

The isolation of these islands presented absolutely no problem for early Polynesian seafarers. The islands were first discovered between 300 and 500 BC and gradually explored and settled. The discoverers called themselves "The Men," (te 'enana) and named the islands the "Land Of Men" (te henua 'enana).

The Men, being somewhat restless, soon began to explore the sea to the north, south, and east. On the basis of linguistic comparisons as well as archeological finds, archeologists are today convinced that Hawai'i was first settled from the Marquesas around the first century AD, and that Marquesans explorers probably reached Easter Island and Mangareva between 400 AD and 700 AD.

This theory is strengthened by the marked similarity between the languages of the Marquesas, Hawai'i, and Easter Island, as well as by similarities in a range of artifacts such as fish hooks made of pearl -shell and bone, and stone adzes. Artifacts from early sites in Hawai'i are nearly identical with those from the Marquesas. When it comes to the date for settlement of Easter Island, we're groping a bit in the darkness, because the archeologists there have focused on the huge moai statues and temples, rather than looking for deeply buried and more obscure early sites without stone structures.

During its more than 1800 years of isolation, the population of the Marquesas grew to about 100,000, until the "second discovery" occurred. On 18 July 1595, a flotilla commanded by the Spaniard Don Alvaro de Mendaña de Neira dropped anchor in Vaitahu on the island of Tahuata. This seafarer was on a voyage to the Solomon Islands, which he had discovered 16 years earlier. He had brought with him everything necessary to start a happy colony: his wife and her family, a detachment of soldiers, a bunch of whores from the South American waterfronts, and some priests.

When he saw the tips of the Marquesan peaks poking up above the horizon, Mendaña first imagined he'd reached his Melanesian goal. The navigation techniques of that era were considerably less accurate than those of today, but even for those days, an error of 3000 miles was quite uncommon. One might characterize it as being not even close enough for government work! In accordance with the custom, Mendaña named his discovery after his patron, the Marqués de Cañete, Don Andres Gracia Hurtado de Mendoza, at that time Viceroy of Peru. And this was the source of the complex name of this archipelago: las islas Marquesas de Mendoza y Cañete, or to put it briefly, the Marquesas.

The next European sail popped up much later, in 1774. This was Captain James Cook, following in Mendaña's wake. Cook also anchored in Vaitahu harbor. The northwestern group of islands remained undiscovered, but not for long, for in 1791 Captain Ingraham of Boston raised the islands of Nuku Hiva, Ua Pou, and Ua Huka, and a month later the French Captain Etienne Marchand landed on Ua Pou. Whalers followed, drawn by the rich hunting grounds not far from the islands.

In 1804, the Russians appeared under command of the famous Captain-Lieutenant Ivan Fedorovich Kruzenstern. A short time later (1813) came the US Navy, under Captain David Porter, who dropped in to refit after a prolonged campaign of raiding British shipping in the Eastern Pacific. Porter made a kind of military census on Nuku Hiva. At that time there were 19, 200 warriors on that island alone. On the basis of Porter's "order of battle" count, as well as a survey of the abundant ruins in every Marquesan valley, the previously-stated estimate of a total population of 100,000 was developed.

It's a safe assumption that at the end of the 18th century, the fertile valleys of the Marquesas had long been overpopulated and that there was a serious shortage of arable land. This population pressure had brought about a state of chronic warfare among Marquesan tribes. These fights took their toll of casualties, as did the results of the battles when human sacrifices were offered to the numerous gods. Cannibalism also played its part. The most aggressive tribe was the Taipi of Nuku Hiva, whose warriors raided throughout the archipelago, earning well their epithet of " Taipi kaikai 'enana" ("Taipi man-eaters").

At this time many European sailors deserted in the Marquesas. They brought with them European diseases, mainly childhood communicable and venereal diseases, leaving unimaginable havoc in their wake. At the same time, these "Rejects of Civilization" taught their receptive hosts how to handle rifles and cannon. They also taught them how to make home-made booze from local products and how to enjoy the intoxicating effects thereof. The Marquesans were devoted students in all these subjects. Right to the present day, alcohol abuse remains one of the biggest problems on the islands.

More European ships followed in the first decades of the 19th century. Among these was a French warship commaned by Admiral Dupetit-Thouars, whose party included well-educated missionaries. They quickly acquired fluency in the Marquesan language and with great diligence began to push for the Christian conversion of the "Heathen." They were only the advance-guard of a French military occupation force which secured the Marquesas for France in 1842. With the help of the military, these early missionaries robbed the Marquesans forever of their culture, their way of life, and accordingly, of their dignity as well.

The work of the occupation forces was not all negative: they stamped out intertribal war and cannibalism. In spite of this, the inhabitants were almost completely wiped out in a series of epidemics which followed colonization. In the small-pox epidemic of 1863–64, two-thirds or more of the population died. This decline came so abruptly that even today, in many valleys, there are only eerily quiet ruins of house platforms, temples, and tribal ceremonial centers. The Marquesan voices have been stilled forever. Of the population which once numbered around 100,000, only 4800 Marquesan were surviving in 1882. Only 3200 people were left at the end of the century, and 20 years later this number had dwindled to 1900, leading to the mournful prediction that the Marquesans would be extinct in 20 years. This prediction (happily) to the contrary, the population has now rebounded to 7400!

At the end of the 19th century, the first scientists arrived to study the Marquesan culture and all of us, especially the Marquesans, are indebted to them. The most famous of these scholars was the German, Karl von den Steinen, of the Berlin Ethnological Museum. In 1896, he visited every inhabited valley in the archipelago and published a superb encyclopedic study in three volumes entitled: Die Marquesaner und Ihre Kunst (The Marquesans and Their Art) Berlin; 1925, 1928.

Von den Steinen's point of departure for his investigation of the culture was Marquesan art, which is not completely unusual, since he was a psychiatrist and dealt in symbols of all types. He described the unique Marquesan tattooing and wood carving in great detail. In these art forms, the Marquesans remain to the present day uncrowned masters of the South Seas: nowhere else in this vast ocean can such artistic works be found. It's to Karl von den Steinen's credit that this art work was preserved. Today, copies of his volumes and his drawings are circulating all over the Marquesas. The wood carver, the tattoo artist, the tapa painter, all use his works for inspiration, even though they can't read a word of the German text. One Marquesan even tried to convince Bob, whose Russian is very good, that von den Steinen's text was written in Russian!

In 1859, the church and the colonial administration outlawed tattooing, dancing, and tapu, because they were connected with the pagan religion, warfare, and especially with fertility rites and celebrations of sexual maturation. These interdictions were a major force in the destruction of the culture.

Tapu is the same word as "Taboo" in English and signifies holy, supernaturally charged, and therefore untouchable, invulnerable, or forbidden. It can be applied to a person, place, thing, or activity. Me'ae *(temples) were tapu places, as were the persons of chiefs and priests. When going on major fishing expeditions, embarking on military campaigns, carving tiki, or engaging in tattooing, various kinds of tapu had to be observed. These most often involved prohibitions on sexual activity and eating of certain kinds of foods. In addition, each tribe had special tapu related to its pa'io'io or guardian spirits. So, for example, members of various tribes or clans would not eat shark or chicken because they were guardian spirits. These prohibitions are often still observed today.*

Tattooing was forbidden by the French not only because it was connected with fertility and sexual maturation, but was also ostensibly viewed by the authorities as a health hazard for the population. This prohibition lasted for more than 120 years, until the former Bishop of the Marquesas, Mgr. Hervé-Marie Le Cléac'h, permitted it to be removed. Among the Marquesans, Mgr. Le Cléac'h has attained the status of living saint, and in his retirement this status has not diminished. He allowed tattoo motifs to be used as decorations in the churches and caused a variant of the well-known atua motif—Karl von den Steinen's "squatting man," a stick figure with widespread legs and up-raised arms to be transformed into the "Marquesan cross." Furthermore, the old dances, especially the haka, are reappearing with new variations. These were supposedly forbidden, but seem to have been always performed, in strictly private parties, far from the eyes of the church and the law.

Karl von den Steinen was the most active ethnologist to visit the Marquesas but by no means the only one. In 1920, the Bayard Dominick Expedition was launched from Hawai'i's Bishop Museum with Edward and Willowdean Handy and Ralph Linton. The Handys further investigated many fascinating aspects of Marquesan culture, including music, string figures, tattooing, legends and genealogies, and social organization. Linton, as the archeologist, produced simplified sketches of major ruins, but never stuck a spade into the ground. He claimed that excavations weren't worth the trouble!

In 1956, the American Museum of Natural History of New York sent Bob to the Marquesas to make the first stratigraphic excavations in these islands. He soon found that Linton was dead wrong. In 18 months of field research on Nuku Hiva, Bob learned that it was definitely worth the trouble to go beneath the surface in the Marquesas. He frequently found rich artifact-bearing layers 2 meters or so deep, and found sites where occupation dated back to the second century before Christ. Bob learned the language and became an impassioned member of the "Marquesas Club."

This is a bit of the history of the Marquesas, but we want to discover these islands with our own eyes.

Ua Pou: Hakahetau and Hakahau Valleys

On this morning, we're the first on deck so that we don't miss the moment when the dramatic silhouette of the island of Ua Pou, the inspiration for Jacques Brel's song "The Cathedral," rises mysteriously out of the morning mists. This silhouette is a wild conglomeration of bizarre mountain peaks walled in by black stone cliffs that plunging directly into the sea foam. Obelisk -like volcanic needles give the island it's name: Ua Pou, in Marquesan, means "Two Columns."

The geology of Ua Pou is different from that of the other islands, not the least because of the unusual types of volcanic rocks found there. The ancient Marquesans treasured the greenish phonolite from Ua Pou: it was good for making flake tools because it was a hard resistant material and held a cutting edge. A further rarity are the "Flower Stones," pebbles with flower like crystals of golden flakes set in a dark matrix. Today, they're much sought-after as tourist souvenirs.

The awe-inspiring appearance of this island hides a rather gloomy past. The inhabitants of Ua Pou were counted among the most violence-prone of all the islands, and that reputation continues to this day, although inhabitants often seem to be driven by the use of marijuana, for which the island is renowned. Although the first European visitor, Capt. Étienne Marchand, received a very friendly welcome in 1791, a British ship was later captured and plundered, and still later a number of sailors were eaten.

The island was also known as the home of the enigmatic living god, Te Atua Heato. According to traditions, he was not tattooed and manifested supernatural powers while alive. He carried on constant warfare against the other tribes of the island and drove off Tahitian missionaries. For today's Marquesans,

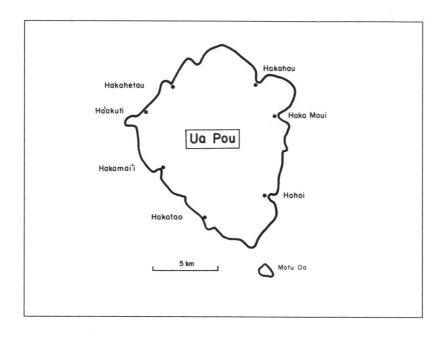

Heato's burial place, Me'ae Te Menaha 'Iaka'oa in Hakamoui, is still the most sacred place on the island. Heato's son, Teikitaiuao, continued his father's campaigns of conquest, and finally succeeded in uniting all the tribes of Ua Pou under his rule. In the history of the whole archipelago, no chief had ever succeeded in conquering an entire island! As is so often the case, however, the joy of victory proved quite transitory: the small pox epidemic soon made the proud chief the ruler of an empty land.

The tribes of Ua Pou are closely related to those of Nuku Hiva, but speak a very different dialect. The difference was once so great that in the mid-1800's a French priest was sent from Hiva Oa to learn this dialect and translate parts of the Gospel and Missal into "the language of Ua Pou," a soft and flowing dialect which has survived to this day.

60

Whaleboats bring us ashore in Hakahetau, a tiny community with a somewhat hidden harbor. Landings here are often a bit chancy due to the strong surf and the swells, because the seas can drive the boats, out of control, against the dock and nearby rocks. Today, however, we're in luck, and the sailors put us ashore without a hitch.

European-introduced pistachio trees afford welcome shade, in which a small market has been set up, offering dried fruits, necklaces and other handicrafts, and "Flower Stones." It's the custom to bring home dried bananas from here, because you can't find anyplace where they taste better. Purses and wallets spring open in response to the first of many attacks.

"Ka'oha nui, Robert!" Greetings come from every side, with hugs and slaps on the back. On our way through the little village, we come upon one of the first stone churches in the Marquesas, built in 1859, a small but impressive fieldstone structure. Dressed tuff and lovingly carved woodwork complement each other harmoniously in the interior. The church is known for its carved chancel, and saints' statues. The turquoise ceiling is, for my taste, a mistake, but I must accept a bit of instruction: its color symbolizes the Blessed Virgin, Queen of Heaven.

Next to the church, and surrounded by flowering hedges, stands the former residence of Mgr. Le Cléac'h. Bob met the bishop some time ago on the dock in Hakahau. Both knew of each other but had never met face to face. Since then, a strong enduring friendship has arisen, rooted in the shared love of these islands and their people.

Three frigate birds circling overhead draw our attention. Bob mutters: 'This is some kind of omen; they're telling us something!" I look doubtfully at my companion, not so ready to believe in mysticism and clairvoyance. "It's true," I'm informed, "the Marquesans still believe in guardian spirits. These can be almost anything: sharks, birds, even rainbows. I've got a good friend, a teacher here on Ua Pou. He's got a frigate bird guardian spirit, believe me!"

"OK, but right now I want to visit the school!" Bob looks at me inquisitively: "Why the school?" I tell him emphatically: "Just because!"

We find the school a short distance up-valley. Not wishing to disturb the instruction, I sit inconspicuously near the door, enjoying the pleasant feeling of tranquility mixed with the murmur of happy children's voices emanating from the classroom. Bob saunters up, looks into the classroom and suddenly two men are hugging, each other, slamming each other on the back, tears running down their cheeks. Old friends, the teacher with the frigate bird spirit and Bob, have once more found each other.

The kids also enjoy the pleasure of a break from instruction. They belt out their song of greeting for the surprise guest with such enthusiasm that other passengers are drawn to the school. The song is an invocation to the ancient Polynesian sea god, and it's believed to bring happiness. Bob, the dedicated nondancer, begins to dance along with the children, clapping happily to keep time, Marquesan fashion. Later, Ioteve Kaiha, the teacher, presents him formally to the class.

The children want to know about his work on these islands, and his life in the USA. The spirited question-and-answer session excites both students and the audience, which is growing rapidly in the meantime. At the end, nearly all the *Aranui* passengers have turned up. They're also infected by the enthusiasm, and the teacher is forced to carry on his instruction on the playground which is also slowly filling with other Marquesans. The kids are dancing, singing, and literally exploding with *joie de vivre*. The boys perform the highly original "pig chant" with praiseworthy seriousness, quite convincingly imitating the snorting and grunting of pigs, stamping the ground in a striking fashion, making threatening gestures all the while. The dainty girls perform the *hakamanu* or "bird dance" solo, imitating the circling frigate birds. Even at this age, they're already capable of very graceful movements and we can only guess what beauty slumbers in these lovely little creatures. All the while, the little pre-schoolers are rushing around, animated by the contagious singing and dancing. With their unsteady steps, they'd like to join in and soon they've conquered all our hearts. It's a beautiful scene of laughing children, proud mothers, the radiant faces of Ioteve and Bob and all of the others, together enjoying a lighthearted and completely unrehearsed celebration of pleasure in each other's company.

At the conclusion, the sea god, *te hatu o te moana,* is once more invoked, and then everyone lines up for photo sessions, but certainly not before diligent mothers have ensured that clothing and hair have all been properly arranged. The clicking of cameras seems endless.

Did the frigate birds have something to do with all this? I really don't know. Perhaps there are places in the world where the boundaries between the supernatural and the natural are thin or nonexistent, and perhaps the frigate birds of Ua Pou really do have wonderful powers!

Afterwards I wander around the village alone, past the hibiscus and *tiare* (gardenia) hedges blooming in brilliant colors. From the shade of breadfruit, pandanus, and mango trees, I enjoy the shiny slate-gray cliffs, that wall in the valley. An encounter with a furious looking Marquesan with wildly disheveled hair snaps me back out of my reverie. He's holding a beautifully colored rooster very tightly under his arm. I suspect the poor bird will soon adorn the lunch table, although he's still crowing with self-satisfaction in this world. My "Ka'oha nui" sounds a bit timid but to my surprise evokes a friendly smile on the face of my opposite number. Pointing to the rooster, I learn the reason for the anger. The cock left the hen house without permission and finally allowed itself to be captured in the cliffs, but only after a lot of effort and sweat, things which the Marquesans don't necessarily like to expend, except when partying. The "Hunter" laughs resoundingly as I tell him what I'm thinking. He calms me with a dismissive gesture: "The hens love this guy too much!" A most unmistakable hand-motion further underlines the rooster's desired activities in the hen house, leaving no room for doubt.

By the harbor, I link up again with the other passengers. Some comb the beach for "Flower Stones," while others watch the sailors loading and unloading the whale boat. The tuff formations which wall in the harbor on the left and right fascinate us, and their reddish brown color is striking. They were formed by a thick layer of volcanic mud and ash which was baked between glowing lava flows to the hardness of fire brick.

There are many forms of tuff in the Marquesas, and because this kind of stone could be cut with stone adzes, it was highly desired. Above all, red tuff, *ke'etu*, was *tapu* ; it provided the raw material for *tiki* figures and great slabs used in temples and chiefs' houses. It was firmly believed that once cut, the stone would actually grow again. The rarer white tuff was only used in temple construction, since white was also a *tapu* color. Looking at the stone more closely, we see small shiny crystals in the matrix; in Hawai'i, these are believed to be the tears of Pele, the volcano goddess.

Back on the ship, we head for Hakahau, a trip which takes an hour. In Hakahau the *Aranui* can come alongside a large pier and tie up. Wearing the customary garlands of flowers, we wander through the village to a welcoming ceremony by a great stone platform or *paepae*. This is a reconstructed temple or *me'ae* of the old Marquesan religion. Beside this imposing structure, tables have been erected upon which various carefully arranged delicacies await us. Of great interest is *ka'aku*, a kind of paste made of breadfruit, taro, or manioc, and served with coconut cream. Then there's raw fish in a sauce of coconut cream, lime juice, and sea water; as well as European-introduced guava and pamplemousse fruits (a relative of the grapefruit), which do especially well here.

Although the foods are unusually delicious, the shady trees are greatly in demand because of the heat, and coveted water bottles are making the rounds. Lancelot alone seems unimpressed. In her inevitable roll-neck blouse, with jewelry and crocodile purse, she courageously defies all the effects of the heat. Her side-kick, the diminutive but equally fashionable Lift-Princess, has long since buried herself deep in the shadows and fans herself with an air of fatalistic resignation.

In the meantime, a music and dance group has assembled before us. With great emotion and many emphatic gestures, we are led through the history of the village and its music by the rotund mayor, but it's the female dancers with their waist -long black hair, their scanty red bras and short *pareu* that really fire up the audience. Their presentations are greeted with warm applause, but soon it looks like we passengers aren't the only ones who are longing for the cool shade: so are the performers themselves. The only exception is the mayor, who drones on endlessly. One cannot escape politicians!

The rush to get to Restaurant Chez Rosalie Tata is unmistakable. Most of the passengers become deeply acquainted for the first time with the more refined specialties of Marquesan cuisine. Tender beef, curried goat, shrimp, and Rosalie's special raw fish in an usual marinade all deserve special mention. The scene in the restaurant reminds me of "Mata Hari" who sat next to me, in the same spot, two year previously. I looked her in the eyes once; then twice; and then even a third time. The somewhat blasé woman actually had eyes of two different colors, one was sea green, the other a watery blue. Margitta was pressing her lips tight together, scarcely concealing her amusement as I tried to formulate my question. Mata Hari looked at me a bit piquedly and asked: "Is it really that noticeable?" Then she stubbornly continued to look out at the world, in two colors! Margitta later told me Mata Hari had lost one of her contact lenses while trying to insert it.

Bavarian souls must react intuitively to the presence of beer. Otherwise, it's inexplicable that a couple from Munich is already working on their second beer before most of the others have even taken their seats. "Where did you find that delicious stuff?" "Two houses further along the road!" In an empty "shopping center," attended by four very friendly sales girls, I manage to get the last can of beer, to my great pleasure. Beyond this can, the total inventory consists only of two cookie boxes, a chocolate bar, and three cans of lemonade. The completely electronic cash register takes minutes, and lots of paper, to compute my "major purchase," but the delay is more than compensated for by the smiling faces of the cashiers, beaming at their achievement with this complex device. And don't worry about the yawning, empty store shelves, because the *Aranui* has arrived, and one of its many containers will also fill up this store again, until in 4 weeks it will be once more empty, awaiting another shipment. *C'est la vie!*

The walk back to the ship in the stifling heat turns out to be more difficult than the walk up valley, which must ultimately be attributed to the very sumptuous lunch. And so I tag along behind my companion who hurries off, disappearing into the local school to meet a teacher, Jean-Louis Candelot. Candelot is a well-known Marquesan author of lyric poetry who also writes excellent articles on the geology and history of the Marquesas. His first novel will soon be published. Jean-Louis, a tall blasé French-Polynesian, tending a bit to the hefty side, regrets that he cannot spend a great deal of time with us. The "Seniors" have announced that they wish to visit the school. The educational possibilities of the island of Ua Pou seem to be of greatest interest to them and it belongs to their often peculiar approach to the world to use the Marquesas to gather precise information about the French school system. The teachers' reactions to this visitation are restrained, if not outright lethargic.

Before the cackling procession can turn the corner, we gratefully turn our backs on the school, and nothing can restrain us from finally taking a well-deserved afternoon break under the shady trees on the beach. A dip in the tempting surf is not advisable because some of Hakahau's sewage finds it way into the bay. Furthermore, the *Aranui* leaks a bit of oil in her old age, and other things which may find their ways into the bay seem even less enticing to romp about in.

The cranes are running at full speed and the sailors are still busy when we return to the ship. Many Marquesans have turned up for gossip sessions, a bunch of children are climbing on the ship's lines where they droop near the water, and there's plenty of very active coming and going on the ship. At 1600, the *Aranui* finally gets ready to let go bow and stern lines; the last kids who've been swinging on these lines make daring dives from their rope perches and swim for shore, as we swing away from the dock, out into the open sea.

The dark shore line of Ua Pou slowly recedes from view; the peaks seem like huge dancing specters, bathed in the ever-shifting rays of the setting sun.

It's a great time to have a lecture, and Bob decides to give a talk on Marquesan stone statues, the famous *tiki,* and the massive ancient Marquesan stone architecture which we'll be seeing tomorrow on our visit to Taipivai. He begins with a lecture in French, for the French passengers, and follows with an English version of the same talk.

Tiki

The Marquesan word for a figure or statue is tiki; (in Tahitian, the word is ti'i, in Hawaiian it's ki'i). In the Marquesas, Tiki is also the name of the Polynesian god who copulated with a sand heap to create the first man. At the same time, he's also the god of carvers, sculptors, and tattoo artists.

Based on the close connection between the god Tiki and art, the word tiki is also used as a verb: "making tiki" means carving, and "inscribing or puncturing tiki" means tattooing. In the ancient Marquesan culture, every figure represented a specific god but was also a representation of Tiki, the "Primal Ancestor" who had created the first man. All tiki are therefore also phallic symbols related to the role which the god Tiki played as Primal Ancestor or Primal Phallus.

The Marquesas had a very long list of gods and goddesses. They worshipped some of the better-known Polynesian deities such as Atea, Taka'oa, etc., but even more important than these great gods were priests, priestesses, and chiefs, who because of their mana (the supernatural power which they had exhibited in life) were honored in life and deified after death. Tiki were carved in honor of these people.

The features of the old Marquesan tiki are extremely unusual and incomprehensible to Europeans. On the one hand, these figures embody the Primal Phallus, but as Karl von den Steinen perceptively noted so long ago, they are also representations of human sacrifices. The great eyes are half-closed, the tongue protrudes from a slightly open mouth, the belly is swollen, arms and legs are drawn up exactly the same way a dead human sacrifice must have looked when brought to the altar, trussed up on a pole. There are tiki of both sexes, two-headed tiki, and small double tiki attached back to back, but all have the same features.

The concept of the creator god as a phallus and a corpse at the same time is hard to understand, but for the Marquesans it was completely natural. Sexuality and human sacrifice played a major role in their religion since time immemorial. Both sexual displays and human sacrifice were intended to please the gods and thereby increase the fertility of the islands. For the old Marquesans, death and sexuality, fertility and sacrifice, all fit together rather well.

Today the word tiki is also employed to designate modern European statues. In the Catholic Church, figures of the Madonna or the saints are all referred to generically as tiki.

Tiki are popularly regarded as the most striking of all Marquesan archeological remains, but in fact, they mainly provide raw material for many often mindless sensationalist theories. Some wish to relate them to prehistoric Peruvian cultures, others see them as remains of the culture of the Lost Continent of Mu, or evidence of ancient Israelite or Egyptian contacts. Therefore, the best way to clarify the supposed mystery is to take a quick look at the results of excavations on tiki sites.

Karl von den Steinen's reports give detailed information on the age of the biggest of these stone figures. The two largest tiki sites in Marquesas are the Pa'eke temple in Taipivai, Nuku Hiva, and the temple of Te I'i Pona in Puama'u, Hiva Oa. Pa'eke, with 11 tiki figures on three large platforms, represents a kind of "pantheon" for the gods of the Taipi tribe. Te I'i Pona in Puama'u is best known for its great size and its 11 tiki, among which is the largest stone figure in the Marquesas. Karl von den Steinen very shrewdly dated this temple in 1896, long before the development of the radiocarbon dating method.

With the aid of five internally consistent genealogies which he collected from descendants of the builders of this temple, it was possible for von den Steinen to quite precisely date the construction of Te I'i Pona and the statues standing thereon, as having been built only 6 generations before 1896, or between 1700 and 1750 AD.

Genealogies had great significance in Polynesia. They provided the basis for one's position in society, mana or supernatural power, rights and privileges, and one's relationships to all other members of the community. Every genealogy began with a god, the primal ancestor, and his wife; and traced descent through the subsequent generations of first-born sons and their wives. These often extremely lengthy genealogies (e. g., 80 generations for a Taipi chief) were committed to memory, and recited in certain ceremonies to affirm or validate the direct relationship of the living chief to the gods. In the Marquesas, the genealogies begin with the god Atea and his wife, Atanua.

Bob's radiocarbon dates from the tiki quarry sites on Nuku Hiva agreed well with von den Steinen's dates. The tiki have been regarded as of high interest by some researchers because it was believed that they would reveal something about the origin of Marquesan culture. In reality none of the tiki are very old, all of them seem to have been made in the 18th century, and they tell us absolutely nothing about the roots of Marquesan culture which is 1900 years or more older than the statues.

The Norwegian adventurer, Thor Heyerdahl, took great interest in Marquesan tiki sites. His logic was disarmingly simple: Peru had stone statues of anthropomorphic (human-like) figures, so did Polynesia; therefore there had to be a connection! It seemed as though the excavations on the temples of Pa'eke and Te I'i Pona during his 1956 expedition might produce support for his theory that the Polynesians are descendants of Peruvian Indians from the Tiahuanaco Period (about 900 AD). According to one of Heyerdahl's diggers, the Norwegian knew about Bob's work in the Marquesas and was apparently afraid of the results Bob might get. But Bob wasn't very interested in statues!

Because of their patron's overwhelming focus on statues, which were all seen as being stamped with "Made in Peru," Heyerdahl's archeologists actually engaged in a narrow-minded "charcoal hunt," looking for that substance or any other organic material that could be dated by the radiocarbon method. With the material they obtained, both of the sites (Pa'eke and Te I'i Pona) were dated to the late 16th century, a long time after Tiahuanaco (900 AD). There's another problem that they never addressed, however. Charcoal from beneath the surface can't tell anything about the age of something standing on the surface. These dates only proved that a Marquesan built a fire on that spot in the 16th century, a fire that was totally unrelated to the tiki now standing on the ground surface. Logically, that which is above ground has no direct or necessary chronological identity with that which is beneath the surface. If that were the case, a gas station built on an Native American Indian site could be used to prove that the native Americans had prehistoric internal combustion engines.

After detailed investigations in Marquesan sites, we know today that the tiki and the monumental stone buildings in which they stand come after the 16th century, and many actually date from after the arrival of the first Europeans. Under the massive stone platforms one often finds

European artifacts such as parts of firearms, iron tools, wine and brandy bottles, and tobacco pipes, all of which support this conclusion.

In conclusion, the ruins and the tiki themselves are all of Polynesian origin. There were no ancient Israelites and certainly no Peruvian raft-riders!

With the conclusion of Bob's talk, we've arrived at the island of Nuku Hiva, where the *Aranui* comes alongside the dock in Taioha'e Bay.

Some passengers take the opportunity to walk about a bit on land or to watch with great curiosity the unloading of the "Problem Backhoe" which has finally reached its destination. When, after much ado, this monster ultimately is deposited on terra firma, one can almost feel an enormous collective sigh of relief. The crane operator and the sailors are once again the heroes of the night. Capt. Taputu personally drives the machine to the place set aside for it. I could easily believe that he was overjoyed to be finally rid of this burden (not to mention how the elderly *Aranui* must have felt, having carried this dead weight for so many hours).

The night is warm; we all sit on deck quite a while longer beneath a sparkling canopy of stars, happy and grateful to be back on Nuku Hiva.

Nuku Hiva: Taioha'e and Taipi Valleys

Before we left Ua Pou, we saw the island of Nuku Hiva on the northern horizon, stretched out like some great prehistoric monster. The western ridge and the slopes of the Henua Ataha, "the deserted land," look like the monster's head, the jagged peaks of the island resemble spines on the giant reptile's back, and a long "tail" extending eastward terminates in a final spike represented by the Cape Tikapo promontory. Nuku Hiva is also the largest Marquesan island, with 340 square km (Hiva Oa has 320 square km).

Within this huge dark "Monster" hides the administrative center of the French colonial administration in the archipelago, as well as the seat of the Catholic Bishopric. Nuku Hiva also has the best harbors (Taioha'e, Hanga Ha'a / Taipi, and Anaho). From Nuku Ataha Airfield on the northeast corner of the island, Air Tahiti runs a regular service to and from Pape'ete.

Nuku Hiva is all that remains of a large volcano that blew apart, in an enormous explosion, millions of years ago. The surf must have been "up" that day! On the western and northern coasts, the walls of the volcanic cone are still visible. The central plateau of To'ovi'i is part of the caldera floor, but the eastern and southern sides of the cone disappeared in that primeval explosion. From the central plateau, rivers flow to Haka'ui valley in the west and Taipi in the east, making these valleys unusually fertile. This island, today the nerve center of the archipelago, was also important in prehistoric times, supporting an estimated population of over 30,000 before the 19th century. Now there are tiny settlements in only 6 valleys. The other valleys are littered with spooky, moss-covered ruins. These ruins, especially those in Taipi valley, are the biggest structures in

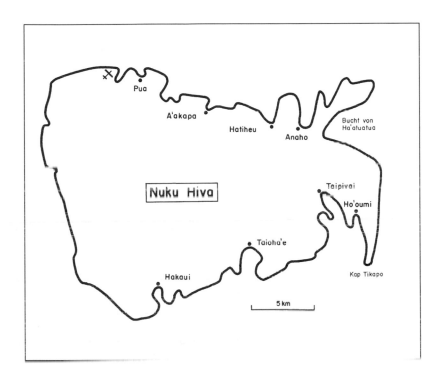

the entire archipelago, a further indication of the vast manpower available on ancient Nuku Hiva and in the old Marquesas.

Captain David Porter, of the US Navy, played an important roll in the history of this island. The terraces on the hill of Tu Hiva, directly opposite the bow of the *Aranui* as we tie up to the dock, were first laid out in 1813 by US sailors and Marines of Porter's command. Porter obtained the right to this hill and the surrounding land from Kiatonui, the paramount chief of Taioha'e. Porter's men fortified the hill with terraces and a barricade of earth-filled barrels, behind which they emplaced a number of cannon. The good captain named this installation Fort Madison, in honor of then-President James Madison. The cannon, removed from British prize ships, played a decisive part in Porter's war against the Ha'apa'a tribe. One of these cannon, a 6-pound carronade, can still be admired in Taipi today.

Porter's last detachment left Taioha'e in 1814. A bit later, the English arrived and took possession. On Tu Hiva hill, Porter had buried a bottle containing a "Document of Possession for the USA" but the British could not tolerate this audacity (particularly since Porter had been so thorough in sweeping British shipping from the eastern Pacific). The British dug up the bottle and used it to plant their own document of possession, this time in the name of the Crown. In 1842, the French, in turn occupied Tu Hiva without any local resistance being offered, and Fort Madison was renamed Fort Collet, the name which it bears to this day. There's little to be seen of the fort itself, but it's still a very popular place for a walk.

In the meantime, the quay has filled up with more cars, containers, and snack wagons, around which the *Aranui* forklifts are skillfully dodging. The crew is working furiously, the cranes swinging and dipping at top speed. This spectacle has such a profound impact on many passengers that they often forego the opportunity to go ashore.

Bob, however, absolutely must set foot on "his" island. He and his wife lived here a long time; he carried out most of his revolutionary research here, his oldest friends still live here, and he speaks the melodious Nuku Hiva dialect with a Taipi drawl. Last evening he was naturally excited to see Nuku Hiva island reposing so clearly on the horizon; a crown of clouds resting on its jagged 1300-meter peaks. He's got plans for side trips to see old friends and I'm happy to accompany him to meet some of Nuku Hiva's personalities.

Because it's going to be a long day, we've got to bring along all the necessities: drinking water, sun block, insect repellent, hats, comfortable clothing, good shoes, and a very alert mind to be able to soak up all the information

In the midst of the hustle and bustle on the dock, we spot the white Landcruiser belonging to Rose Corser, a long time resident of Nuku Hiva. Rose is the president of the Shim Nuku Hiva Owning Company which holds Hotel Keikahanui. She arrived at this island many years ago with her husband, Frank, who died in 1992. Like so many others, they both succumbed to the charm of these islands. Today, following a total renovation, the Hotel is operated by Air Tahiti. This gives Rose the opportunity to devote herself to her all-consuming hobby which is the study of Marquesan archeology, art, and culture.

We drive with her to the house of Teikivahiani Puhetini (his name means "sky-splitting prince"), a gifted wood-carver and one of Bob's old companions. Together they team-taught a successful class at Windward College, in Kane'ohe, Hawai'i, introducing the students to Marquesan culture, art, and history. Bob lectured in English, and then translated for Teiki, who interpreted the deeper meaning behind his carvings.

Teiki Puhetini is a *tuhuka ha'atiki*, a master carver, and I've had a strong desire to obtain one of his carvings for a long time. Now I've got the chance, but instead of one *tiki*, two are awaiting me. I've got a real problem making a choice between these beautiful sandalwood artworks and so I take both. It's also impossible to resist some elaborately carved armlets of rosewood, decorated with Teiki's distinctive breadfruit designs.

Marie Antoinette Puhetini, the master-carvers wife, receives us. A lively little Marquesan lady, her bubbly manner of speaking is marked with such emphatic gestures and mimicry that I hang fascinated on her every word and have all I can do not to imitate her. Constantly, I catch myself as my mouth forms words right along with her. It's thus not hard for me to sense that her husband, Teiki, lies seriously ill in the hospital, and that I've just gotten his last artworks. This news hits both Bob and Rose rather hard. It's quite clear how much respect they have for their friend. Almost worshipfully, I pack these valuable pieces in my backpack and wish that I could say more to this lovely lady than just: *"A pae!"* ("Good bye!").

We gladly take Rose's suggestion to visit the renovated Hotel Keikahanui, which was named after Keikahanui ("Big Coconut Husk"), a legendary Marquesan chief and warrior of great prowess. During the drive to the hotel, I'm shown the house platform of the last "Queen" of the Marquesas, Vaekehu. This massive *paepae* platform stands in the middle of a long ceremonial plaza along the beach road. The history of this Queen, her King, Te Moana, and their family is quite interesting and deserves to be told.

Te Moana, born in 1821, was the chief of a sub-tribe of the Te I'i tribe of Taioha'e. During a tribal war he had to flee the island on a European ship and spent a bit of time thereafter in England. He later shipped aboard a whaler as a cabin boy, but returned to Nuku Hiva in the company of a Protestant missionary. He then converted to Catholicism in order to curry favor with the French, who hoped to install a "king" for the entire archipelago. Moana saw himself as the person best suited to bear that title.

He wasn't a good choice, despite the fact that he could show an illustrious collection of ancestors in his genealogy, which is generally the most important prerequisite for a chief or "king" in Polynesia (aside from being a good warrior). Moana was considered to be cowardly and revengeful, possessing a character that was once described by an English sea captain as deserving "neither esteem nor respect." He was also more than a little attracted to alcohol. He died in 1853 after an inglorious life. It was bruited about, and perhaps not without good cause, that he had fallen victim to a poison plot by his enemies in nearby Haka'ui valley.

As Karl von den Steinen remarked, Moana's wife, Vaekehu, was by far "the better half." She lived until 1903 and her peacemaking efforts exerted a strong positive influence on the entire strife-ridden archipelago. The couple had no children of their own, but adopted several from the family of the chief of Haka'ui. Bob knew two of these adopted children: Taniha (Great White Shark) Taupotini, a former chief himself, and Te Ui'a (Lightning) a quite egocentric woman, tall and slender, with an extremely aristocratic air and a strikingly penetrating eye. She was well known by virtue of her *pekio* (secondary husbands) of which she had seven, all totally devoted to her. The *pekio* lived far apart from each other, in separate houses in the western and northern valleys of Nuku Hiva. Each house consisted of a dwelling house and a cook house. The *pekio* served as watchmen in the noble lady's absence, but couldn't enter the dwelling house, since Te Ui'a controlled the keys. The *pekio* lived in the cook houses! When the mistress of the house came by on her grand tour, they cohabited in the dwelling house. The favored *pekio* gladly provided her with the affection that she needed until she decided to leave, at which time the door was again shut, she went off on her merry way to visit other *pekio*, and he returned to his quarters in the cook house. The men were quite proud of their positions and quite satisfied to serve such a noble woman.

Pekio relationships with secondary wives and husbands were quite normal and entered into openly. These relationships were also often valuable in tribal politics. The male and female *pekio*, frequently traveling to and fro between valleys on their conjugal visits, could and did serve as an alternative to what we today term as "official channels" or intelligence services. These visits were the "channels" for circulating information in a somewhat roundabout but nonetheless efficient way.

Another variety of Marquesan interpersonal relationship was the name exchange or *ikoa* ("name"). It was done like this: men who were good friends, or wanted to be good friends, exchanged their names, and in so doing exchanged their identities. Naturally, access to each other's wives was often the real motivation for the exchange, as well as the acquisition of all other rights and privileges. But there was a "down side" to all of this, too. Obligations were exchanged with the privileges, and some of these obligations were not so pleasant, such as responsibility for revenge in blood feuds, caring for orphaned children or performing various costly rituals and feasts. Marquesans could have many *ikoa*. For example, Mr. Smith might become Mr. Jones but might also be Mr. Brown, Mr. White, and Mr. Green, if other attractive opportunities presented themselves. Since Marquesans have many names to exchange, the cycle could extend quite far; and it's no wonder that town clerks' offices were unknown in the old Marquesas. Capt. David Porter exchanged names with so many that he had to start giving out names of his relatives. To this day, there is still a family on Nuku Hiva proudly bearing the name of Porter.

In the meantime, we've reached the other side of the bay and are mounting the hill to the hotel with its picturesque bungalows which snuggle stylishly into the landscape. In front of the central building, housing the reception, dining room and bar, lies a truly extravagant swimming pool which appears to overflow directly into the bay below. Ornately carved *tiki* and other traditional Marquesan carvings of rosewood decorate the rooms.

Narrow, well-kept paths connect the individual bungalows, all of which offer an overpowering view of the bay and the surrounding heavily-wooded mountain ridges with their deeply incised valleys. We're still enveloped in the *Aranui* atmosphere, but it seems like we've suddenly entered another world. This is especially true when the doors of one of the bungalows are opened to reveal a very special ambiance composed of stylish French decor with native-style furnishings and design, all blending in perfect harmony. The wide bed, decorated with a tasteful tapa print, and the sparkling clean bathroom arouse strong desires to stay for a while. But then I have to think about my little brown friends, with whom I've managed to work out an uncomplicated group time-sharing arrangement, and I decide to return, happy and satisfied, to the *Aranui*, which has, in its own special way, become just as unique and homey, if not more so, than the Keikahanui.

Back by the Taioha'e inner dock, near Tu Hiva, stands Fare Mama "The House of the Mothers." This is an open pavilion, where we meet up with the rest of our group. The house got its name because it is ruled by a group of older rather emancipated women (Marquesan women were and are quite often *very* emancipated). The Mamas' dance exhibitions on various holidays really delight Taioha'e audiences.

Handicrafts and various native products such as coconut oil, fruits, sea shells, attract the curious. This tends to retard the departure and the division of our group among the various trucks that have been assembled for our tour. We climb in with Toma, for whom we've been looking for a while; he's a slender young fellow who looks more like a Latino than a Marquesan, and he's known as a talented musician, photographer and snack bar owner. Margitta jumps in beside him in the front seat and I can imagine that it's going to be a very pleasant ride for both of them. Uschi and Karl have made themselves comfortable in the back seats, while Dagmar, Bob, and I prefer the free air of the truck bed.

The bumpy trip begins; it's a pleasure; but of a decidedly strange sort, and that "pleasure" will rise to a crescendo during the course of the day. To warm us up a bit, the first leg of the trip only lasts the few minutes it takes to reach the Cathedral of Sts. Peter and Paul, an edifice unanimously acclaimed as the most impressive church of the entire archipelago.

The Cathedral precincts are entered through a huge stone gate. This gate was the front wall of the old church, which had been built in 1843 on the ruins of the Mauia tribal ceremonial center, where human sacrifices had previously been offered. When the Cathedral was built in 1973–77 under the guidance of the former Bishop Mgr. Le Cléac'h, the old church was razed, all except for the facade, which was retained as an impressive gateway, and a monument to the first missionaries.

Tall pandanus and breadfruit trees surround the paved area before the cathedral. Across from the entrance stands a row of carved wooden figures in traditional Marquesan dress. In reality these represent David, Solomon, Isaac, and Moses from the Old Testament. The exterior walls of the Cathedral are of roughly-dressed rectangular stone blocks; here and there among these blocks we note large irregular stones with parallel grooves. These stones were used to sharpen and polish the stone adzes in pre-European times. The sharpening stones were and still are considered to be *tapu* and have been gathered here, with other stones, representing all of the islands of the archipelago, to the glory of the Church.

The entrance to the sanctuary is flanked by statues of Sts. Peter and Paul, the patron saints of this church, carved in *temanu* wood *(Calophyllum inophyllum)*. The two sturdy apostles are shown in Marquesan attire with skirts of *ti*-leaves; on the right, Peter holds a net with fishes, while Paul, standing on the left, holds a spear.

In the interior of the church genuine miracles of Marquesan woodcarving done by leading carvers await us. The unique carvings harmoniously portray Biblical figures and events in terms of Marquesan culture traits and surroundings. Especially noteworthy is the Chancel with the four Evangelists, John, Matthew, Luke, and Mark; represented respectively as an eagle, an angel, a bull, and a lion. Also deeply moving are the baptistery with its large carved panel showing Jesus, as a Marquesan, being baptized in the Jordan, and the Tabernacle on which a huge richly carved *koka'a*, a bowl normally used to prepare *popoi*, the Marquesan staple breadfruit paste, invites communicants to: "Come, eat ... !" *Temanu* wood has been used for most of the carving, creating a uniformly calming atmosphere with its warm brown tones.

On the slope at the end of the plaza before the Cathedral stands a statue with a bishop's miter and crook. This is Mgr. R.-I. Dordillon, who compiled the first Marquesan dictionary and grammar at the end of the 19th century.

We slowly straggle back to the trucks. Despite the shadowy trees which invite us to tarry a while there, and the musicians who are unceasingly doing their best, the nearby latrine has developed into a major attraction. The Seniors, once again operating as a closed private party, engage in a collective use of the facilities, effectively monopolizing them. This naturally arouses similar desires elsewhere in the group and the line soon reaches out to the street. Those who don't have the urge organize a protest movement: "Hey, what the hell? Damn it all, the first one is going in again, but the last one has just finished! And what's wrong with our French friend over there? Does he have to use the ladies' room too? Why isn't a tree good enough for him?" This rather original Bavarian sentiment finally reaches the ears of one of our hostesses, who decides that it's definitely time to move out. Despite jammed zippers and open flies, no more excuses are accepted, and the long-awaited trip to Muake Pass finally starts.

After about a kilometer on the main road, the autos turn onto a bumpy track that leads to Taipi Valley. Steep serpentines weave back and forth up the thickly wooded ridge sides. We've left the concrete far behind and a light coating of dust settles indiscriminately on everyone. Little brooks cut gullies across the track and give those of us on the truck beds a little bit of extra "bounce" to enjoy. Big paddle-shaped leaves of the *kape* plant, a wild relative of taro, bestow their comforting shadows on us. Now and then, we catch a glimpse of the Muake Peak above Taioha'e. On this peak, in the 13th century, the Taioha'e tribe erected an impregnable fortress. Today the remains of this extensive installation are scarcely recognizable, its place having been taken by TV and radio antennae, which are visible from afar.

On the high plateau, about halfway to Taipi, we reach the picnic spot. Tormented backs and sit-downs enjoy a well-deserved opportunity for recovery. Having had enough of truck noise, dust, and crowds, I split off from the group, following a path that leads a bit down hill to a sort of promontory from where I have a good view over the "Valley of Tears," a kind of neutral ground, where in times past the chiefs and warriors of the opposing Taioha'e, Taipi, and Ha'apa'a tribes used to meet to discuss questions of war and peace. The tangle of underbrush climbing the mountainside, with its prickly-leaved pandanus trees, acacia, and ferns, spans the spectrum of hues from dark olive to delicate light green. Caught in the sun's rays, this verdure produces a marvelous profusion of color, while the warm breeze and the silence permit a feeling of almost reverent calm to take possession of me.

In contrast, the groaning board of the cold buffet which Yoyo and the kitchen staff have set for us in the middle of this wonderful remoteness, seems somewhat out of place. But when I look at the happy faces chewing with such gusto, I seem to be in something of a minority. It's all a matter of opinion, I guess.

It's almost a genetic characteristic of the Marquesans that music is required; everywhere, and on all occasions. And that's the way it is today! Concerning the seemingly inexhaustible repertoire of the musicians and singers, I'm told: "In the more traditional songs, they sing about everything. Quite often it's about sex. With improvised lyrics, they mock the tourists' behavior, or each other, referring to their own well-known funny experiences." A particularly well-known chauffeur, with a tummy the size of a prize pumpkin, is the local matador of today's scene. He tries to get the ladies dancing, then encircles their hips and enthusiastically grabs hold when the hip joints seem a bit too stiff. That he's the son of the honored carver, Teiki Puhetini, brings forth a sigh from Bob: "My God, what's going on? This apple has certainly rolled a long way from the tree!"

We leave the group and look out over Taipi valley, lying there beneath us. This valley has received world-wide and lasting fame as the setting for Herman Melville's first novel: *Typee: a Romance of the South Seas*. Having mentioned Melville, I now get the "straight story" on his visit to Taipi.

Melville really did live in Taipi; not for six months as his novel claims, but for about six weeks. In writing his book, he took considerable information from earlier visitors, such as Kruzenstern and David Porter (although he explicitly denies using Porter). *Typee* is therefore neither a historical document nor an ethnography ; it is, exactly as Melville himself put it, a romance, and a very good one at that, for it's time!

When you read Melville's description of his wanderings in the mountains of Nuku Hiva, it's immediately apparent to anyone familiar with the area that his account is pure fiction. The ridge on which Melville supposedly climbed out of Taioha'e is impassable, and when he writes that he stood on the Muake Peak, he would have been standing in the middle of the Te I'i fortification on that spot. Approaching that fort, he would have been captured and either ended his days in an earth oven, or returned to the ship from which he deserted, in exchange for weapons, ammunition, or alcohol. The terrain on which he and his friend Toby supposedly wandered was fully imaginary and in no way reflected the existing terrain.

On the other hand, that Melville lived in Taipi is virtually certain. He was given lodging by the clan of Hou, deep in the end of Taipi valley, on their tribal ceremonial center, Te Ivi o Hou. Melville's story squares quite well with the traditions which Bob recovered in 1957–58 when he lived in Taipi with the Clark family. Heiku'a Clark was a descendent of Melville's beautiful girlfriend, Peue ("Fayoway" in the novel). Heiku'a had heard a lot about Melville from her grandfather who clamed that Melville's fair skin, auburn hair, and hazel eyes ("like a cat's," they said), had created a sensation among the Marquesan ladies.

Peue loved Melville dearly because of these characteristics, and defended him vehemently against all her competition. Bob's archeological excavations on the ceremonial center of Te Ivi o Hou certainly found nothing that could be directly linked to Melville, but did find proof that the latest structures on the center had been built after the arrival of the Europeans. A tobacco pipe of whale ivory, and an early-1800s Stiegel-ware glass bowl from Pennsylvania showed that the site had been occupied at the right time for Melville to have been there.

In our shady little depression, protected from the wind, my thoughts wander upwards toward Muake peak. We must forego a visit to this lofty perch today, but I recall our visit there in the 1997 trip. Back then, a warm soft breeze and an absolutely fantastic view rewarded our tenacity in enduring the discomfort of the wooden benches in the truck beds. Beneath us lay the *Aranui*, well sheltered in Taioha'e bay. The jagged ridges flanking the harbor on both sides were brown and lacking in live vegetation. The deep blue of the sea, the white ship, the brown cliffs, with the green foreground of the valley floor, all complimented each other in a very effective play of colors.

The view with its interplay of colors wasn't the big Muake attraction back then, however! All attention was focused on a richly ornamented two-meter long representation of a phallus lying very nicely in the grass. This monument; which we called the "David of Muake" was carved out of the hard white volcanic tuff bedrock, and bore the name: Te Kohu. I turn to Bob: "Didn't you say that Brutus the sailor's real name was Kohu? Could he really...?"

The answer comes with a broad grin: "Yep! Could be!", to which I can only respond: "Oh, noooooooo.!" as another image crumbles.

It's well known that the peak above the pass is a popular spot for tourists and so a decision seems to have been made for a typical Marquesan-style advertisement. The locals are very en-

84

thusiastic about it. "First things must always come first," is their grinning explanation of this monument. As we've already written, the *tiki* is also a phallic symbol, and a *tiki* decorates the Marquesan flag, and so, while the Germans have their Eagle, and the Japanese have their Rising Sun, the Marquesans, ever refreshingly frank, have their phallus.

That the people here are fascinated by sexuality in all its forms and permutations is certainly no exaggeration. Before the Europeans arrived with their all-forbidding missionaries, these islands had a culture which was among the most erotic in the world. Nudity was common ; men often wearing only a string to secure the foreskin. Public sexual activity was the rule during many major ceremonies, and even today, phallic symbols pop up everywhere. The modern *tiki* carved for tourist consumption are often quite well-endowed, although sexual characteristics of the archeological *tiki* were rudimentary at best. No need to advertise what everyone knew! Long narrow objects, even the surveying stakes on Bob's archeological sites, were quickly transformed. Handles of knives, files, and other tools, as well as fish spears and walking sticks were also often adorned.

"I'll tell you a story on this subject," says Bob. "Back in 1956, one of my men, a fellow about 58 years old, asked to discuss a confidential matter with me. His face was marked by serious concern and sorrow. ' Robert, I've got real problems. I can't make it 10 times a night anymore!' Shocked, I could only stammer: 'Oh really? Hmmmm, that's terrible... ahhh, certainly not normal ... but, ahhh, just keep trying, maybe you're a little tired' I thought to myself: 'My God, what a concern, at age 58!'"

Two years ago, this monument on Muake peak was the source of a lot of nervous tittering and excitement. One of the indefatigably faithful French passengers thought it was highly original to be photographed from all sides with the voluminous status symbol between his wide-spread legs. The women's enthusiasm remained well within the bounds of decency, however. When she saw the nature of the object that was attracting so much attention, Marie-Claire, a somewhat puritanical American, dropped her otherwise always-ready camera with dismay and pivoted, turning her attention to the relatively harmless view of the *Aranui* rolling gently in the harbor below, and deliberately avoiding visual contact with the demonic entity lying in the grass.

In the meantime, we have climbed back up on the trucks and are now back on the road to Taipi. This road, cut through the bush in a swath as wide as our own main roads in the West, seems like a senseless assault on nature. Any government which shares our proud European environmental consciousness must certainly realize how imprudent such projects are. One only hopes that nature will permit the healing of the damage man has inflicted.

Heat, dust, and well-jolted body parts are increasingly taking their toll. A number of photo stops at least provide a chance to grab a cool beer from the drink truck. The concrete bridge spanning the Taipi river is a welcome relief to our rather abused sit-downs. At the same time, this bridge is a part of governmental development projects and looks a bit out of place.

The Taipi river is the biggest and longest of the archipelago, fed by several waterfalls at the western end of the valley. Several years ago, the stream in the high plateau that feeds the most beautiful and biggest of these waterfalls was diverted into a turbine to supply electricity to the valley. Naturally, the river reacted to this diversion. The water level dropped, in many places the stream has dried up, and its bed has become polluted. The time is long past when schools of little neon green fish and big eels played in its deep cool waters, and swimming was a pleasure.

In Taipi village, the group divides: one group wants to visit Pa'eke, the ancient temple with big stone *tiki*, located high on a steep finger ridge, far up the valley. The other group will return to the *Aranui*, by whale boat. I ask some German tourists why they decided to go back to the ship and they respond with a bored air : "Oh God, we've already seen it all!" I wonder about such jaded people: they've gone back and forth all over the world and the Marquesas simply can't touch their hearts.

With Toma, we jolt up-valley on Taipi's washboard "main drag." On the right, Bob points to a wide empty lot where the foundations of a house are still visible. This was the house of the Clark family which we've referred to above, where he and his wife Rae lived in 1957–58. This family then numbered 19 people, including a number of adopted children. Adoption was a matter of course for the Clarks and most other families; when a girl became pregnant, offers were immediately made for adoption. No child ever went unwanted in the Marquesas. These relationships lasted for life: Hu'uveu, the *Aranui* supercargo, was an adopted son of the Clark family and maintains the closest contacts with the entire Clark clan to the present day.

Heiku'a, the lady of the Clark house, called cadence for the whole household. This meant that the day began at 0530 with family prayers, followed by enormous breakfasts of fish, meat, fruits of all types, bread, and Heiku'a's famous Marquesan coffee. This was made by filling a long narrow cloth sack with ground native coffee, and pouring boiling water through the sack. The coffee thus obtained was then poured back through the sack repeatedly, until the resulting brew was like ink. A bowl of this high-octane liquid would be enough to keep anyone working right through until noontime, with the heart thumping away so merrily that there would be no thought of fatigue.

In the Clark house, everyone, right down to the smallest child, got their chores to do. Everyone except Charley, the husband, a Tahitian of American whaler ancestry. He sat in regal splendor before the house, his only job being that of overseer of Heiku'a's rather vast holdings in the valley. Once a tourist, noting his demeanor, asked him if he were the chief of the valley: "No, I'm not the chief; I'm just the owner!"

We leave the autos and begin a short hike through a palm grove, then up a steep zigzag path leading to Pa'eke. We intentionally set a fast pace in order to be the first on the site and thus be able to shoot the *tiki* without other tourists milling about. The rest of the group follows along behind, huffing and puffing. Once everyone's there, Bob and Sylvie begin the explanation of the site: he speaks English and she translates in French and German. It's great to listen to the two of them; the close harmony that exists between them can be seen and felt. We listen attentively to the interpretation of these ruins and the silent, staring statues, while the last rays of afternoon sun wrap the site in a diffuse light making the scene seem all the more mysterious.

This temple is a kind of pantheon for the gods of the 11 Taipi sub-tribes or clans. It was still considered *tapu* into the early 20th century. In 1813, Porter was told that 3,500 warriors, i.e., men between the ages of roughly 18 to 40, were living in Taipi. This squares with the legends of a total valley population of 10,000 at its peak in the late 18th century. Today only about 200 people live here and the *tiki* keep watch over them for eternity.

Each visit to this site is a strange, unfathomable experience. The Marquesans call such places *vahi mana*, sites with supernatural power. We find ourselves between rows of moss- and lichen-covered *tiki* whose expressionless faces gaze out over the broad valley. Lizards dart about over the heedless figures. Phaeton birds float silently, in wide circles above the valley. Were the *tiki* always here? No one can say with any certainty. It's possible that they were brought here after the collapse of the culture, merely in order to protect them. It's further possible that Pa'eke was a cult site that was first built only in the 18th century. In any event, old photos show that the site has been restored several times in the last century. The names of several of the *tiki* seem to indicate clear connections with tribal groups or clans such as: "God of the Shadow People" (a two headed *tiki*), "The House of

Pandanus", "The House of the *Ti* Plants." On the other hand, names such as "The Void" or the "Red Earth" are a bit harder to explain. We examine the two-headed figure, which is in fact female. It probably belonged to a clan or sub-tribe which occupied the area close to the beach. American naval officers visiting Taipi in 1825 noted a two-headed idol on a temple site near the shore. It's an interesting question whether there's a connection between this double-headed *tiki* and the famous double-headed poi-pounders of these islands. No one knows at present, and for the archeologists it remains an unsolved riddle.

So much for the explanation of the site, which toward the end was accompanied by the unmistakable humming of video cameras. The all-powerful photographer's soul will always force it's way to the surface, but it's quite understandable that people try to capture this most emotionally charged atmosphere on tape. That Eveleyn stands before the temple and shows no intentions of disappearing drives Mr. Bean to despair. His: "*Allez, vas t'en, retires toi* !" (Hey, let's go, back off!) fades away unnoticed. Without achieving his goal, he finally abandons, in a great huff, the photographer's vantage point to which he climbed with so much effort.

The mystical mood still clings to us on the return to the autos. We literally stroll along, taking so much time that the only place left for us is on the edge of the truck bed. Luckily Toma halts about halfway to the beach to carry us off to his snack bar, which he proudly declares he personally built. The limited selection, consisting only of a few cans of Coke and 7-Up, is more than made up for by the presence of his beautiful wife, who causes the gentlemen passengers to forget the slim menu. As is often the case, her father worked for Bob, back in "the old days."

And then, for the last time today, we're off again on dusty, bumpy roads, holding tightly as we bounce repeatedly into the air. Everyone has had enough; the sight of the waiting whaleboat is comforting, although the sandy mud through which we wade is less so. Because it's the last boat, the sailors make short work of packing us in. Bob, the last man in the boat, is bundled aboard by Tino, who puts him on the gunnels, where he presents a rather pitiful sight with one leg dangling in the water astern and the other leg and arms drawn up under him in awkward positions. Any lasting damage is avoided, but only because the trip is short and because the sharks who inhabit the bay apparently have other things to distract their attentions at the moment. At the end, everyone is longing for a refreshing shower, to remove the reddish gritty dust of many kilometers of Nuku Hiva roads which now covers us all.

This evening at table we present a very colorful mixture of languages, during which a tiny French woman and Frau Helvetia duel for the loudness prize. Tired of the racket, we steal away into the salon and then to the lee side of the ship, where we can follow the *Aranui*'s departure for Hiva Oa in a more peaceful atmosphere.

Hiva Oa: Atuona Valley

This morning my gymnastic session on deck is especially re-freshing due to a fantastic sunrise. The decision to begin the session early seems to have been quite wise, because the photographers are already crowding the rails. They don't want to miss our entrance into Traitor's Bay, on the south coast of Hiva Oa. At 0700 the *Aranui* comes alongside the pier in Taha'uku, the harbor of Atuona. Opposite the bay, the outline of Tahuata, the island of the Spanish "discovery," can be seen in the rays of the morning sun. On the port side, the sharp peak of Mt. Te Metiu thrusts itself 1276 meters into the heavens, its tip shrouded in its famous garland of clouds.

Hiva Oa is one of the younger islands in the archipelago. On a map, it resembles a huge sea-horse whose head faces the sunrise. The mountain chain running the length of the island, from southwest to northeast, attains heights of between 800 and 900 meters, with three peaks surpassing 1100 meters. Toward the east, the crest of the island slopes downward a bit, plunging into the sea at Cape Matafenua. With Nuku Hiva, Hiva Oa is the only Marquesan island to have an interior central plateau. The clouds hanging low above the highest peaks supply enough water to the many streams to make this island a flowery oasis.

After breakfast, Te Ui'a, the son of the seriously ill Madame Pélagie Clark, is waiting to bring us to her. Mme. Clark suffered a stroke which has left her hemiplegic and forever confined to her bed. Once known for her beauty, and admired as a dancer and teacher of Marquesan traditions and lore, she was also famed as an expert in Marquesan medicine. Her intellectual powers helped her to attain the highest respect throughout the islands. Beloved by everyone, she was nonetheless branded as somewhat of a backslider by the church, where her illness was seen as

the appropriate punishment for her supposedly heretical activities.

A bumpy ride of about 10 minutes brings us to the Clark house, which stands in the midst of a colorful proliferation of flowering plants. Chickens and dogs bustle about among the shrubs and bushes in unusually good fellowship.

We cross a verandah into an airy room. White curtains move gently in the breeze. The room is lovingly decorated: knick-knacks adorn wall shelves; pictures and photos decorate the walls. A closet of *temanu* wood with carved doors dominates the back wall; it's the master work of Mr. Clark who won a prize with this piece in a furniture exhibition. Two comfortable rattan chairs

92

and a small matching table complete the furnishings. The floor is covered with light beige and brown speckled tiles, lending an additional element of comfortable coolness and cleanliness to the room.

Pélagie lies on a hospital bed, beneath snow-white sheets which remind one of the old white Marquesan *tapa* barkcloth, formerly signifying a person of *tapu* rank. Her eyes are closed, her face is gaunt. The once thick curly hair is now thin and in strands. Her powerfully-built but gentle husband sits quietly, like a guardian, almost motionless at the foot of the bed. He sees us and arises without a word, extending his hand to us. His deep kindly eyes speak far more than words: they tell us how pleased he is over our visit.

"Robert, Robert!" Pélagie's thin arms reach out toward Bob. Tears flood down her wrinkled cheeks. He leans over her and embraces her with great feeling. They alone understand the words which are exchanged in this embrace; but we all feel, in a most moving fashion, the depth of the friendship which binds these two people together.

I accept with gratitude the chair which is offered to me and sit down beside the bed. Pélagie is now calm; she holds Bob's hands, asks about our trip, and is quite eager to learn all the details. After a while, Te Ui'a leaves us, but we stay on.

The gentle voices, the delicate perfume of the *tiare* gardenias that wafts through the room, the all-pervasive calm, all lull me into sleepiness. Most of all, I'd just like to close my eyes, to lose myself completely in this state of complete peace of mind. How much time I spent in this condition I don't know, but I do know how difficult it is to return to the present and to remind myself of the days' program that we have set before us.

The parting brings great pain, but I also have a sense of deep gratitude for the opportunity to meet this unusual woman. For a long time we go on in silence until Bob begins to tell me how Pélagie once helped him with her clairvoyant powers. He was in

Taioha'e, with a nasty intestinal infection, a high fever, and no medicine. In the evening the phone rang: it was Hu'uveu, calling from Tahiti. With urgency in his voice, he stated: "Ropea, the Old Lady (Pélagie) called me and told me that you were sick and needed a special medicine."

"Which Old Lady?" asked Bob not sure as to what was going on. The response was quick: "Oh, you know, the one on Hiva Oa. You've got to take the medicine exactly as I tell you, and don't make any mistakes, you hear?" Hu'uveu had never used this tone with Bob before. He proceeded to explain to Bob how the medicine was to be used and told Bob that his daughter, then living in Taioha'e, would arrive at Bob's place, at 1730 sharp, with the first dose. And true to her father's words, the young girl appeared precisely on schedule! That was even more of a surprise, because "Punctuality" in Polynesia is a rather elastic concept, meaning anything from hours, to days, weeks, or even months of delay.

For the next two evenings, Bob obediently continued treatments with the medicine which Hu'uveu's daughter always delivered, precisely on time! His condition improved markedly and a few days later he was able to continue to Tahiti, where he once again stayed with Hu'uveu. One of Bob's first questions was: "Hu'uveu, how did Pélagie know what kind of illness I had?" "She saw it," came the matter-of-fact response. Bob bored in: "What do you mean by 'saw'?" Hu'uveu looked at Bob as though he was more than just a bit slow in the head: "She sees, you know, she *sees* for everyone, and when she can't help them, she sends them to the French doctor." "Oh, *Ua hei, Ua hei* (OK, OK)" Finally Bob understood how Pélagie had "diagnosed" his problem and had taken it upon herself to organize his treatment by telephone. When he detailed the illness and the medicine to his doctor in the US, the doctor admitted, without a trace of professional jealousy, that Pélagie had cleverly diagnosed and effectively treated this illness, at quite a long range!

À propos M. Paul Gauguin

Hiva Oa is, above all, known as Paul Gauguin's last island. His paintings of the South Seas belong to the classics of the Post-Impressionist period, and grace the most famous art museums and collections of the world. As a man, however, he was certainly not an endearing figure, but more of a bluffer and opportunist with a tendency toward provocation and polemics. "He craved adulation and would sacrifice anything, do anything, to become the lion of the hour." Such was the verdict of the American art historians Wingert, Upjohn, and Mahler, regarding Gauguin's behavior in Tahiti and the Marquesas. After a careful reading of his books "Noa Noa" and "Avant et Après," as well as his correspondence, we most emphatically concur in that judgment.

Most of Gauguin's best-known South Sea canvasses were done during two long residences in Tahiti. Some of these scenes were not done from life: postcards or photos served as his models. His book, "Noa Noa," the supposedly autobiographical account of his life in Tahiti, contains a long text which Gauguin claimed to have copied from an old manuscript in the possession of a girlfriend's family. The text was actually plagiarized from a book published in 1837, by J. A. Moerenhout, a Frenchman serving as a counsul in Tahiti.

In his letters and books, Gauguin loved to refer to himself as a "savage" who sought the company of other savages, but strangely enough, he avoided contacts with real savagery, which was readily available in Africa or the tropical forests of South America, choosing instead to remain in close contact with Europe his entire life, pursuing the discussions of the day about artistic theory and technique, and raging over his artistic detractors, something a savage would have never done. He was understandably much concerned about money as well. This "petty bourgeois savage" spoke neither Tahitian nor Marquesan and had little interest for the art of the islands: his pictures fail to reflect any elements of native art styles.

In 1901, at the end of his second stay in Tahiti, Gauguin decided to relocate to the Marquesas. First, as a "savage," he wrote that he wanted to reside on Fatu Iva because, as he claimed, there were still cannibals there. This claim was no longer true but may have impressed some people. Instead of Fatu Iva, he settled instead in Atuona, Hiva Oa, the seat of the ecclesiastical and colonial in the midst of the European colonialist milieu which he professed to hate. This settlement apparently offered the "savage" a far more comfortable life.

At the outset, he politely ingratiated himself with the Bishop and the civil officials, passing himself off as a solid conservative French Catholic. At that time, only the mission disposed of cheap land for house construction, and he needed to beguile the missionaries to acquire the desired real estate. His plan worked: the Catholic mission rented him a piece of land in the narrow valley of Atuona, under the shadow of the giant green Te Metiu, the Matterhorn of the Marquesas, where he built his "House of Pleasure." There he spent his last years, accompanied by a series of women, the last of which was supposedly the 14-year old Vae'oho.

Scarcely was the house finished, however, than Gauguin turned on the church. And not against the church alone, but against the colonial administration and police as well. This was not a smart move in the "Spain of Polynesia!" He posed as an anarchist and brave defender of the Marquesans; a fearless hero, locked in endless conflict with the colonial functionaries, the bishop, and the gendarmes. Once again, Gauguin wanted to be "the lion of the day," but this goal completely eluded him. The French colonists saw him as a nuisance and for the Marquesans, "Koke" (his name in Marquesan) was just another crazy whiteman. They had already met a few.

He stopped painting almost completely, led an increasingly licentious life and became addicted to alcohol and drugs (recent excavations in the immediate vicinity of his old house site brought to light a dazzling collection of broken wine, liquor, and drug bottles). He danced away many nights with his friends in the House of Pleasure. "I need everything. I can't have it, but I still want it. Just let me get my breath and when I've recovered, I'll shout out: fill the glass, fill it, pour it out again! To run until I'm out of breath and die raving. Wisdom ... you bore me, make me yawn unceasingly." So spoke "Koke," and wisdom made room for his overwhelming boredom.

During his stay in 1956, Bob learned a bit about Gauguin's life in Atuona. One of the painter's daughters was still alive, and he spoke with several older people who had known Gauguin during their childhood. An older Marquesan recalled that during the Sunday Mass Gauguin and some of his girlfriends would sometimes pull up in a wagon before the church. When the congregation streamed out of the portals, they began provocative sexual displays.

On 8 May, 1903, Paul Gauguin died, alone and ill in his House of Pleasure. It's said that he died from an overdose of drugs and / or alcohol but it could have been from any number of causes, including suppurating infections on his legs and body. Corpses decompose rapidly in the tropics but Gauguin decomposed more rapidly than most, so the church and the administration rushed to put this unlovable rebel under the ground forever. After his death, the House of Pleasure reverted to the church. Inside, church authorities encountered a mural of Gauguin's enemy, the bishop, en flagrante, with the housemaid of the Residence. Mgr. Tirilly, who was bishop in 1956, thought that the portrait was apparently a good likeness of his predecessor. That is surprising, because Gauguin rarely painted portraits. "If someone had been able to sell the painting, then the mission could have realized a tidy sum, but what could we do?" the bishop said, raising his hands in resignation. "We had to burn down the house."

A chair from Gauguin's "House of Pleasure" also ended up in the Residence in Atuona. It was stuck away in a corner somewhere. Years went by and no one remembered which chair had come from the painter's house. This was unfortunate, because otherwise it would certainly have been enshrined, if not converted into francs. Sic transit gloria mundi.

Gauguin lies in the cemetery, high up on a ridge above the village, his grave covered with vesicular basalt stones. Next to it, stands a statue of one of his sculptures, entitled "Oviri." In typically romantic overstatement, this statue has been often eronneously described as the "Polynesian goddess of death". In the Polynesian cultures there was no such thing as a death goddess: *Oviri* is a Tahitian word meaning "Wild One," which nicely expresses the artist's ideal conception of a woman: "I love women when they're round and wicked," he wrote, "but it bothers me when they're intelligent, the kind of intelligence that's too clever for me. I've always wished for a fat mistress and never found one. It's funny, but they're all too flat for me."

The grave is in the shade of a big *tipanie* (*frangipani*) tree, the blossoms of which are known as the flowers of the dead in the Marquesas. This morning, a fresh branch of red bougainvillea adorns the grave. And here's another final twist to the Gauguin story: it's not certain that this is really Gauguin's grave! Since the painter had left the bosom of the Church, he was buried just outside the hallowed ground of the Catholic cemetery. Only in the 1920s did the French administrator, Doctor Louis Rollin, begin to seek the grave. Bob met Rollin in Tahiti in 1956. The Doctor described how he found the grave outside the cemetery limits, but how Rollin identified the skeleton remained unclear. Protestants, assorted sailors, soldiers, and miscellaneous foreigners were buried outside hallowed ground; further, there was no information available on the dentition of the painter and DNA analysis was still unknown. A new debate is now going on as to whether Gauguin was interred in Atuona's red earth with Protestant or Catholic rites. What possible difference would that make for the man whose canvasses today bring millions?

In close proximity to Gauguin's grave is that of the Belgian singer Jacques Brel. The tombstone is decorated with a sculpture of the singer and his lover. Brel was quite famous and highly regarded in the Marquesas. A real individualist with significant financial resources, he had many admirers in the islands, not the least because he employed his twin-engined aircraft for the benefit of all the Marquesans, making emergency runs and carrying mail. One of Brel's last compositions is entitled: "The Marquesas," it's a strange composition, which nevertheless manages to capture the many contrasts of this enigmatic culture.

The lives of two talented Europeans came to their respective conclusions here. Did they simply burn themselves out in the Marquesas? For Gauguin, the Marquesas was only the last stop on an increasingly sad *journey, an ever-tightening death spiral. In his letters, he always expressed the desire to find a paradise with hot women and free food, where he could live as a "lord," without the obligations of the European lifestyle, but paradoxically in close contact with it, and enjoying all it's privileges. He never found his paradise: it does not exist.*

Before Gauguin's restored "House of Pleasure," which is not too far away from the site where the original house stood, Brel's Beechcraft aircraft, "Jojo," rusts in the tropic humidity. It's regrettable that there are no originals of Gauguin's masterpieces in the adjoining museum gallery. The walls are adorned by copies done by a charming Frenchman who spent some time in a French prison for his Gauguin counterfeits. French police apparently identified these counterfeits without much difficulty. The same counterfeits, now sold as "copies," are a lucrative source of income for him today, as are his published memoirs, available at the museum.

Arriving at the Museum yard before the rest of the group, we encounter a contingent of Marquesan women who are spreading out their souvenir wares. *Pareu*, pandanus hats, shell necklaces and ornaments, and flower *hei* (wreaths) are all neatly set out for the *Aranui*. visitors. Bob draws them into conversation; the initial distance disappears, and they begin to laugh and joke with him. I learn that they are joking about the tourists and imitating their behavior. The Marquesans are keen observers of all human behavior, with a very good eye for idiosyncrasies! Not long after, however, the first tourists arrive and a metamorphosis overtakes the Marquesan ladies: professional charm takes the upper hand, white teeth sparkle from humble laughing faces, their *pareu* are absolutely tight-fitting and revealing! Suddenly, they're in business!

In the Museum next to Gauguin's house, there is an interesting exhibit of archeological artifacts including adze blades, stone poi-pounders for the preparation of the "Marquesan staff of life" and mother-of-pearl fishhooks. Unfortunately, there are no labels, so it's impossible to know when or where these artifacts were found, and how old they might be. There are many types of stone adzes which were used for specific tasks in woodworking and stone sculpture. A one-shouldered stone adze blade awakens Bob's interest. I learn that this type of adze is well known from excavations on remote Pitcairn Island. This obviously raises the question: what were the early relationships between Pitcairn and Hiva Oa? Was Pitcairn settled from Hiva Oa, was there a trade in adzes going on between Pitcairn and Hiva Oa in prehistoric times? Pitcairn had fine-grained basalt deposits, excellent for making adzes, but so did the Marquesas. A lot more work is needed on both islands before these questions can be answered.

It's no exaggeration to designate Atuona as a Garden of Eden. The magnificent banks of flowers lining the roads and decorating the yards and gardens surely rank among the most beautiful and exotic displays that nature can offer. The flamboyant trees, with their flame-red blooms inspire me once again. The wish to embrace this beautiful riot of color with wide open arms and to take it all home with me is overwhelming.

Here, as everywhere, we meet people who greet us cordially. As we go along, Bob shows me the house in which he lived in 1956. Just across the street, there's a vacant lot which is the actual site on which Gauguin's oft-cited House of Pleasure once stood. As we stroll along, each new vista prompts a stream of anecdotes and tales of earlier times, flowing into each other without interruption.

It's becoming quite warm and a snackbar sign appears to be heaven-sent. But, as always, where there's lots of light, there's also lots of shadow. The ice-cold lemonade can't be excelled for taste, but there's unbearably loud Rock music in the snackbar, playing for the benefit of a bunch of lounging Atuona teens.

The cacophony soon drives us out again from the shady back yard into the noonday heat.

I get a sudden yearning, and ask: "Is there honey in the Marquesas?" "Certainly," Bob says, "and it's very tasty, too!" I suggest that we get some honey and at the same time find some shade in a store. The heat is becoming quite oppressive.

In the tiny "business district" of Atuona we come across not only Hu'uvcu, but a jar of the much sought after dark brown Marquesan honey, sitting on shelves amidst a jumble of merchandise. TV sets, toilet seats, baby nipples, underwear, and sanitary napkins, light bulbs, household articles, and clothing, are stacked around patent medicines, small ice boxes, eyeglasses, cosmetics, and canned foods. At the cash register, we are overcome by the tempting aroma of fresh pastries on display there: these are the tasty *pain chocolat*, a light and flakey pastry shell filled with chocolate. The temptation is not to be denied, and with delight, and sticky fingers, we consume one of the oven-warm delicacies, right on the spot.

At noon we're to meet the party in the Hoa Nui Restaurant. With a crumpled-up map, we start off on our search, but are distracted almost immediately in front of a strikingly well-groomed house and yard which rivets our attention with its symmetrically arranged oval windows, surrounded by tastefully planted flowers and trees, all combining to make the whole structure seem as though it had been lifted out of a fairy tale.

"And who owns this jewel?"

"Oh it's belongs to Te Ui'a, you know, Pélagie's son. He's a road builder in Hiva Oa."

At a closer look, I see two rather well-concealed backhoes and other construction equipment.

"Did that all come here on the *Aranui*?"

"Everything that you see here, the machines, the materials for the house; everything came on the *Aranui*; everything except the flowers."

101

When we arrive at the Hoa Nui, Uschi and Karl beckon us to join them. The coolness of the verandah effects us like bubbly champagne and the ensuing lively discussion with this couple is a real treat.

Slowly, all the passengers wander in, including the chubby little Frenchman, stewing in his own juices, his inseparable video camera firmly fixed on his round naked tummy. His pouting mouth droops a bit more than usual, his gait is a bit more draggy. His long-suffering wife, who arrived before him, doesn't even give him a second look: their well-advertised marital problem must have escalated on the streets of Atuona. He searches out a place quite far from her and she lets him go.

The buffet opens with an explanation of the dishes, and this time we're assured that there's a lobster for everyone. This is quite important to avoid a battle at the buffet table. Last trip, you see, the desire for lobster overcame all bounds of good manners, and those who came away from the table empty were quite angry; they included, for example, the Frenchman who graced me with the growl of: "Merde!" because by oversight I wound up in the wrong line and somehow cut him off from the lobsters. But all I wanted was some rice! Greedy guts didn't understand: I don't like lobsters at all!

We belong to the happy few who refuse the proffered delicacy. Bob wound up in the Taioha'e hospital a few years ago after eating lobster. When he began to feel a bit better, he found the hospital atmosphere quite remarkable, with lizards skittering around the ceilings and walls inside, while outside chickens cackled and loose dogs passed the time away barking. Attractive French nurses clad in T-shirts and short bike pants, discharged their duties with great charm. In the evening, Marquesan friends arrived with their families: "We heard that you were here, so we brought you something to eat!" "God bless you all!" But the pamplemousse and coconuts didn't fit too well with his prescribed diet or his ravaged stomach.

Was it a good idea to head back to the *Aranui* on foot after lunch? Two stories made the trip a lot more interesting than expected. "Makemake" seemed like a somewhat unusual name for a snack bar. I ask: "Does that mean something?" "Sure does" comes the reply, "it's the name of the high god of Easter Island!" Bob explains that according to Heyerdahl's fantasies, this name was of Peruvian origin and appeared nowhere else in Polynesia. This claim was torpedoed by the German ethnologist-philologist, Dr. Horst Cain, of the Ethnographic Museum in Berlin. Cain's expertise in Austronesian languages led him to a diametrically opposite conclusion after his own research on Hiva Oa. He found that Makemake is definitely a Polynesian name, and is actually Marquesan in origin, once belonging to a god from Nuku Hiva, as well as to an important deified ancestor from Atuona. In the remote past, a small side valley in Atuona was named in honor of this ancestor, and the snackbar stands in this valley.

Makemake from Hiva Oa was the ancestor of chief Hotu Matu'a, who discovered Easter Island, according to legend. Cain believes that Hotu Matu'a started out on his voyage of discovery from Hiva Oa, referred to as "Hiva," in the Hotu Matu'a epic, and ultimately came to Easter Island. Cain's thesis is further buttressed by the fact that the same name appears for gods in Tubuai in the Austral Islands, as well as on some of the Tuamotus. He concludes that these islands were also settled by Marquesans on their voyages of discovery toward the south.

We go around the point to Taha'uku where the ship is tied up. "See that crooked old house up there?" asks Bob "that was once the home of an English scientist whom we called him Lord Jim. A sad story!" Bob relates that Jim had fallen head over heels in love with a Marquesan woman, and wanted to marry her on the spot. His main problem was one of simple communication: he couldn't speak a word of either French or Marquesan and his intended didn't know any English! So he asked if Bob would make a marriage proposal on his behalf. Bob initially refused, it would have been too embarassing for him. But Lord Jim was in torment, and he kept on pleading for Bob's help. Bob finally gave in, and on the shores of Taha'uku Bay he played matchmaker, telling the truly beautiful girl of Lord Jim's love and his desire to marry her. The mutual embarassment was enormous. The lovely girl cried, declaring that she couldn't possibly love Lord Jim. That hit Jim really hard, but he still didn't give up. Having seen how this proposal thing was done, he kept repeating his love, until the girl fled to Tahiti. Only a short while later, Lord Jim also left with a broken heart, never to return to the Marquesas. In fact, he simply disappeared. Since that time, the crooked house over Taha'uku Bay has been uninhabited.

Dog-tired and sweat-soaked, we finally make it back to the *Aranui*. Even the combined charms of Bob and Te Ui'a are not enough to move me to inspect the Hanake'e Pearl Cottages Hotel property, high on the ridge overlooking the bay. The desire for a good shower and some reading on deck easily wins out. I'll later regret this decision because a trip to Ta'a'oa was planned, following the visit to Hana Ke'e. In Ta'a'oa, Hu'uveu has his vacation house, in what I'm assured is the most beautiful and most peaceful valley of the entire Marquesas archipelago. Ta'a'oa has many archeological sites, including the ruins of an enormous ceremonial complex, the largest in the islands. One also encounters many unusual birds among the valley's unusual hardwood forests. Ta'a'oa has another interesting if slightly disturbing feature. On land and under the sea, volcanic sulfur hydroxide gas leaks forth from deep in the earth's mantle, lending an often perceptible taint of rotten eggs to the scent of gardenias and frangipani. You see, after 3 million years, Pele still occasionally rolls over in her sleep. West of Ta'a'oa, the island is now uninhabited, but in earlier times, many tribes made their homes there and there's also plenty there to occupy archeologists.

Since noontime, Margitta has been on deck, inconsolably mourning her sunglasses, which were lost in the surf. She doesn't brighten up, not even when I remind her of the story of the "the neon strip light." On my first trip, she led me one night to the C-Deck, where the big dormitory compartment with its bunk beds is located. Because her bunk strip light had given up the ghost in the evening, the tube belonging to her neighbor, Funés, suddenly became a very tempting target for her the next morning. The swap (or theft!) seemed to be taking place smoothly, until Funés unexpectedly reappeared on the scene of the infamous deed. Frightened, Margitta threw the coveted object back onto the bed where it rightfully belonged, and tore her own bed curtains in so doing. Complete chaos reigned, but Funés, ever the gentleman, handled everything quite well. He comforted Margitta, put the curtain back on its track, and mounted his own strip light over her bed. There was great mutual rejoicing over the functioning bed light. That Funés' own tube went out that evening disturbed him no end. Mumbling, he crept to his bed in the darkness while, next to him, Margitta read on and on, in total comfort.

The afternoon comes to an end and Yoyo's "Miracle Cocktail" very nicely facilitates the smooth transition from a stressful day to a most relaxing evening. Once more, the sun plays its games of light and shadow on the lush soft shoreline to the west, where Ta'a'oa Valley blends into the gathering darkness. At 1900, we leave Hiva Oa on course for Fatu Iva, where the *Aranui* arrives at 2300, dropping anchor off O'omoa. A glittering star-filled canopy spans the heavens, the sea gleams as though sprinkled with silver. It's very difficult to wrench myself away from this spectacle.

Fatu Iva: O'omoa and Hanavave Valleys

Fatu Iva is the most isolated and southernmost island of the Marquesas chain, and for many people the most beautiful and wildest, with its spectacular terrain. It is not only the unusual panorama, or the sure-footed wild goats wandering on the precipitous moutainsides which make this island so unusual, but the deep green of the forests which extend over lush valley walls and narrow ravines right to the edges of the almost vertical sea cliffs. With its dangerous-looking shore, Fatu Iva appears as a fortress, a black-walled green castle in the middle of the Pacific.

At present about 500 inhabitants live on this island. They are divided between the valleys of O'omoa and Hanavave. A century ago, when Karl von Steinen visited the islands, six valleys were still inhabited by the survivors of the nine tribes which had once settled the island. The geologically youngest of all the Marquesas, Fatu Iva arose from a volcanic cone which exploded about one million years ago. Today, the island is composed of about a quarter of the ancient cone and a portion of the caldera bottom.

Over the years, many legends and much speculation have been woven around the name "Fatu Iva." French and English mariners recorded the island's name as Fatu Hiva, but today there's good reason to believe that this is incorrect, and possibly attributable to a lack of knowledge of the Marquesan language, or to an early poor transcription of the name. Both French and early English-speaking visitors had problems hearing and pronouncing initial "h" sounds. Although they often dropped them out completely, they also sometimes added an "h" where one should have never been.

In the Polynesian languages, a single word can have many different meanings and one must go on context. *Fatu,* for ex-

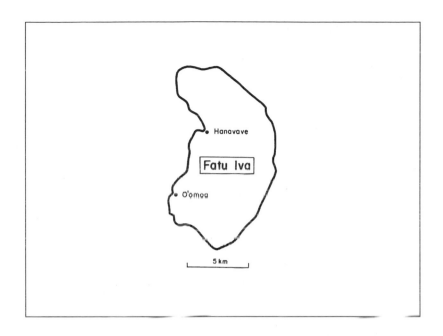

ample, can mean lord or god, but also family or clan, rank or file of soldiers, stick of roof thatch, peak, or as a verb, to tie up, or to double. *Hiva* means side of the valley, dark, roof peak or ridge pole; but *iva* is the number "9".

So what does Fatu Iva or Hiva mean? A relatively new interpretation sees the origin of the name in a legend, according to which the god Atea built his house over the entire archipelago, and each island was a part of the house. For example, Ua Pou formed the two house posts *('ua pou)* for the god's roof; Nuku Hiva was the rear slope *(nuku)* of the roof *(hiva)*, Hiva Oa was the long *('oa)* ridgepole *(hiva)*, and Fatu Iva was the ninth or last layer of leaf thatch *(fatu)* on the roof covering the house.

This legend is quite popular in the modern Marquesans, but is sadly of rather doubtful authenticity. It was reported by the American linguist Sam Elbert, who was not exactly an authority on the Marquesan language and was the only one who ever heard this legend. Karl von den Steinen diligently collected Marquesan legends, but never mentioned anything even remotely similar to the Elbert legend. It's likely that the words: "Fatu Iva" do not refer to the ninth row of thatch on Atea's house but refer to the nine peaks on the island's crest or to the original nine clans which settled the island. In fact, the name could also refer to the nine bands of warriors which these clans could put in the field.

The island has also become widely known through Thor Heyerdahl's book: "Fatu Hiva — Back to Nature." He describes his not totally happy attempt to live a life in a paradise of primitive simplicity. In this effort to achieve harmony with nature, free from all the pressures of the world, the Heyerdahls soon became ill, because in their Fatu Iva "Elysium" the "back to nature" drill got out of control. Wandering around scantily clothed and dining on plants and herbs proved to be less advantageous on a long-term basis than plain sensible living, the way the Marquesans themselves do it. It didn't take long for the first traces of vitamin deficiency to appear, and the pair had to be rescued by the missionaries.

From a priest who was involved in the rescue, it was learned that the brave adventurers were in rather depleted condition. The good Father Victorin, later Bishop of the Marquesas, was still a bit astounded, some 18 years later, to reflect on the couples *naiveté* when he asked rhetorically: "How can any one live half-naked in the forest, without eating sensible foods, and still expect to survive? They were malnourished and covered with insect bites!"

Even the most casual visitor only has to look at the Marquesans themselves: to live as they do is hard work! An unremitting grind of fishing, hunting, gardening, cutting copra, as well as maintaining canoes, houses, and tools, is certainly no one's idea of a tropical bourgeois idyll. Heyerdahl himself seeks to blame the failure of this experiment less on himself than on the evil spirits that made their lives difficult, which is an amusing but typically dubious claim. Maybe a few of those evil spirits were only young Marquesans lurking in the brush, who would certainly have enjoyed a look at a semi-clothed European female. Who would find their behavior unusual?

At 5 AM, the *Aranui* is already vibrating with frenzied activity coming from a little market which has been set up in the salon and the reception area. Fatu Iva women, mostly from Hananave, always come aboard to sell *tapa*, *pareu* wrap-arounds, and woodcarving. Karl von den Steinen deserves a debt of gratitude that these old Marquesan arts motifs have been preserved. If he hadn't recorded the motifs used in tattoo and carving in such painstaking detail, nothing would remain of the old art style. Right to the present day, his pen and ink drawings serve as models for the hard-working *tapa* makers of Fatu Iva.

The business practices of these ladies have changed considerably the last few years. In the beginning, the ladies of Hanavave greeted the passengers with their famous distant adversarial posture; their faint sneers sending a very clear message: "I'm here to sell: if you don't want to pay my price, then go to hell!" Here and there, hesitant customers were cursed or insulted (always in Marquesan). Which is better? Is it really an improvement when the ladies try to "con" their customers, as they do today?

Not too long ago, several men managed to break through the female phalanx; they're quite friendly and sell their *tiki* and bowls. The nicely carved masks which they offer, however, reflect the art traditions of Africa or New Guinea and really have nothing to do with Marquesan traditions!

A sweet voice asks: "Would you like to purchase something? C'mere, I'll help you!" I'm almost drawn into an effort to expand my collection of Marquesan curiosities, but Hu'uveu hands me a lovely piece of *tapa* cloth imprinted with a turtle; it's an especially beautiful piece of work and I leave the bazaar with all my wishes fulfilled.

The turtle is accorded an important place in Marquesan traditions. In their voyages of exploration, the early Polynesians followed turtles, knowing that these would lead them to ideal beaches, where turtles laid their eggs. These fascinating animals also are believed to guide Marquesans in the other direction, leading the canoes of dead souls westward, back to Hawaiki, because only the turtles know the course. Yes, turtles were also slain from time to time, to obtain their shells to make ornately carved crowns, but their importance is shown to best advantage when one reflects that they were also sacrificial victims with the same value as human sacrifices.

We leave the ship on the first whale boat, just to have enough time to become better acquainted with O'omoa. Left and right along the village street, we see nicely decorated houses, one of which, far back from the road, belongs to the Grellet family. It's the place where Bob was invited for a shower, on his first day on Marquesan soil. The Post Office and the mayor's office are close by. Officially one speaks of the Mayor, but for the Marquesans the term is still "chief" *(haka'iki)* even though the chiefs are no longer hereditary but elected.

Our way leads us to a community center where a *tapa* demonstration is being held. In place of a speech, for once only a culinary welcome awaits us. A long table has been covered with an amber-colored *tapa* cloth, tastefully decorated with traditional tattoo motifs. The table sags under an array of colored glass plates on which slices of papaya, pamplemousse, melon, banana, mango, and coconut meat make an appetizing and colorful rendezvous spot. Wide-leafed lilies, hibiscus flowers in red and delicate yellow, and fresh-cut pineapple slices complete the stylish arrangement, which is really far too beautiful to be devoured by our hungry crew.

In a shady corner of the house, a friendly Marquesan woman takes her place to begin the *tapa* demonstration. Her toothless mouth and the many folds that crease her expressive face indicate an advanced age. Nonetheless, her ability to make *tapa* from the bark of the paper mulberry, breadfruit, or banyan trees is really astounding. She uses the soft inner layer of bark, which she strips out, soaks in water, and then beats with a long grooved beater of ironwood, to ultimately produce a fabric in much the same way as felt is produced. This fabric is painted with black pigment, produced in the old way from the soot of burned candle nuts or coco shells, mixed with coconut oil. A bundle of hair serves as a brush.

Traditionally, Marquesan *tapa* cloth was never decorated with painted designs unlike tapa from Hawai'i and Western Polynesia. It was allowed to retain its natural color or was soaked in turmeric, to dye the entire cloth. The only decoration was a kind of water mark, the pattern left by the grooves in the *tapa* beater. In excavations in dry guano caves on the west coast of Nuku Hiva, Bob found a piece of a white *tapa* loincloth which dated back to 1250 AD. This material was very soft and looked surprisingly new, and the parallel lines of the wooden beater could still clearly seen. Such water-mark decoration was also used among the Proto-Austronesians before they left the Asian mainland nearly 7000 years ago. Stone beaters with similar parallel lines have been found in ancestral Austronesian archeological sites in China.

The hikers who have decided to take the mountain jaunt from O'omoa to Hanavave, leave us and head off on their journey. This time, only eight people set out on the 16 km march. Obviously, a lot of good intentions went overboard during the night. The stories of heart attacks, heat, thirst, and aching muscles, have obviously had a chilling effect on not-so-youthful enthusiasm.

There have been several accidents on these hikes, but all of them can be attributed to three causes: carelessness, false pride, and people's tendencies to over-estimate their own abilities. The tour is not recommended for those who are overweight or suffering from heart disease, but it's definitely worth the effort for people in average good health.

We head off toward the Museum in the two-story Grellet house. "No, Oh no! She's got it all wrong!" murmurs Bob, disturbed by the museum narrative of one of the ship's hostesses, who is putting out some highly inaccurate information. "Come on with me," he says, "I'll show you what's really genuine and what's tourist art!" And so I have the pleasure of a special guided tour through the house of the Swiss family Grellet, and many passengers join us.

François Grellet, the founder of the family, came to Fatu Iva in the late 19th century and married one (or several!) Marquesan women. In the first volume of Karl von den Steinen's Marquesan art study, there's a photo of him, regally enthroned and attended by Marquesans. A glass of coco toddy firmly clasped in his hand, he stares off into the distance in deep contemplation.

Grellet had already begun his collection of Marquesan art by the end of the 19th century, and it's a safe assumption that Karl von den Steinen brought some pieces of the collection back to Berlin with him, where they may still be found in the Ethnological Museum. Grellet himself died not long after von den Steinen's visit, but the family remained in friendly contact with the German ethnologist. We're indebted to them, because they subsequently supplied von den Steinen with the striking photo of a temple platform that he used in the first volume of his study. The basalt boulders of the decaying platform and its sacred banyan tree were guarded by a crowd of gleaming white ancestral skulls. This was the way such sites still looked when Bob arrived a half-century later.

The Grellet family grew to quite respectable size, by dint of the labors of the founder and his descendants. Today, it's distributed today over the entire island of Fatu Iva, and if you yell:

"Hey, Grellet !" on the street in O'omoa, you'll certainly see many people turn around.

The main attractions in the Museum are undoubtedly the big, beautifully carved *koka'a* bowls. In these vessels, the famed Marquesan *popoi* breadfruit paste received its final preparations and was served. Paddles, clubs, and spears, as well as stone adzes, poi-pounders and well-preserved *tiki* complete the collection. Yellowed fading photos of the Grellet family decorate the walls, along with certificates from the Legion of Honor and several decorations. But among these photos we unexpectedly encounter a white ceramic plate with images of snow-capped mountains, half-timbered chalets, and girls in traditional Swiss costume, images which contrast sharply with the Marquesan antiquities. Does this relic bear mute testimony to a never-ending longing for a homeland left behind?

Bob takes over the second group of passengers to visit the museum, devoting special attention to the *koka'a* bowls whose outer surfaces are so beautifully decorated with mysterious designs. The complex motifs are quite similar to those which were used in tattooing and remotely resemble the designs found on bronze vessels of the Shang and Chou Dynasties of Bronze Age China. It seems possible that remote Proto-Austronesian ancestors of the Marquesans and the Shang and Chou Dynasties may have long ago shared artistic influences from the same sources.

Beneath shady pandanus trees rustling in a gentle breeze, I fall into conversation with Eveleyn from Kassel. Before we know it, the routine details of everyday German life have caught us up and won't let us go until the group comes out of the museum and heads for a friendly Marquesan woman who is about to give an outdoor demonstration of the manufacture of *kumuhei*. These are little bundles of fragrant herbs, flowers, leaves, and sandalwood powder. They are worn around the neck as substitutes for *eau de toilette*, scented soap, or deodorant. Marquesans also often use coconut oil mixed with sandalwood powder or turmeric for the same purpose; the turmeric has the added benefit of having long been considered as an aphrodisiac *par excellence!* The scent of the pandanus fruit was also greatly admired for the same quality.

In the past, the Marquesan girls painted their bodies with black, yellow, red, and green pigments. These were produced from the juices of plants and flowers mixed with coconut oil. It's a bit hard today to imagine how the girls would have looked with such "highlighting." These colors proved hard to remove from the clothing and uniforms of 19th century ship's crews who associated quite closely and *en masse* with the attractive and highly accessible young girls. In 1825, a humorless American Navy officer visiting Nuku Hiva found it necessary to decree that unless these beauties came aboard without their body paint, all traffic between the sexes would cease! Ah, Discipline! The refuge of the narrow military mind! Perhaps for such odd reasons, it's been many years now since these cosmetics were dropped out of use.

Following this informative morning, we wend our way back to the whale boats, into which we are loaded unscathed, despite the slippery, algae-covered cement of the wharf. As the *Aranui* sets a course for Hanavave, the passengers sink into sleepy indolence following an ample lunch washed down with some of the *Aranui's* good wine. Only a few enjoy the wild cliff-bound coast between O'omoa and Hanavave.

Late in the afternoon, we arrive off enchanting Hanavave, whose name has given rise to much unseemly conjecture. In Marquesan, the name translates rather prosaically to "Surf Bay," but the French have named it *Baie des Vierges* (Bay of Virgins). Since the shores of the bay are crowned with several natural tuff and basalt pillars, some people who have read too much Freud (and a little bit of Freud is too much for most) claim that the original French name was *Baie des Verges*. "*Verge*" has a number of meanings, but in French slang, the term is an impolite reference to the male genitalia, which we will here more politely translate as "phallus." By this translation, Hanavave becomes the Bay of Phalli. According to this tale, outraged missionaries smuggled an "i" into the French name, thus transforming the phalluses into virgins *(vierges)*. To be sure, in 1844, nuns were among the first arrivals in the course of the Christian visitation of the Marquesas, and these religious were known in Marquesan as *virikine* or "virgins." In Atuona today, the convent school is known as the *papua virikine*, literally the "virgins' or nuns' enclosure." And so, other fortunately less Freudian people think that they can just as easily see nuns in these towering pillars. After all, even Freud himself once said: "Sometimes a cigar is just a cigar!" Perhaps sometimes a nun is also just a nun.

Even though the Marquesans have a decided preference for sexual interpretations, the pillars in question are actually viewed in ancient Marquesan folklore as the bones of a huge eel from Nuku Hiva who ran aground and died on Hanavave shore, and the Marquesan name "Surf Bay" has no sexual reference at all (at least for normal people)! The names *Baie des Vierges* or *Baie des Verges* are purely French designations and it's clear that we're dealing here with a case of a French play on words, decidedly after the fact! Bay of Phalli, Bay of Virgins, or Bay of Nuns? Whoever is willing can rummage through the annals of the mission, or the French Navy, to ultimately decide whether phalli, virgins, or nuns was intended. One thing is sure, however; the responsibility for this name can't be pinned on the Marquesans!

In Hanavave, hefty powerful Marquesans await as always the freight which the *Aranui* disgorges. On the shore, dogs of every shade and children romp about among containers, boxes and sacks, while the *Aranui* sailors once more go about their work with total dedication.

The road up the valley beckons to us, leading us between the pillars? phalli? virgins? or nuns? This is without doubt one of the most beautiful valleys in the Marquesas. The peaceful atmosphere is only broken by the murmuring of the stream and the melodious twittering of the birds. Dense underbrush on both sides of the river forms a unique deep green roof, beneath which the water meanders around cliffs and mighty boulders, here and there collecting in glass-clear pools. At the inland end of the valley, the inner wall of the ancient caldera rises, dark and mysterious in the slanting afternoon sun.

In the midst of this idyllic landscape live the people of Hanavave. Unapproachable, taciturn, and cold, many of them live their lives in complete withdrawal and leave an impression of veiled hostility. They don't respond to our: "Ka'oha Nui," often avoiding even eye contact. Little children beg 100-Franc pieces on the streets: "*Cent francs, cent francs ...!*" Some of the kids get nasty; one group of girls actually tries to stop a passenger from entering the church. Explanations have been sought for this odd but well-known behavior. A psychiatrist who once toured the valley with Bob said that he'd never seen so many clinically depressed people in one place. Some say the problem is genetic, a result of inbreeding. That is possible, but it's also likely that the church in this valley is maintaining very tight control: we hear rumors that close contact with foreigners is discouraged, that the flock is being led more by xenophobic prohibitions and threats of Hell, than by injunctions to good works, compassion, and love. But aren't we on the brink of the 21st century?

We recall Arthur Baessler's description of Hanavave in his book; *Neue Suedsee Bilder (New Pictures of the South Seas),* which appeared in 1900 with the Riemer Press in Berlin. Baessler, a South Seas ethnographer with the German Ethnological Museum in Berlin, arrived in the Marquesas in 1896, shortly before Karl von den Steinen. The two ethnographers knew each other very well and worked closely together. Arthur Baessler founded the Baessler Archive, an academic journal which remains to this day an excellent source of ethnographic information on all societies of the world. Baessler wrote the following about Hanavave:

"Hanavave is a very picturesque valley, one of the most beautiful of the group. It rains here far more frequently than in the northern islands. Plenty of crops could be raised here, if only someone would plant them. A completely successful attempt was made to establish coffee here, even though the coffee plants were neither planted under shade trees, as is normal practice, nor well tended. Since the people here are still satisfied to go around clad in little *tapa* loin cloths, and coconut palms and breadfruit trees are standing around in abundance, it's going to take a long time before they get themselves motivated to make any innovations connected with uncomfortable work."

It looks like very little has changed in Hanavave, except for the loincloths! A kind of lethargic peace still reigns throughout this not-so-happy valley

On our way up-valley, we encounter the first hikers. Haven't they found the "Olympic Pool?" Memories of our own first voyage suddenly return: two years ago, we were among the first to leave the ship. The cloudless sky, the sea in its incomparable ultramarine, motivated us to set out with great enthusiasm. The hiking boots were firmly laced on, and backpacks were filled with picnic lunches and water bottles. To be sure, there were also those optimists who set out relatively unimpeded, taking only a shopping bag and wearing a pair of rubber sandals!

On that day in O'omoa two years ago, we decided to skip the *tapa*-making exhibition and the museum visit, because we wanted to get the first and steepest section of the hike over with and far behind us before the noonday heat became oppressive. Later, a bit higher up the slope, we strolled happily along through shady quiet mango groves and it was decidedly more pleasant. We were constantly climbing toward the crests, but at a comfortable rate of ascent. Below us, the houses of O'omoa dwindled in size, finally becoming almost impossible to distinguish. The splendid view cast an increasingly powerful spell. Every rest stop was a delight, not only to quench our thirsts but to simply enjoy the much desired quietude and the vistas offered to us.

As we climbed, our group of hikers did not remain compact, but began to stretch out along the trail, everyone taking it at his or her own pace. Although the clear, fragrant air made breathing quite easy, the sun beat down mercilessly on us and forced us to save our strength for the long haul. Nevertheless, we often forgot the path that wrung the sweat out of very pore, because the unique views of the interior of Fatu Iva were so inspiring. Precipitous mountain slopes and narrow side valleys constantly revealed to us strange new worlds. In the slanting light, against the background of dark cliffs, the palm, pandanus, banana, and ironwood trees that lined our route were transformed into masterpieces of natural beauty. With little or no warning, we often found ourselves standing on mountain sides cloaked in dark green verdure, teetering on the edges of precipices which plummeted vertically into dark abysses. Far below, recognizable only as a tiny white spot, we occasionally glimpsed the *Aranui*, pitching its way along, on course for Hanavave.

We enjoyed our picnic lunch in a shady grove, with a view of the endless breadth of the Pacific; enthralled and overwhelmed by the power of this scene of untouched nature. Water was on everyone's mind, because by this point it seemed we'd lost several liters of it through sweat. In the heat of high noon, we reached the highest point on the trail, at which time the vision of the much advertised "Olympic Pool" (a dammed-up stretch of the Hanavave river) at the end of the hike was quite understandably becoming an increasingly inviting prospect. Finally, we saw the house tops of Hanavave below us and all that remained was to conquer the steep zigzag trail descending into the valley. This was the last serious challenge to calf and thigh muscles, worn-out knees, and overall conditioning.

The tempting vision of diving right into the cool delicious wetness of a river disappeared like a puff of smoke. Wherever we looked, there was no sign of the pool. Our party of seven held wildly divergent opinions as to which direction to take: "Further up-valley?" "Better to head back?" "Left or right?" Everybody wanted to be a pathfinder, but no one knew the answer. An exemplary and uncomplicated solution to the problem was demonstrated by the chubby little Mr. Pickwick-Brown of England: a rather meager brook near the path sufficed to provide him with just enough water to timorously splash over his back. Then, his clothing very neatly folded near him, he lay down in the midst of his own private water-course, happily relaxed, with hands folded on his tummy. Meanwhile, all around him, the Germans and the Swiss were arguing directions ever more stridently.

Thanks to a guide from the ship who came along to keep an eye on things, we finally got to savor the pleasure of the "Olympic Pool." Even though it stank of rancid copra, the cool shade finally presented us with the well-deserved refreshment we had fought for.

We decide to head back toward the beach. It will still take time before the last containers are loaded. We pass the time with a repertoire of German songs, which Bob acquired long ago in New York's Columbia University. It's a rather astounding alternative program to put on in this remote, scarcely inhabited island. "Die Lorelei" is always a good opener, the "Alte Kameraden" (Old Comrades) isn't bad either, but at first no one can precisely recall the melody of the Macki Messer song from Bert Brecht's "Three Penny Opera" (*Drei Groschen Oper*). When we finally get it down, it runs through our heads the rest of the evening.

Back on the *Aranui*, everyone is up on deck; they don't want to miss the marvelous spectacle, as the constantly changing colors of the setting sun illuminate the mighty pillars (whatever they represent!) of Hanavave and the surrounding steep cliffs and wooded mountain ridges. Only when the sun finally sinks into the sea with its last valiant golden rays, can we escape the spell in which this island has held us prisoner the entire day.

Hiva Oa: Puama'u Valley,
and Tahuata: Vaitahu Valley

Thick clouds cover the sky this morning; the sun rarely shows itself, and the sea is accordingly stormy. This means that the whaleboats and sailors will be challenged today because the harbor at Puama'u is well exposed to the tricky actions of the relentless waves. Even in calm sea states, the boats must be carefully maneuvered between a mighty rock and the dock / sea wall. With today's strong surf, it's a very intricate and risky game to choose the right time to come alongside the dock. But Tima'u, the dark-skinned coxswain, plows with stoic calm through the agitated seas and brings the boat masterfully alongside. Happy as ever, Iakopo, Pahutu, Ta'utu and Tino heave the passengers out of the boat onto the dock. The timid faces of the ladies and the courageous little hops and skips of the men permit one to assume that there are definite limits to the trust which is being placed in these normally most reliable sailors. Once more, Iakopo grabs Lancelot with her crocodile purse in his tattooed arms, whispers a not-too flattering compliment in her well-powdered ear (in Marquesan, of course), and sends her on her way, with an explicit gesture.

Everyone is free to chose whether they will ride or walk from the dock to the archeological site, the temple of Te I'i Pona. We decide on the jeep, chauffeured by the chief's cousin. Unfortunately Bob's neck isn't decorated with the usual flower wreath which he normally is given upon arrival. We had long since planned to use this wreath today for a very special purpose. A brief chat with the chief's cousin seems to restore everything to proper order. His *"E! E ho'i"* (Yes! Certainly!) sounds most trustworthy. Shortly thereafter, the ride is briefly interrupted and the chauffeur disappears into a nearby house. After a few minutes, he returns smiling radiantly: *"E, ua hei; koana te hei, OK?"* (All's well, you've got your wreath, OK?)

At the end of a dusty road lies Te I'i Pona, the most famous archeological site in the Marquesas, overshadowed by huge breadfruit trees and decorated with red and green-leafed *ti* *(Cordyline)* plants which were said to possess supernatural powers in the old culture. For this reason, *ti* plants were used everywhere, not only to decorate houses and tribal ceremonial plazas, but also to make skirts for dancers. When mature, the roots of *ti* were prized for their delicious sweet taste plants and were baked and eaten. Today, they yield a sweet syrup which goes very well in coffee.

The site lies at the foot of the large volcanic pillar, To'ea, whose crest as crowned with another temple. The rough vertical rock face of Toe'a is honeycombed with nooks and crannies of all sizes, which were used, in the old days, as depositories for the skeletal remains of departed Na'iki. The temple site of Te I'i Pona itself consists of two large and two small platforms ascending a gently rising plane. These platforms are home to a very interesting collection of 11 *tiki*, among which are the giant Taka'i'i and the strange Maka"i Tau'a Pepe. These two statues have imparted a certain degree of fame to the island, because they remain a cause of speculation, to the present day.

Te I'i Pona was well known since the middle of the 19th century, but reports of the site were published only in the last decade of that century by Alfred Baessler, Karl von den Steinen, and Frederick Christian. It has been confirmed that the site once belonged to the Na'iki tribe. In the 18th century, the Na'iki captured a chief of the Etu'oho tribe, a gentleman named Tiu'o'o, whom they cooked and ate in a rather nasty fashion (apparently there was no nice way to do such things). This caused bad blood to arise between the tribes, leading to a war in which the Na'iki tribe was driven out and their lands occupied by the Te Pa'aha

Tai, another tribe from the shore-line area of Puama'u. The Na'iki sought refuge all over the archipelago; some fleeing to nearby Hanapa'oa, others to the south coast of Hiva Oa in Atuona valley, others to Nuku Hiva in the northern group, and yet others to Ua Pou and Ua Huka.

We have to thank Karl von den Steinen that we know more about this site than about other monumental sites in the Marquesas. The two meter tall statue of Taka'i'i ("Red with rage"), the symbol of the site, is also seen as the protector of these sacred precincts. It supposedly took three months of tugging and hauling to move this chunky gentleman from the quarry where he was carved to the site where he was finally installed.

The reclining, or more accurately, prone statue known as Maki'i Tau'a Pepe represents the "Butterfly Priestess," wife of Manuiota'a, the famed Na'iki sculptor to whom we have dedicated this book. She is shown as she lay dying in childbirth. The word *maki'i* is a verbal participle used as an adjective meaning "writhing in agony," which is a fitting description for this *tiki*. In addition to many other *tiki* on the site, Manuiota'a carved this statue in memory of his beloved Butterfly when she was deified after death.

Through the years, many wild-eyed adventurers have seen all sorts of things in this rather poignant memorial, including various mammals, and even amphibians. But as in the representation of Tau'a Pepe. But as in so many cases in the Marquesas, it is Karl von den Steinen who brings clarity to the picture. In 1896, he learned the story of Tau'a Pepe from the elderly Pihua, the only living man who knew the names of the *tiki* on the temple site.

As noted, the adjective *maki'i* in Tau'a Pepe's name, as well as her body position, show clearly that she is writhing in agony. Although now lying on her stomach, she was first discovered lying on her back and was intended to be so displayed. Arthur Baessler, who visited Te I'i Pona shortly before von den Steinen, wrote with irony: "Beneath the feet of the statues, an uncarved section usually extends from the block. This section is to be used to erect the statue in the ground; under the woman (Tau'a Pepe), however, there is nothing, which is a sign that she was always lying down and had not fallen due to old age."

The canons of Marquesan art give absolutely no possibility of realistically depicting anything, particularly anything as complex and emotionally loaded as the death of a beloved woman in childbirth. The sculptor therefore had to depart from the canons in order to express his ideas. As a result, this *tiki* is much more powerfully expressive than all other Marquesan statues. The anatomical details of such a scene, which would appear to be obviously necessary to Europeans, had no relevance at all to Marquesan logic or art and therefore are not shown.

In this connection, it's important to note that Marquesans were very much afraid of the spirits of women who died in childbirth. In every valley, there were *tokai*, shrines on which offerings were made to the spirits of these women, and in some cases such women were "elevated" to the level of tribal goddesses as was Tau'a Pepe, who forthwith took her place in the Na'iki pantheon. She was not only worshipped in Puama'u on Hiva Oa, but on Ua Huka as well, where a very badly damaged smaller version of her is found in a temple in Hane.

Even more typical of the confusing swirl of misinterpretations about this statue is the vain controversy about the animal figures on the sides of its protruding stomach block. You can see a quadruped on her left side, quite clearly a dog, with a long tail curving up and over its back. A debate has raged for years, however, among romantic theorists, concerning the identity of this animal. A European writer, apparently a believer in the Heyerdahl myth, seized on the curving tail to identify this figure as a llama, a supposition which he accepted as definitive proof of Heyerdahl's theory of Peruvian settlement of Polynesia. Unfortunately, llama tails are short, thick, and curve downward;

it's anatomically impossible for a llama tail to curve up and over the animal's back. Heyerdahl himself has always held the view that the figure is one of a puma, an animal equipped with a nice long tail. He professes to see claws on the figure's feet, which is a real stretch of the imagination but ignores the three (!) straight-up ears which make this the strangest puma ever. It's rather remarkable that on the left side of Tau'a Pepe's tummy, the outlines of the enigmatic animal are very clearly and deeply carved, while the figure on the right side of the stomach is so heavily weathered that it's hard to know if it's an animal or not. Has someone perhaps rather recently "retouched" the "South American" version of the figure on the left side? Heyerdahl himself admits that he "restored" the figure in 1956. How far did the "restoration" go? And did one of the "restoration artists" goof with that third ear?

One thing is certain: for the Na'iki tribe, the figure of a dog was by no means unusual, because dogs were numbered among the totem animals or guardian spirits of this tribe, and dog figures appear wherever the Na'iki went. Scientific investigations once more contradict the theories of the adventurer. The other standing *tiki* in Te I'i Pona (there's also a rare sitting statue here) have mysterious names, such as "Cave of the Twilight", "the Inciter of the Na'iki," and "the Stone-breaking God." Some *tiki* are only heads, the sinister *upoko he'aka* or "victim heads," representing the heads of human sacrifices offered at this temple.

At the right, at the far end of the upper platform, is the victim head of Tiu'o'o (Strong North Wind), whose death ignited the bloodfeud between the Etu'oho tribe and the Na'iki. The head shows Tiu'o'o his mouth gaping, teeth and tongue protruding, just the way he must have looked when his body was removed from the earth oven and beheaded.

The largest of the victim heads from Te I'i Pona (82 cm high, 90 cm in diameter) has been absent from Te I'i Pona for over a century. As we stated in the dedication, this head has been named

Manuiota'a, after the master sculptor who made him, Tau'a Pepe's talented husband. After a very long sea voyage, Manuiota'a stands today in the Ethnological Museum in Berlin. He's definitely a victim head, but the original victim's identity is unknown, lost in the mists of time, and so von den Steinen gave the head the name of the sculptor. Manuiota'a looks quite similar to Tiu'o'o, with his teeth and tongue jutting forth through opened lips beneath a triangular nasal opening, like that of a skull (apparently noses didn't endure the heat of earth ovens too well!). On his cheeks are the dog tattoo motif and the little stick figures with upraised arms and wide-spread legs, known to the Marquesans as *etua*, or god.

When Karl von den Steinen came to Puama'u in 1896, the Te I'i Pona site was the property of Rev. James Kekela, a Hawaiian Protestant missionary who had planted the entire site with coffee plants. Kekela lived from 1853 to 1903 in the Marquesas, and during his remarkably long life, layed the foundation of a very large family whose descendants are today found everywhere. He did much good, on one occasion even rescuing the captured mate of an American whaler whom the Marquesans were preparing to roast in an earth oven, to avenge themselves for an offense committed by an earlier European visitor. For his bravery in this affair, Kekela received an engraved gold watch from President Abraham Lincoln.

Von den Steinen was able to capitalize on his friendship with Kekela and purchase the above-mentioned victim head for the Berlin Museum. It took 15 Marquesans, strong as oxen, to carry the head from it's stony bed in the quiet temple grove down to the beach where a five-meter square raft awaited him.

A German trading schooner sufficed for the rest of the trip, and after an adventurous voyage, the victim head finally came to rest in the Ethnological Museum of Berlin where he survived two wars without injury. Alone and forsaken, uprooted, he stands there to this day. During my last Museum visit, a youngster came up to him, stuck out his tongue and hissed: "Yuk! You're like, really ugly, dude! Phooey, baahhhh!"

We head back to the beach on foot. The short walk does me good and the quiet is very refreshing. My wish to go swimming is decisively vetoed: "Believe me, it's dangerous ... the surf ... the sharks!" I protest: "Sharks? That's just a fairy tale!" But there's arguing with experience: "No, it isn't ! Please stay here." Our exchange is interrupted: my wreath has arrived! Mint leaves and light yellow *pua 'enana* flowers (*Fagraea* sp.) have been woven into an intoxicatingly fragrant and colorful necklace. "*E hoa, ko'uta'u nui! Ua koakoa 'oko 'au, o mea kunahao 'oko te hei!*" "Thanks, my friend! You've made me very happy with this wreath!"

"Delicious, delicious!" is the adjective applied to this marvelous wreath by one of our German fellow-passengers. It's doubtful if this is really the most appropriate adjective, but maybe she's only expressing envy at not having gotten one herself. "Please Iakopo, load me gently into the boat; don't let anything happen to this wreath!" Iakopo picks me up and lifts me into the whaleboat with the touch of an angel.

After lunch, it's time to consign the wreath to the sea. Months ago, in Berlin, I promised the lonely Manuiota'a that I'd send him a floral greeting from his homeland, and the wreath goes overboard in accordance with that promise. We watch the flowers for a long time, playfully bobbing around on the waves, until they finally disappear, tiny green and yellow flecks, into the infinity of the Pacific. Spontaneously, we resolved at that moment to dedicate our travel book to Manuiota'a.

During the trip to Tahuata, many people express interest in a lecture on traditional Marquesan tattooing. This comes unexpectedly, and Bob has no 35 mm slides to use. The new encyclopedic work on Marquesan tattooing by Pierre and Marie-Noëlle Ottino is quickly pressed into service for a good presentation on this intriguing native art, which was developed to a higher degree in the Marquesas than anywhere else in the Pacific.

Since 1858, the French colonial authorities forbade tattooing in the Marquesas, but the art, with its traditional motifs, was once again permitted after 1985. Over many years of painstaking work, Marie -Noëlle Ottino researched the history, significance, motifs, employed, and technique of this art. The research on the names of the motifs was quite time -consuming, because these names often varied from valley to valley, and even between individual tattoo masters. Marie-Noëlle carried out her exhaustive work most precisely, so that this wide-ranging book goes far beyond a treatment of tattoo as art. It provides detailed information on the terminology used by the tattoo masters, and approaches the entire traditional life style of the Marquesans through their tattooing.

The original tattooing was done with narrow needles of bird bone and mother-of-pearl. Mounted on a wooden handle at a 90-degree angle, the needle was placed on the skin of the client and hammered in with a small baton of iron wood. Then the wound was wiped with the pigment; a mixture of coconut oil and soot from burned candle nuts (*Aleurites trilobata*). Did it hurt? Certainly! The tattoo master usually needed four helpers to hold the legs and arms of the client.

For the "customer," tattooing was also an expensive proposition, because he (or she, since women were also tattooed) had to build a special house for the master and his helpers and had to support them with food for the entire length of the "treatment" as well as the *tapu* period that followed. And by the way, the *tapu* restrictions were unpleasant, usually requiring the customer, the master, and his assistants to abstain from sexual relations and to avoid specific types of food that normally would have been standard fare.

As models and inspirations, the tattoo masters used the distinctive Marquesan *tiki* figure and face, the stick figure "squatting man," and images of animals which played a roll in mythology, such as lizards, turtles, sharks, etc. In some cases, these animals were revered as guardians or totems. In earlier times, it was considered the best of good form (when it could be afforded) to have one's entire body covered with tattoo designs. Chiefs, priests, and warriors quite often were tattooed from head to foot with elaborate designs. Some of the elite even had their intricate tattoos gradually filled in, transforming the motifs into a series of solid blue-black panels. This was a very ostentatious statement great wealth in Marquesan society, where nudity or semi-nudity left very little to the imagination. Women were normally tattooed on the arms and from the hips down, with occasional small motifs beneath the ears and tiny vertical lines around the mouth.

Since the renaissance of tattooing, around 1985, this traditional art has undergone some alterations. If you're crazy enough, you can still be tattooed in the old style, with bone and pearl shell needles, which are almost never cleaned. Most prospective customers seem to prefer the speedier and more hygienic devices which the inventive Marquesans have developed from old electric shavers. Most recently these have often been replaced by good European tattoo equipment. Nonetheless, it's best to approach tattooing with a good deal of care. Many of the talented new masters may not fully understand the warnings about AIDS, hepatitis and other blood-borne diseases, hence may not be too careful about cleaning their equipment. Trish Allen, an American tattoo expert who has held seminars in the Marquesas and elsewhere in French Polynesia, has done her best to make the tattoo masters aware of the very real modern dangers which exist in the practice of this art, but these warnings may not have been taken seriously in all cases.

In the meantime, we've reached Tahuata. The boats deposit us on a slippery dock near the black sand beach of Vaitahu valley. The rustic image of the village is enhanced by fruit-bearing avocado, pamplemousse, and mango trees, beneath which lounge hairy black pigs and barking, yelping dogs. Serious, rather morose Marquesans hurry along the road to and from the dock. The bucolic village scene opening before us hides a bloody, violent past, however.

In 1595, the Spaniard Mendaña "discovered" this island, coming ashore at the present-day football field, where a large tribal ceremonial center then stood. Taking possession for the Spanish crown, the new owners celebrated a Mass, and thereafter continued slaughtering Marquesans, a bloody pasttime which they had already begun while they were still scouting the shorelines for a place to come ashore. In the ensuing 8 days, more than 200 Marquesans were killed, some dying only because the soldiers of the expedition wanted to test the effects of their muskets. The terrorized inhabitants of Vaitahu fled to the mountains, raining down rocks on the heads of the pursuing Spaniards. Pedro Quiros, the expedition pilot and a devout Catholic, was horrified by the brutal killings, but could do nothing to stop it. The soldiers ran wild, only answering to the psychopathic *Maestro del Campo* (Camp Master), Pedro Merino Manrique, who answered to no one. Manrique literally came out of nowhere to join the expedition: nothing is known of his background except that he was a constant source of trouble from the moment he set foot aboard.

In accordance with the pious Spanish custom, the islands were baptized with religious names: Tahuata became Santa Cristina; Hiva Oa became La Dominica, Fatu Iva was called La Magdalena and the massacre site in Vaitahu Bay, in a final supreme irony, was dubbed *Baio de la Madre de Dios*, or Mother of God Bay! Luckily for the Marquesans, the other islands of the southern archipelago were spared a Spanish visit in person; the only victims on those islands were the poor unfortunates who came out in their canoes to check out the Spanish ships, only to be shot for target practice.

Mendaña was a totally incompetent commander; before departing from Peru he had eked out his supplies by committing serial acts of piracy against Spanish ships along the South American coast, acts in which he was greatly aided by the skills of Manrique and his thugs. One of the expropriated ships carried a cargo owned by a Spanish monk. In fury, the monk pronounced a curse on Mendaña and his whole expedition because of this criminal deed, but this did not dismay the intrepid adventurer.

After Mendaña left the Marquesas, he sailed on toward his hoped-for but never attained destination in the Solomons, finally landing on Santa Cruz in the New Hebrides. On the night of his arrival, the ship stolen from the Spanish monk disappeared with all hands. Mendaña had hoped to establish himself as viceroy of a new colony, but once ashore in this verdant hell, the expedition members were opposed by hostile inhabitants who were surprisingly good fighters. They also encountered deadly diseases, and a lack of food and potable water. Under these stresses, the proud expedition collapsed in a leaderless shambles; factions formed, and internecine warfare began. Manrique attempted to assassinate Mendaña, and was in turn killed by Mendaña's wife and brother-in-law. Only Quiros, the pilot, Mendaña's wife, and a few hardy survivors managed to reach Mexico, after a lengthy detour through the Philippines. Behind them lay more than 200 graves and two of the four expedition ships. The Marquesans were avenged, and the monk's curse was fulfilled.

Almost 200 years later, in 1774, Capt. James Cook called into Vaitahu, following Quiros' reports of the Mendaña expedition. Shortly after his arrival, his men shot and killed a Marquesan who was trying to steal a metal fitting from the ship. It was excused as an accident, the fatal shot supposedly having been intended to scare the man off. Whatever lay behind the shooting, this attention-getting entrance must have immediately recalled local memories of Mendaña's cruelty, which had certainly been enshrined in local legend and passed down from generation to generation. As a result, the inhabitants of Vaitahu were not at all happy to see Cook and seem to have largely evacuated the area. In view of this hostility and the derogatory comments of his Tahitian "interpreters," who portrayed the Marquesans as degenerate savages, Cook was unable to get much accomplished, and set sail for "civilized" Tahiti after only four days.

Dreamy Vaitahu valley was later the scene of even more violence. In 1793, the American skipper Roberts called in at Vaitahu. With the help of the Marquesans, he had a ship built for himself, giving the chief the impression that the people of Vaitahu would share the use of the ship with him and his crew. When Roberts tried make a clandestine departure, the Marquesans erupted and there was further killing, once more with Marquesans victims. In the late 1700s and early 1800s, Vaitahu was for some reason the preferred refuge for many deserters, mostly Americans, who were quite often well-armed. They ruthlessly terrorized the population of the valley and brought with them European diseases.

When French Admiral Dupetit-Thouars called in at Vaitahu in 1838, the Marquesans finally saw their chance to cast off the deserters' yoke. In the belief that the French had finally freed them, the Marquesans gave the French their trust. At least until they realized that they had only changed the identity of their overlords. Earlier, it had been the deserters who acted as laws unto themselves; now it was the French, also ruling by their own laws. On 7 September, 1842, a bloody uprising erupted in Vaitahu with casualties on both sides, less on the French side, however, than on Marquesan side. Today a memorial tablet stands on the beach at Vaitahu commemorating the few French casualties in this mortal combat. Of the Marquesans who died in an unequal fight against trained French colonial infantry supported by naval and land-based artillery, there is no mention.

The church standing on a low rise behind the present day football field was constructed with the direct financial support of the Vatican. It bears the name of "Our Lady of the Infant

Jesus." The portals of this very imposing edifice are decorated with traditional lizard motifs, and multicolored bundles of sunbeams stream through the beautiful stained-glass windows into the interior. It's unusually cool and peaceful in the sanctuary, but the mild smile of the Marquesan Madonna above the altar somehow doesn't touch my heart. During the course of this afternoon, far too much anger has accumulated deep within me over the arrogant brutality of the "civilized" Christian invaders of all nations who have successively wreaked havoc in this valley. And the Catholic Church, with it's own politics, has not helped. In retrospect, this church, designated as "a gift to the people," is almost an insult.

It is, however, a bit of a relief to know that the history of Tahuata has not been indelibly imprinted with only violence, misery, and death, but has had its humorous side as well. The Protestant missionaries, Harris and Crook, came to Vaitahu in 1797. The chief invited Harris to his house, giving him food and shelter, while Crook was sent to another valley. Unfortunately, Harris lacked the most fundamental knowledge of Polynesian customs of hospitality, and so didn't know that a chief's guest was normally offered the company of the chief's wife or some other female member of the family. Totally unsuspecting, Harris ate well and bedded down for the well-deserved rest of the innocent. He apparently crudely rejected the proffered Marquesan version of "welcome wagon service," much to the consternation of the chief's wife. She met with her lady friends, discussed the matter, and concluded that there was something a little odd about the guest. Was there a female body beneath the missionary gown? For Marquesan women, this possibility also was not exactly lacking in interest, since casual bisexuality is not uncommon. A decision was quickly made: "Let's get the facts!" The ladies subjected the sleeping preacher to a most thorough physical exam, the results of which must have heightened their consternation! Even a sleep blessed by the Lord can't be deep enough to enable someone to survive such a bodily assault. Harris awoke to find himself quite uncovered, in the Biblical sense, and surrounded by naked giggling beauties; he fled in panic to the beach. Crook found him there the next morning, half naked, shivering and in shock. Harris was sitting on the dwindling remains of his once formidable baggage, most of which had been pillaged during the night. He supposedly never quite got over the experience, but is said to have lectured on it to enthusiastic puritanical congregations for many years! What price glory?

One might ask, however: how did Mr. Crook deal with the same situation? He almost certainly got the same offers!

We visit the Museum in the Vaitahu chief's office, with its neat displays of artifacts excavated by Prof. Barry Rollet of the University of Hawai'i at Manoa, in a site on the south end of Vaitahu beach dating back to 900 AD. Rollet's museum was a first in the archipelago. He felt, and we strongly agree, that the Marquesans should know of their own heritage and so he established a display with artifacts, diagrams and photos, all labeled in French, English, and Marquesan. There is still nothing like it elsewhere in the archipelago. After this visit we go to meet another Teiki, this one a bone carver who produces exquisite works in beef and pig bone. Some of these duplicate the ancient Marquesan miniature *ivi pou* carvings which were done in human bone, while others are interesting creations, combining ancient and modern ideas and concepts. Some of these works are bought and resold sold at very high prices in Tahiti, their value often enhanced by totally fictional tales of their age, origin, and meaning. Prospective buyers are often told some version of the following: "This was secretly removed at great risk from an ancient burial cave; it belonged to a famous chief and supposedly still has magical powers!" But Teiki the bone carver is a man of the 20th century, he's got a very well equipped shop, and distributes his attractive business cards quite freely.

134

The clear light of the late afternoon sun brings sharply into focus with unusual clarity the jagged sawtooth peaks of Tahuata's mountain spine. The wooded slopes, illuminated by the slanting rays, the ink-blue sea, the gleaming white *Aranui* riding at anchor combine to present an idyllic setting that no photography enthusiast could withstand! At such a time and place, the growls of the boat crew are of no avail, and the all-important seating order, ensuring trim in the whaleboat, is turned on its head as people scramble for good camera angles.

This evening, the wine is especially delicious, the food is as always excellent, and the dialects of the German speakers tumble over one another in happy confusion. There's Trudi with her Viennese sarcasm, Helmut the Bavarian, Sybille from the Tyrol, Evelyn and Ed from Kassel and in the midst of all this Nancy from Boston, Bob from Boise and myself from the Black Forest.

Helmut smiles across the table at Bob and speaks in his colorful Bavarian dialect:

"Here's to your health, Bob! No misunderstandings between sailors, right? You recall the big sea battles? Hell's bells, those were crazy days! We shot the bejeezus out of each other, damn' projectiles whizzing back and forth! C'mon, tell us a lil' bit more, but no hard feelings, OK, no hard feelings!"

Helmut and Bob, a Munich native and a Connecticut Yankee, are still-enthusiastic old sea dogs from two once-opposing navies. Then and there, the recollections of sea battles in the South Pacific and elsewhere flare up: we hear names of strange islands, straits, officers, ships that were sunk or those that managed to survive. The eyes light up at the names of naval figures such as Bob's childhood hero, the debonair and totally non-violent Count Felix von Luckner and his raider "Sea Eagle." Then the conversation switches to Count Admiral Maximilian von Spee's surprising 1914 appearance at Taipi Bay on Nuku Hiva, Spee's brilliant victory at Cape Coronel and his death at the Falklands, where he went down with his ship rather than strike his flag.

There's no end of talk about World War II. We hear names such as Coral Sea, Midway, the "Slot" off Guadalcanal, and Surigao straits. And we sit, ask questions, translate for the two sides, to and from High German (Bob doesn't fully understand the Munich dialect; Helmut isn't comfortable with Hochdeutsch) and laugh ever louder, as the sailor yarns are so energetically spun.

The only ones for whom this discussion doesn't seem to fit are an older couple. It was already painfully clear when they sat down that they weren't especially overjoyed to be among us Goths, but all other tables were unfortunately occupied. And so they sit, staring at their plates with consternation and frustration. Bob, truly neutral in this situation, tries repeatedly to engage them in French, hoping to break the ice. In return he gets back only pained: *"Oui, merci"* or *"Non, merci."* The lady sighs endlessly, wearing an expression as though she had simultaneously eaten a lemon and smelled something foul. With jaws firmly set, lips pursed and nose elevated, she chokes her food down with obvious effort.

Does anyone want to talk about Franco-German friendship? The basis of the oft-cited *fraternité* (brotherhood) comes lamentably to grief in such cases, and it's not only on this evening.

After dinner, our curiosity brings us back to the lee side of the ship, where the sea is alive, with schools of fish flashing silver in the glow of the ship's lights. These shiny little visitors provide the sailor-anglers with a welcome respite from their separate menu. At 2400 the *Aranui*'s diesels come to life, and we're off on a course toward Ua Huka.

Ua Huka: Vaipa'e'e and Hane Valleys

The night is short, and about 0300, I decide to go on a search for the Southern Cross (*Te Peka* in Marquesan). This constellation has exerted a magical attraction on me, ever since my childhood when I devoured adventure and discovery books.

Despite the fact that the ship's interior is well lit, I'm seized by an uncanny feeling: it's unsettling to be up and around, all alone, in the "wee small hours of the night." The darkness on the bridge is interrupted only by a few tiny isolated indicator lights, blinking here and there, which doesn't make it any better. My rather tentative "Hallo?" is lost completely in the sound of the ship's engines. Slowly, I reach out for the door and stagger up against a figure coming in my direction. The last bit of courage disappears, and the carefully rehearsed: *"Bonsoir Monsieur, vous serait-il possible de m'indiquer le Croix du Sud?"* (Good evening sir, can you possibly show me the Southern Cross?) ends in a terrified stammer. It's Steve, the 3rd officer, who has a hard time repressing his laughter. "OK! Follow me!" he says, and we climb up to the weather bridge. Dead on target, he points the way into the heavens where, directly above me, the long-sought Southern Cross blazes embedded in a sparkling myriad of stars! There's no way to mistake this constellation! I can recognize the Milky Way, blazing a broad, glowing phosphorescent path across the sky. The heavens have always been a great mystery to me, they have engulfed me and will never let me go.

The night wears on, the stars begin to fade. Delicate streaks of light appear on the horizon, announcing the beginning of a new day. Cloud banks transform themselves into fairy-tale beings, fabulous shifting shapes of light and shadow. Fantasy and reality are indescribably, inseparably, intermingled.

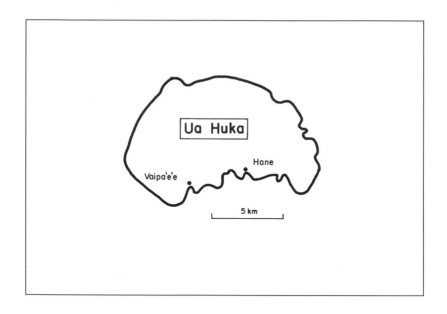

I'm awakened from my trance by the first curious fellow-voyagers popping up on the bridge and the deck. They're there at this early hour because no one wants to miss the complex evolution when Théodor, our first mate, turns the ship 180 degrees in the narrow fjord-like bay of Vaipa'e'e, a feat that many consider to be beyond any skipper's capabilities. One of these skeptics was an officer of the German merchant marine, who gruffly and emphatically pronounced his authoritative opinion in one word *"Unmoeglich!"* (Impossible!). He was quickly humbled, however, having underestimated the skill of the *Aranui* crew, and above all, Théodor's shiphandling mastery that enables him to execute this end-swapping maneuver even in the tightest environments. The German merchant skipper stomped off in a huff, but rendered no more professional judgments for the rest of the trip!

Perfect coordination between the bridge and the whaleboat crews is essential for the success of this evolution. The bow and stern lines are put to good use, and aided by the ship's own engineering plant, the *Aranui* once more turns obediently on its own axis. Getting up early to see this spectacle really paid off !

Théodor's proverbial expertise doesn't permit him to indulge in the slightest bit of self-pride. He calmly waves aside the congratulations of the onlookers, but his warm smile shows that he really appreciates the cheers and applause. This outstanding navigator, astronomer, and chess player, whose open honest face evidences his European forebears, is perhaps the most relaxed member of the ship's company. No one knows better than he the maliciousness of the Pacific, but his love for these islands has continued unbroken through 30 years as sailor and officer.

During my last trip, I often sat reading up on the weather bridge. One evening, Théodor called me over and pressed an old portable radio against my ear. I'll never forget my astonishment when I found myself listening to a news broadcast on the Swiss radio station, DRS, ending with a report from the Bern Federal Parliament! Little kindnesses like this, added to his superb ship-handling abilities, make Théodor absolutely indispensable to the *Aranui*.

We go ashore in Vaipa'e'e with whaleboats, and set foot for the first time on Ua Huka. Once more jeeps and trucks bring us to an assembly area where we are welcomed by lovely young ladies with *hei* flower wreaths and the traditional cry of welcome: "*Mave maiiiiiiiiiiii, Mave maiiiiiii* (Come hecere, come heeere!!) With completely normal reflexes, many masculine heads bow a bit deeper to be encircled by the floral garlands.

The usual ceremony begins with singing and dancing. Because of the beauty and grace of the dancers, the performance produces an exquisitely strong reaction on members of the masculine gender, especially the Tahitian dance known as *tamure*. In this dance, the solo female dancers seem to be inviting onlookers to love play, using unusually provocative hip movements which simulate certain normally quite private activities. The dancers start dragging passengers out to dance, and suddenly and mysteriously, Bob disappears! No *tamure* for him!

Unfortunately, the women of these islands are often only beautiful in their youth. Their relaxed, beautifully proportioned facial features and their gracile figures all change quite rapidly as they grow older, and this aging process is accelerated in the tropics by the normal Polynesian diet. Werner Krum discusses this in his book *Suedsee* (*South Seas*):

"Among the girls who are still young, one is often tempted to notice a certain Mongol slant of the eye, perhaps a memory of their ancient origin in the Far East." The unique girls of Ua Huka remind me very much of this Far Eastern origin, so remote in time.

Along with the music and the dancing, the mayor's speech is a part of the welcoming ritual, and as is everywhere the case, it's quite longwinded and filled with lovely gestures. Politicians must be genetically identical, the world over, regardless of race or nationality! That this community leader goes by the exceedingly un-Marquesan name of Lichtle is really his most interesting aspect. Has another Swiss left traces here? Correct! Mr. Lichtle's features give no hint of his lineage, however, for he's a true son of the island, loves to hear himself talk, is dark-skinned, tattooed, and weighs in at a cool couple of hundred pounds.

The thoroughly self-absorbed diligence that his Swiss forefather devoted to the fruitful increase of the local population has paid off handsomely, for as we soon learn, just about every third person on the island is linked to the Lichtle clan, in one or another fashion.

Framed by flowering bushes, a one-story house stands directly adjacent to the site of our welcoming ceremony. This building houses the museum, an institution under the direction of Josef Te Hau Va'atete, whom I would have liked to meet. Regrettably, he's away in a Tahitian hospital, news which fills Bob with concern for his friend.

140

On this island, Joseph Te Hau Va'atete takes foremost place among the woodcarvers and stone sculptors. His much sought-after works are mostly small *tiki,* and beautifully carved bowls, houseposts, and paddles. But his greatest artistic feats were first revealed in the monumental stone *tiki* he carved from the sacred soft red tuff, known as *ke'etu.* These red giants have made him truly famous. Many of his works in stone are quite difficult to differentiate from actual archeological finds. Josef has made great contributions to the reputation of Ua Huka as the Marquesan "mecca" for woodcarving and stone sculpture, and we're happy to learn that he's now training students to follow in his footsteps!

It seems to me, however, that he has also accomplished great things as a museum curator. The museum pieces, including a full array of stone adzes of all types, small stone *tiki,* fishhooks of pearl shell and other implements are well-displayed and labeled, as are the war clubs and paddles mounted on the walls. There's a very informative display of a traditional Marquesan kitchen, with poi-pounders, a thick heavy *hituku* or poi board, as well as a coconut meat grater and assorted bowls. In the rear of the museum, the display of ancient burial practices doesn't fail to exert a strange effect. The small, boat-like coffins interest me. It makes me shudder to realize that they were coffins for the bones of the dead, who had first been exposed and allowed to decay, but even more disconcerting is the thought that in ancient Marquesan society, it was women who had the delectable task of massaging the decaying cadavers with coco oil and ultimately cleaning the bones!

A large panel on the wall by the entrance concisely sets forth the history of the archeology of the Marquesas. Bob's name leads the list of contributors. He modestly acknowledges that fact: "Yes, I guess the people know about me." Although small, this museum is the best in the archipelago in terms of the size of its collections and the design of its displays.

On my first trip, the unusual architecture of the village church in Vaipa'e'e impressed me. Built of hard stone blocks, and crowned by a triangular red tower, it's quite striking by virtue of its columns and balustrades, it's decorated facade, and the windows painted in the Marquesan "national" colors of red, white, and yellow! The colorful little church stands on a plain of reddish sand, behind which only bald mountain tops rise into the blue sky. It seems to be the last stop on a road leading into loneliness and isolation.

Maybe it's only the pleasant coolness inside the church, or the influence of so many prayers of the faithful, but it does wonders to be able to leave the hectic activities of the day and briefly enter into a meditative atmosphere, which is enhanced by the beautiful wood carving!

The rest of the trip is left up to the passengers: one may either ride in jeeps, or make the trip on horseback. For us, riding is not an option; aside from the fact that we aren't equestrians, the graphic descriptions of the results of prolonged exposure to the Marquesan carved wooden saddles and the temperamental island horses exert a certain influence on our decision.

The dusty bumpy ride begins along the southern coast of the island, which is the floor of an ancient volcanic caldera. A short time later, we overtake the riders who don't seem too happy judging from their facial expressions and rather tense "seats." Only Mr. Bean, the perennial shutterbug, seems to be comfortable as he snaps away. Quite otherwise is Little Bean, who waves to us with undisguised discomfort as she brings up the end of the column.

The coast of Ua Huka is almost treeless at present, contrasting sharply with the 1813 observations of Capt. David Porter. Sailing by Ua Huka, he enthusiastically reported heavy vegetation, streams, and fruitful, well-populated valleys. Since the arrival of the Europeans, however, the environment has suffered greatly. The forests have been cleared and free-ranging horses, goats, and donkeys have transformed the landscape into a wasteland. Long periods of drought separate the increasingly infrequent rains.

Along our way we encounter some of these same horses, goats, and donkeys: they're steadfastly munching away, further reducing the sparse grass and greenery and drinking the last water holes dry. Some of them are little more than skeletons. Many bleached rib cages and long-bones scattered along the roadside attest to other animals' hopeless fights against drought. The blooming flamboyant trees, unfolding their vermilion splendor here and there, provide the only welcome color in this land of monotonous brown and gray.

Despite this rather bleak picture, we have Mayor Lichtle's immense energy and motivation to thank for the fact that Ua Huka has an extensive botanical garden in Papuakeikaha Valley. True, it's struggling to survive, poorly supported by a watering system which appears to be marginally operational.

For this reason, the desire for a guided tour in the garden is easily controlled. Some of the passengers make the tour in small groups, while others take a quick siesta in the shade outside the garden entrance. Native plants constitute a large part of the specimens in the garden, but they are joined by many exotic genera and species. The native plants include bamboo, breadfruit, banyan, pandanus, ironwood, rosewood, hibiscus of several varieties (including non-native types), *temanu* (*Calophyllum inophyllum*), *ti* (*Cordylinia terminalis*), and even the mysterious native intoxicant, *kava* (*Piper methysticum*). The active ingredients of this innocuous-looking plant attack the central nervous system. They are calming, but definitely habit-forming. Repeated use will ultimately lead to mental confusion as it did for many Marquesan chiefs and priests of old. Today's Marquesans, who will tell you they drink to get drunk, don't like *kava* because of it's soporific effect. When they drink, they want dance, gab, maybe fight a bit, and do a few other things as well. *Kava* immobilizes you; it makes you want to seek total peace and quiet, in other words, it's no fun at all! Soooooooo: pour out the wine, whiskey, Hinano beer, and let's tie one on! In addition to the native plants, there are also a wide range of introduced tropical and semi-tropical trees and plants, such as teak, croton bushes, passion fruit, guava, and more than 30 varieties of citrus fruits. The garden is also home to many types of birds, including the endangered ultramarine lorikeet, the reed warbler, and the fruit dove.

Our next stop is Hokatu valley, east of Hane. Hokatu,well known for the quality of the local carvers, offers another chance to load up with choice handicrafts. Our fellow- passengers storm the handicraft emporium. Even paddles and clubs almost two meters high find buyers, but I've got to wonder how in God's name these unwieldly, heavy items will ever find their ways safely back home. Certainly not in overhead luggage racks!

The best sellers are, and will probably remain, the very useful carved *koka'a* rosewood bowls. For one of these, admittedly a real masterpiece, an American passenger drags $ 2000 out of his pocket and gaily counts out the bills on the table. From the astounded glowing faces across the counter, it's safe to conclude that the sellers have just made the biggest sale of their lives.

On a short walk not far from the crowded clamor of the handi-craft shop, we encounter a big outrigger canoe which appears to be almost complete. A delegation from Ua Huka is going to sail this craft to Nuku Hiva for the Millennium celebration, at which time groups from the entire archipelago will participate in a three-day marathon celebration of the event. Regrettably, there also will be a three-day prohibition on alcoholic beverages to minimize casualties, but once the 3 days are past, look out!

Finally, the last lingering customers make up their minds on souvenirs, and we head back to Hane. After a short ride, we at last stumble into the Chez Fournier Restaurant, dust-streaked, sweating, and thirsty. The table is well set, with sweet and sour

144

pork, raw fish, shrimp, beef with vegetables in coco milk, curried goat, breadfruit, cooked and raw bananas (which go well at all meals), and a number of other delicacies. There's also the standard red wine, and mineral water, the most desirable item on the menu at the moment. The fried goat cutlets are the specialty of the house; highly spiced and crisply fried, the meat comes right off the bones. The dogs begging in front of the porch love these bones. A scroungy lot of highly indeterminate breed, they look at us with sad starved expressions, as if telling us that every cutlet should find it's way directly to them, intact, just to relieve any pangs of conscience on our part. Their happy leaps and barks thank us for the bones which wing their ways into the waiting jaws.

Although the heat and the wine heighten the fatigue, a substantial number of archeology enthusiasts join us on a hike up-valley to the ancient temple of Meiaiaute. The road leads straight up the valley from Chez Fournier. We soon reach the end of the paved road, and continue on a rocky, muddy path, weaving ever-upward through a dense palm grove. Copra is produced in groves like this; this commodity still has some importance for Ua Huka and the Marquesas, and as we climb, sacks of copra from this and other groves are being loaded onto the *Aranui* by the busy whaleboat crews.

We reach the top of a finger-ridge, after climbing a steep serpentine path. Bob points out many ancient *paepae* house platforms long the ridge top. On the surface of the damp earth lie thousands of basalt flakes; the debris of stone adze manufacture in the prehistoric past. My eyes have long since been focused on the ground in the hope of finding some interesting artifacts, but thanks to Bob's help, I soon find a piece of a stone adze and then, to my great joy, a nice pear-shaped stone net weight.

Concrete stairs, another of the mayor's great ideas, help us up the last 30 meters or so to the temple terrace, where we finally stand, a bit out of breath, on Me'ae Meiaiaute. The temple consists of four badly damaged stone pavements, on a narrow artificial terrace. On the left stands a low altar with four *tiki,* one of which is a small scale version of Mak'i'i Tau'a Pepe, the unfortunate priestess whom we already met in Puama'u. It's a shame, but someone has beheaded this statue, and only the body and part of the legs remain. Tau'a Pepe's presence here confirms that the Na'iki tribe not only fled to Nuku Hiva and Ua Pou, but to Ua Huka as well; spreading the fame and worship of Manuiota'a's wife. In fact, ethnographic data also indicate that the Na'iki were here.

By contrast, the other *tiki* occupying this platform represent the typical style of the southern archipelago. They are carved out of slabs of tuff, are relatively small, but with proportionately somewhat larger heads than northern *tiki.* One of them displays an unusual tattoo motif on the cheek, indicating that the figure represented possessed a higher degree of supernatural power than the others. The names of these other figures have been sadly forgotten, however.

Thanks again to the mayor, the trees on the seaward side of the temple platform have been cleared, providing an inspiring view of the bay of Hane. Far below us, we spot the *Aranui,* riding at anchor. Cargo handling operations are in full swing, whale boats, hurrying back and forth, shuttle freight ashore, and bring copra and other cargo aboard.

On the way down from the temple to the beach, we make a short stop at the open-air studio of Joseph Te Hau Va'atete, the museum curator. Here he creates monumental stone *tiki,* which are often quite phallic in form, in keeping with Marquesan style and attitudes. There's also an almost full-scale copy of our friend Maki'i Tau'a Pepe. She would be a great decoration for my garden at home, but how would I ever bring her back? She certainly doesn't fit in the category of hand luggage.

In order to reach the landing at the end of the beach, we have to cross a huge dune behind the beach. This dune happens to hide the point of origin of a scientific polemic which endures to the present day, and Bob tells me the story.

He finished his work on Nuku Hiva in 1956–58 with results that drew plenty of attention. It was possible for him to describe the entire prehistory of the archipelago. Each period was clearly identified in terms of artifacts, house types, etc. and dated by the radiocarbon technique. The finds from the 125 BC site on Nuku Hiva's Ha'atuatua beach played an important role in these results. In this site, Bob discovered the first pieces of pottery ever found in Eastern Polynesia. At the time, there were two other archeologists, self-appointed guardians of the Polynesian legacy, who proudly demanded the right to interpret the results of all other's research work in Polynesia. And these fragile egos couldn't find it within their hearts to recognize Bob's results from Ha'atuatua; especially the early dates and the pottery. For these authorities, theory was more important than fact; and these facts, including very genuine pottery sherds, just didn't fit with preexisting theories. Therefore, the facts had to be denied!

Even though Bob maintained constant contact with both these archeologists, he was quite well aware that they were carrying on a campaign of slander behind his back, crudely calling all his work into question. One of the adversaries finally set out for the Marquesas, to get his own naturally indisputable results. He selected the Hane site for a dig. He found pottery there, too, and so the attacks on Bob's pottery ceased abruptly.

But instead of clarifying the situation on the age of early Marquesan settlements, the so-called research brought about total confusion. The radiocarbon dates from Hane were several centuries younger than Bob's from Ha'atuatua! How could this be? Through the power of omniscience, the answer came instantaneously: Bob's dates had to be in error!

Using dates from a site on one island to correct dates from another site on another island, was not only laughable, it was ridiculous. Since Ua Huka and Nuku Hiva are about 30 miles away from each other, who is to say that both sites should have been occupied at precisely the same time and would yield identical dates, anyway?

In the end, the whole "scientific" spat degenerated into the old children's game of "Mine is better than yours is!" But then it became known that a very large systematic error had appeared in the results from the inexperienced laboratory where the first Hane radiocarbon dates were processed. A new set of samples were submitted and these samples gave roughly the same dates as Bob's dates from Ha'atuatua! The omnisicent ones never acknowledged this, however, and the smear campaign continued. This was difficult for Bob because he saw his own honest work continually called into question. The second series of Hane dates was duly published, but without any comment, in the apparent hope that the scientific community, many of whom don't read much, would not take notice of the 600 year disparity between the dates for the lower levels of the site!

After several years, it was finally possible for Prof. Patrick V. Kirch, the dean of American archeologists in Polynesia, to resolve the contradictions, as an impartial judge. After a long, careful analysis of the tangled records and results from the Hane site, Kirch came to the totally objective conclusion that Hane had been occupied in the second century before the Christian era and possibly even before that. The previous digger had for some strange reason never attempted to date the earliest levels of the site, apparently having an allergy to early dates! Based on his study and results from other Marquesan sites, Kirch also believed that the archipelago had been settled as early as between 300 BC and 500 B.C. Finally, the word is now out in archeological circles that no one, most especially the original excavator himself, knows exactly what was really found in Hane. The final definitive statement from Kirch supports Bob's Ha'atuatua results in an impressive fashion, and destroys the theories of the two omniscient ones, according to which Hane was occupied between 400 AD and 700 AD (depending on which day you asked them). Beside Ha'atuatua and Hane there are now other sites on Hiva Oa and Ua Pou which have yielded dates in the late BC-early AD period, and so Hane has found it's rightful place in Marquesan prehistory.

I think that this sorry chronicle shows once more that even the so-called great figures of science are ultimately only human and blessed with all of the human frailties.

While we wait for the whaleboat, a pretty woman approaches Bob and engages him in an animated conversation with many gestures. His: "*E! E hoi!*" (Yes! Certainly!) comes with spontaneous laughter. From then on, he is the protector of two huge and cumbersome *'u'u* war clubs and some *koka'a* bowls, all to be delivered to Rose Corser 's Museum in Taioha'e.

In the meantime, the heavens are closing in again and the desire for a swim has gradually disappeared. The first passengers head to the boats. With his massive clubs packed in Tahitian newspapers, Bob looks like he's heading off to a tribal war. Tahitian newspapers, so I'm told, are used only for packing in the Marquesas. There are no newspapers in the archipelago, and no one is really interested in the Tahitian newspaper, "*La Depêche*," because this publication arrives too late and doesn't devote much attention to the Marquesas, in any case.

In the course of the afternoon, an imposing cross-section of the Hane population has assembled on the beach to watch the cargo-loading activities. It's a real pleasure for them, but for the leading performers, the sailors and the tourists, it's less of a pleasure. Because of the stubborn unpredictability of the seas in this bay, it frequently happens that onrushing waves seem on the point of burying the boats with their passengers, as well as those who are waiting to be hoisted aboard. None of the participants see this as a lot of fun. It takes plenty of ability, muscle, and nerve on the part of the sailors to defend against the impact of these rollers. This is especially true when the passengers crowd into the pitching, rolling boats with their awkward and bulky handicraft purchases, threatening the heads, ribs, and other body parts of everyone around them.

With his heavy freight, Bob's loaded last. "Aren't these clubs too heavy to be used as weapons? Wouldn't the old Marquesans themselves have problems swinging them in the midst of a raging fight?" "Sure!" Bob replies, "The real clubs were made of iron wood and had long thin handles. You could use those weapons easily. But actually, it's better that these are art works and are heavier than the real articles!" "But why is that?" "Nobody's going to be tempted to try them out on a neighbor's head!"

And finally the bowls are loaded. The pretty woman, quite happy to be rid of her wares, yells a hearty: *"Ka'oha nui!"* as the outboard motor begins to rumble, and we head though the surf for the *Aranui*, loaded to the gunnels.

While we were ashore, the ship has been transformed. The pool deck has sprouted palm leaf decorations for "Polynesian Night," and there's a buzz of activity, far more than is usually the case. There's a Polynesian Night on every trip, often in Anaho on the north coast of Nuku Hiva, but sometimes in other harbors. The decision as the location for the festivities depends on the skipper's itinerary. But wherever it takes place, Polynesian Night includes an exquisite cold buffet, music, dancing, and plenty of good company, and it's the highpoint of the cruise.

Once more, we're under way, and passing westward along the bleak cliffs of Ua Huka's south coast, we approach three so-called "bird islands." These odd-shaped, spectacular chunks of lava jut up out of the sea, looking even more mysterious in the evening light. Many bird lovers come to the islands of Motu Manu, Himeni, or Teuaua because around 40,000 brooding redfooted boobies and sooty terns have found a home on the flat tops and lofty vertical cliffs of these huge rocks. The waters around the islands are also regularly visited by numerous dolphins, the famous "spinners" whose antics always please the passengers. Loud toots from the ship's whistle are supposed to arouse the birds to flight, but we really can't say that spectacular swarms of our feathered friends rise to greet the blasts. This greatly disappoints the video film buffs, who have positioned themselves along the rail. Isn't it possible that the poor birds have finally developed an immunity to the ongoing bi-monthly irritation of the ship's whistle? Might they not be sitting calmly on their nests, snug in their thick downy coats, secretly amused by the humans who so desperately hope to goad them into flight?

A favorite Marquesan pastime is to either swim or canoe to the islands to collect sea bird eggs. These taste, and smell, like sardines, and have dark orange yolks, but when you need a bit of variation in a diet of raw fish and breadfruit, a sardine-flavored omelet goes down quite well, as Bob can testify from lengthy experience.

Leaving the bird islands, we shape a course toward Anaho bay on the northeast coast of Nuku Hiva, about 70 km from Ua Huka.

Around 1900, the "Night of Nights" begins. *Pareu* of every description are the favored attire, paradoxically topped off with hand-knitted sweaters against the rather strong breeze. Wooden hair pins from Ua Huka and flowers from the morning appear in carefully arranged hair-dos. In spite of the *pareu* trend, the varying degrees of freedom in costume go far beyond questions of the permissible weight of earrings, spanning the full spectrum from Parisian summer evening dress to clothing representing a complete disdain for the unique nature of the evening. Some people are wearing the very same clothes they've worn for a week! The men scorn the *pareu*: their attire generally consists of conservative trousers and shirt. Bob sports his Philippine *"barong tagalog"* shirt. To be completely in style, he says, the wearer of this filmy white shirt of pandanus or pineapple fiber must carry a *balisong* knife in his pocket. He accepts as a good alternative my suggestion that the all-important "traditional" dress item be replaced with a Swiss Army knife. Such a knife might get a scornful laugh in the bars in Subic or Olongapo, but it's still quite a weapon. The Seniors show up *unisono* in the "Country-Look" of the fancied Frontier days. Dug in behind a redoubt of plastic deck chairs, they huddle in a corner of the pool deck for their usual secret evening meeting.

The transit to Nuku Hiva is calm; the contours of Ua Huka gradually fade behind us and we see the broad silhouette of Nuku Hiva bulk up on the horizon. Two hours later, we're still chugging toward the coast of Nuku Hiva in deep darkness. The impatience level of the assembled passengers is rising rapidly. The hysterical laugh of a tiny French lady is getting on my nerves, just as much as is the cool wind, which is chilling me right to the bone through the loose clothing. But the outlines of Nuku Hiva are gaining detail and definition and the ship is perceptibly slowing down. Finally we enter Anaho Bay! There, on the starboard side, we recognize the tiny, weak lights of the houses of the approximately 20 inhabitants of this valley. This tiny settlement stands in sharp contrast to the once-blossoming prehistoric tribal population of Anaho.

About 2100 the lights on the pool deck are turned on. In next to no time, a brilliant buffet is laid out, a buffet which would calm the ravening appetites and satisfy the refined tastes of all gourmets. Still, the long delay has exerted a negative effect on moods, and when the entertainment program begins, it's greeted with little emotion.

Anniversary couples are heartily welcomed, as are a number of birthday boys and girls and honeymooners. But tonight, we celebrate a very special occasion: it's the golden wedding anniversary of the constantly-battling French couple. This provides more irony than entertainment, but it shows that even under such conditions it's possible to live together. After the ensuing award ceremony, conducted by the hostesses and featuring the mock-solemn address of a burly crew member (I think it was the cook) who is always used for such occasions, the couple retreats once more into the shadows, where they continue to dispute, with energetic gestures, as to who did what, to whom, when, where, why, and how.

With celebrations over, the buffet is open for business, and a stampede takes place, but this time the Seniors are caught behind their impregnable deck-chair Maginot line. They can't move out of their positions fast enough, and wind up at the end of the chow line. Bob recalls an old military adage that's quite applicable here: "If the enemy can't get in, then you can't get out!"

The sailors are truly a sight to behold. All decked out, they're a wonderful collection of masculinity. Only Brutus, whose virile hips are decorated with a yellow and red *pareu*, has lost a bit of his attraction. The macho look of 1997 with the dangerously tight jeans and the black *Aranui* crew T-shirt gave him a bold aspect, making him the most irresistible conqueror of the whole crew.

In Bob's opinion, this evening is a fringe benefit for the sailors: "They've had enough time to check out the pretty gals among the passengers, lifting them in and out of the whaleboats, and now they have the chance to get a bit closer." This is typical male logic, resting on somewhat shaky ground. It seems to me that the choice foods, wines, and beer are far more tempting than the rather sparse selection of attractive young women. With the strains of the *Aranui* band, and in the company of my industrious little roommates, this day comes to a peaceful and leisurely, if slightly chilly, end.

Nuku Hiva: Anaho Valley

"Anaho: this sheltered bay with its white sand beach and inshore reef, is the most beautiful that we've so far seen in these islands. The bay combines, in a charming fashion, a broad, gently curving expanse of tropical beach with the surrounding nearly naked peaks and ridges. The surface of the turquoise waters reflects the sunlight in unique and impressive ways, while the dark green shades of the wooded shoreline enclose the bay, adding a touch of mystery. Anaho seems to be the realization of a South Sea dream: isolated, protected, empty and primitive. It is beguiling in its beauty." (Excerpt from my 1997 Journal)

The *Aranui* lies at anchor; the surface of the bay is an almost glassy calm. In the early morning light, big manta rays and the occasional shark cruise slowly and deliberately around the ship.

Anaho bay is spread out before us; it's like a huge bowl, walled in by volcanic peaks and from the sea by small peninsulas. The only coral reef in the entire archipelago extends in the shallows along the palm-shaded beach on the western bay shore. Despite the few houses clustered behind the beach, everything seems to be untouched and forsaken. Opposite the beach, the eastern shore is formed by a grim line of layered basalt cliffs incessantly assaulted by ranks of white surf.

In the south, like a giant gray-black obelisk, the grim and almost threatening peak known as Tukemata (The Eyebrow) juts up 800 m above us. This morning, its tip is shrouded in mist and cloud. From the side of this obelisk, a huge black *tiki* eye stares out over the bay. The Marquesans named this peak well! What seem to be long gossamer veils of cloud, extending down the face of the obelisk, are actually narrow torrents of water dashing into the valley below, carrying moisture from the rain-laden

154

clouds that hover over the peak. These falls have given Anaho the reputation of having the best water on all of Nuku Hiva.

This bay seems to be the fulfillment of a tropical paradise fantasy, but it's had a very turbulent past, rich in drama and human suffering. When Captain David Porter, USN, arrived at Nuku Hiva in 1813, the Marquesans told him a fascinating and significant legend which he recorded for posterity. According to the legend, many centuries prior to 1813, a two-masted ship had called in at Anaho. The ship's crew were said to have looked like Marquesans; that is, they had brown skin and long black hair, but they were not tattooed. The strangers asked the Marquesans for pigs, and gave their Marquesan hosts pieces of iron in return. This was the first time that the Marquesans had ever seen this metal.

The racial description of the visitors, the absence of any mention of monks, soldiers, or firearms, and the fact that no Marquesans lost their lives in the encounter make it certain that the ship was neither Spanish nor Portuguese. Further, the date of the contact seems to be around 1200–1300 AD and there were no Europeans in the Pacific at that time. Since South America can be ruled out, the only other source for iron is Asia or Southeast Asia. Was this ship perhaps a *prau* of one of the Indo-Malaysian seafaring peoples such as the Bugis from Sulawesi, or the Madurese? Or could it be a junk from the South China coast, where pigs were very much an item on the menu? Was the reference to long hair really a reference to pigtails? Whoever these visitors were, their arrival cannot be precisely dated, but if they came from Southeast Asia, they must have come before about 1400, when Islam was getting established in that area, because pigs would certainly not have been sought by Muslim sailors.

The ruins which fill Anaho's quiet palm speak of a very large population. In fact, when Porter arrived on Nuku Hiva, there were four tribes in the valley. According to information which he collected, Anaho could put several thousand warriors into the field.

It is said that the Anaho tribes tended to be treacherous and very much attracted to cannibalism. The stories tell of an honest, trusting Marquesan from Hiva Oa who was lured there, captured, and sacrificed. In memory of this deed, it is said that the full moon often bathes the bay in a blood-red glow. A "stick-figure" petroglyph on a seaside rock on the southeast bay shore also commemorates this unhappy event.

The last officially-recognized case of cannibalism on Nuku Hiva took place in 1867 in Anaho, not far from where the *Aranui* picnic is held. On this lovely shady beach, the victim was cooked alive in an earth oven and devoured. While 1867 marks the official end of cannibalism, this practice, always a form of human sacrifice, continued in the southern archipelago until much later and did not end on Nuku Hiva until 1925. In 1956, Bob was led to a small cave above Ue'a valley, on the now-deserted west coast of Nuku Hiva, where the skull of the supposed actual last victim of cannibalism had been deposited, 31 years earlier. The skull, that of a child about 10–11 years old, was definitely quite new, and the account given by the informant was so vivid and detailed, that it seemed as though he himself might have participated in this meal.

Because of its ideal situation and features, Anaho was already widely known among mariners in the latter part of the 19th century, and visited by many European and American ships, seeking the advantages of its secure anchorage and it's water. These visits brought great tragedy to the inhabitants of this fertile valley and ultimately to the entire archipelago.

In 1862, "Blackbirders" (slave hunters) called in at Anaho. They tempted the unsuspecting inhabitants to come aboard their ship and not a few accepted the invitation. Plied with alcohol and drugs, the Marquesans passed out, awakening from their stupor to find themselves prisoners, headed for a life of slavery in the Guano Islands off the coast of Chile.

The French colonial administration made immediate and successful protest to both the Chilean and Peruvian governments. The Marquesan captives were freed and placed aboard the ship *"Diamant"* to be returned to their homeland, but a smallpox epidemic was raging at the time in Chile and Peru, and the Marquesans had already been infected. They reached their homeland in moribund condition, bringing the dreaded disease back with them. The infected returnees came ashore in Taioha'e; those who were still able returned to their families in Anaho, and the adjacent valleys of Ha'atuatua and Hatiheu. Shortly thereafter, a smallpox epidemic broke out across the entire archipelago. In only three short years, the disease carried off more than 66% of the population. The valleys of Anaho, Ha'atuatua, and Hatiheu were almost completely depopulated. It's safe to assume that the losses were even greater than stated, since the official census reports were never really precise. Bob's 1956 field research team came upon many places in the deep forests where human bones were lying on the ground surface, proof that often there was often no one left to bury the dead.

In 1888, not long after the smallpox epidemic, a famous and quite peaceful visitor arrived in Anaho. This was the Scots author, Robert Louis Stevenson, aboard the schooner *Casco*. Stevenson was enchanted by the magnificent sunrises above the eastern ridge wall of the bay. He often walked along a particularly isolated stretch of beach, collecting small seashells for his wife, lost in deep contemplation of the beauty around him.

Stevenson knew that he only had a short time to live and was searching for a place to spend his last years. He felt quite comfortable among the people of Anaho, but because of his bad health it was impossible for him to remain very long in the Marquesan environment. With a heavy heart, he left Anaho on course for Micronesia, ultimately dropping anchor in Samoa, where he spent his last days as a respected guest. His Samoan title was *"Tusitala"*, or "Storyteller." Not far from Apia, he was finally laid to rest. The modest inscription on his grave is perhaps one of the most beautiful ever written:

> Under the wide and starry sky,
> Dig the grave and let me lie,
> Gladly I lived and gladly die,
> And I lay me down with a will.
> This be the verse you grave for me:
> Here he lies where he longed to be,
> Home is the sailor, home from the sea,
> And the hunter, home from the hill.

Anaho was also not spared in World War II. During that conflict, Rear Admiral Richard Byrd USN, the famous Arctic explorer, was sent on an expedition to locate ideal sites for airfields on the islands of Eastern Polynesia. US Naval Intelligence gave him a tip to check out Nuku Hiva, which was known to offer suitable terrain for such construction. This information was provided to Naval Intelligence by the ethnologist, Edward Handy (himself a former naval officer); the Polynesian linguist, Sam Elbert, who had worked in the Marquesas and was then a serving Lieutenant in Naval Intelligence, and the British entomologists Adamson and Mumford, who knew the environment of Nuku Hiva down to the finest detail.

The Byrd Task Group, with the official title of "Special Presidential Commission to the South and East Pacific" set out from Balboa in Panama aboard the cruiser, *USS Concord*. After calls at Easter Island, and islands in the Tuamotu Archipelago (including the future French nuclear test sites Mururoa and Fangataufa), the Task Group arrived at Nuku Hiva., The French Administration officials were at that time Petainist Nazi-collaborators. Not surprisingly they were not overjoyed to see these visitors, with their awe-inspring six-inch guns, reconnaissance aircraft, and auxiliary vessels.

For six days, US Navy engineer construction personnel scoured the island, guided by catapult-launched recon aircraft from the cruiser. The *Concord* called at Taioha'e, Taipi, Hatiheu, and finally Anaho, which was recognized as the best harbor in the entire archipelago.

On 7 October, 1943, as the *Concord* was leaving Anaho, she was rocked by a terrific explosion: fumes from aviation gas, leaking from tanks deep in the ship had been ignited by sparks from the electrically-operated rudder. The explosion buckled the afterdeck, killing the "XO" (Executive Officer), and 25 sailors. The ship was saved only by the valiant efforts of damage control teams.

Since that tragic day, 26 Americans rest on the sea floor, just off Anaho, along with a large number of powerful anti-submarine depth charges, which had to be jettisoned from the *Concord* to prevent total destruction of the ship.

In spite of all this drama, the Anaho that greets us today is a small-scale tropical paradise, and almost no one has any idea of this valley's turbulent past.

Before we go ashore with the whaleboats, we must satisfy the desires of a number of passengers to visit the engine room. That the *Aranui* at one time was known as the "Bishop of Bremen" becomes quite clear during this tour. All the information, instructions, and placards are in German. As a product of high-quality German technology, she has superbly confronted all the challenges of the Pacific Ocean and never strayed from her course. Thanks to her engineering plant, screws, and thrusters, she is extremely maneuverable. Naturally, she rolls a bit now and then, but that's only because she's always sailing diagonally across the trade winds and the swells that come with them.

The chief engineer, a tall quiet, but friendly Tahitian, is almost never seen on deck. To meet him you must descend into "his world," a world that is scrupulously clean and well-organized. The deafening background noise can't be helped, of course. After 20 years, this is his last cruise on the *Aranui*. Will he actually leave the ship? I hear a remark: "After that length of time aboard ship, he's got sea water in his veins! He'll soon be hankering for the smell of diesel fuel again. Those engines are like unforgettable mistresses, he'll always be yearning for them ...!."

After the tour, the whale boats bring us to Anaho beach. Most of our shipmates use this magical day to relax; some explore the deep blue depths of the bay, others wander along the gently curving beach, still others lie under the shade of rustling palm trees, completely abandoning themselves to the enjoyment of these surroundings. People dream about places like Anaho on cold winter days in Europe and North America!

The more active passengers join those who are interested in archeology, gathering with Bob off to one side of the beach for the hike to Ha'atuatua valley. Before the hike begins, certain precautions must be taken to ensure that a beautiful day doesn't end up unhappily. These precautions include applying a sufficient quantity of insect repellent against the vicious little *nono* flies (we'll discuss them later). We must also ensure that everyone has full water bottles, that sun block cream has been liberally applied, and that long trousers and long sleeve shirts are worn. Although I'll later have to atone for my light and rather frivolous clothing and my smirks at such precautions, I still can't quite avoid the impression that our well-wrapped hikers look more like they are heading for the Himalayas rather than going for a hike on a South Sea beach.

We set off behind Bob on the path to Ha'atuatua, leading through an open palm grove, littered with fallen coconuts. Many of these nuts are giving off shoots and will soon be taking root as new trees. If one of these nuts happens to fall on your head,

160

it would certainly put an abrupt period to all the lyrical thoughts you might be enjoying as you swing along the path!

We pass a small house cluster in a clearing on the beach; this is a missionary youth vacation camp, and several years ago, it was Bob's base camp for three months when he was last working at Ha'atuatua. At that time, he slept on the floor of a large dormitory room with other crew members, lulled to sleep night after night by the rhythmic crash of surf against the rockbound east side of the bay. Like Stevenson, he was awakened every morning by the sun coming out of her house beneath the sea, peeking over the eastern ridge, bringing the day to him and his crew. The floor of the dormitory area always had to be defended against incursions of beetles, cockroaches, centipedes, mice, and rats, but it seemed worth the annoyance when every evening you could lose yourself in an enchanting sunset, and end the day under the glorious gleaming South Sea heavens.

Next to the camp site, we discover a tiny chapel with seats made of coconut trunks set vertically in a white sand floor. This chapel is used every Sunday by the few remaining inhabitants of Anaho valley, who meet with their prayer leader to chant parts of the Mass.

We reach a promontory and another beautiful beachscape stretches out before us. This is Stevenson's favorite beach, where he roamed and collected seashells for his wife, Fanny.

The hike is enchanting; we stroll along lonely expanses of beach backed by basalt cliffs sculpted in bizarre forms. It seems as if nature had once built a playground for giants here. The exertion of the climb to the low saddle leading into Ha'atuatua valley is not even noticeable because of the captivating landscape and the mysterious peace that seems to emanate from this valley. Suddenly a new view opens up before us: there, like an untouched jewel, is the beach of Ha'atuatua. Silvery sunbeams flit over the dark forests enclosing the white sandy beach on both sides. The endless vista of the Pacific, the surf, and the wind that blows across the dunes all combine in other-worldly perfection.

On the other side of the surf, we recognize Ua Huka in the distance, a black volcanic cone set in the middle of a seemingly infinite ocean. On the right of our vantage point, a gray black cliff rises into the heavens, supported by thin, sharp volcanic dikes standing out from the cliff face like flying buttresses. These geological formations have given Ha'atuatua its name: "Sharp Ridge Bay." The buttresses and the cliffs separate Ha'atuatua from the neighboring and once-allied valleys and tribes of Taipi and Ho'oumi to the south. The peak on our left, almost 300 m. high, forms the back wall of Ha'a Ta'i Ve'a valley on the north-eastern tip of the island, where the great *tiki* quarry is located.

The path to the beach leads through an eery hibiscus grove, winding around and over helter-skelter, criss-crossed fallen trunks, which look like the beginning of some cosmic game of jackstraws. The footing is not always sure. Suddenly everything is much quieter: only the strangely muffled sound of the surf penetrates our ears. The Marquesans believe that spirit drums can often be heard in this grove, and they regard it as a *vahi mana*, a place with a charge of supernatural power.

Many of the Marquesans are actually afraid of this valley, and it's rare that anyone lives here for a long time. Can they sense the tragedies that have occurred here? Even in the time of Karl von den Steinen, in the late 19th century, the only residents were two old women, and now the valley is empty.

Bob was drawn to Ha'atuatua in a rather special fashion. In 1956,when he was visiting Hatiheu valley west of Anaho, a Marquesan casually asked if he'd ever been to Ha'atuatua. When he responded in the negative, the Marquesan quietly advised: "You really ought to go there and look around, there's a lot of pig bones on the beach." That was enough to launch Bob to-ward Ha'atuatua the very next day. He didn't find many pig bones, but he found many human bones, as well as a large assortment of artifacts: basalt adzes, fishhooks and ornaments made from mother of pearl, basalt flake tools of all sorts, and many coral files used for shaping mother of pearl hooks.

A few weeks later, he returned and began his excavations. Soon he realized that the sprawling dune, 750 meters long, hid the remains of an entire ancient community, including a low temple platform and burial ground in the middle of the beach, and a series of house clusters extending along the dune crest to the north and south of the temple.

The excavations were considered a great success, partly because of the rich collection of artifacts, but also because of the human skeletal remains recovered. These showed that the early Marquesans were quite different from their modern descendants. The first settlers were generally of shorter stature, but had extremely muscular physiques and were long-headed (18th century Marquesans were among the tallest of the Polynesians and were round-headed). Their dentition was absolutely beautiful. There were signs of endemic arthritis, however, even among teenagers, and many indications of violence, including fractured skulls, and in one case evidence of a successful trepanation. This person had suffered a fractured skull: a piece of bone pressing on the brain had been successfully surgically removed, and the individual had lived long enough for the bone around the wound to grow smooth again.

The structures on the beach were not elaborate. The temple platform was a roughly rectangular pavement of breadloaf-sized beach pebbles. On the inland side of the temple was a broad dance floor surfaced with gravel. The houses were small, simple huts, built directly on the sand without any paving. They all had an elongated oval, or boat-shaped, ground plan, similar to ancient houses excavated on Easter Island, in early sites in Hawai'i, and in western Polynesia. Thanks to radiocarbon dating techniques, it was possible to date this ancient village to at least 125 BC, and this was another great step forward. As stated above, however, the radiocarbon dates posed a real problem for those who steadfastly believed that these islands had only been settled for a few centuries, as well as for a few other theorists.

Bob's second season in 1957–58 was even more successful than the first. On the very first day after returning to Ha'atuatua, he found potsherds in the vicinity of the temple. This was another sensational find: up to this time pottery was completely unknown in Eastern Polynesia! Even where it had been found in Western Polynesia it was always assumed to be the result of trade with Fiji. As noted above, this find was quite a shock for the Guardians of the Flame of Polynesian Archeology, a shock from which some have yet to recover!

To assess the significance of this find, we have to take a brief detour through Polynesian archeology, and talk about the Lapita culture. This is the culture of the ancient ancestors of the Polynesians. The story of the Lapita people, revealed over the last half-century, is one of the most fascinating tales of modern archeology. This story is regrettably found only in the professional literature and is quite unfamiliar, even to the informed public, many of whom think that the wild fantasies of Thor Heyerdahl represent the current state of knowledge of Polynesian prehistory.

The Lapita people, ancestors of the Polynesians

Since 1958, we've learned much about the prehistory of the Polynesians, and on the basis of the work at Ha'atuatua, it's been possible to get a far more complete picture of the settlement of Polynesia. The finds at this site allowed us to connect it directly with the original culture from which all Polynesians societies have descended.

In 1952, while excavating on Lapita Beach in New Caledonia, Prof. E.W Gifford of the University of California at Berkeley found pottery with impressed decorations. He sent charcoal samples from the site to be dated by the radiocarbon method. To be sure, these highly decorated sherds had been known elsewhere in the Pacific since 1908, but their age had always remained a complete mystery. It was only after 1948 that the radiocarbon dating technique was finally made available to archeologists, and it was this method which happily established the full significance of Gifford's work at Lapita: the strata containing the strangely decorated sherds was dated conclusively at 846 BC, far earlier than anyone had ever anticipated in that part of the Pacific!

There are two types of Lapita ceramics: the best known is the highly decorated type with its unusual geometric motifs, big-eyed tiki faces, geometric designs, and occasionally lizards. These motifs, now believed to represent tattoo motifs, were impressed in the wet clay before the pots were fired, using what seems to have been tattoo needles. Because these pots were rather poorly fired and soft, archeologists suppose that they could not have been used for cooking and were probably made by males, for strictly ceremonial purposes. Today in Melanesia only women make pottery for household uses.

The second type of Lapita pottery is that known as "Polynesian Plain Ware." This is an undecorated utilitarian household ware. The vessels were thin-walled, very well fired, hence quite durable. The finds at Ha'atuatua are of this type of pottery.

As early as 1960, in his first book: Island Civilizations of Polynesia, (NY, New American Library), Bob had already drawn attention to the significance of the Lapita Culture as the most probable ancestral culture of all Polynesian civilizations. It was only 10 years later, however, that anyone took any deep interest in this culture. The resulting excavations, mainly under the leadership of Drs. Patrick Vinton Kirch and Roger Green at Lapita sites in Melanesia, New Guinea, and Polynesia have finally illuminated the hitherto shadowy prehistory of the earliest Polynesians.

Today, we know beyond a shade of doubt the Lapita culture originated at least 1900 BC in Eastern Indonesia-Western Melanesia. The Lapita seafarers were an off-shoot of a single widely-spread group of peoples, all speakers of the so-called Austronesian languages. Through the course of several millennia, this group had filtered out into the Pacific from coastal Mainland China and Taiwan, into the Philippines and Indonesia and along the coasts of Vietnam and Malaysia. It was the Lapita peoples, a later branch of these Austronesian speakers, who developed the ancestral or proto-culture of Polynesia.

Lapita was a seafaring culture: the Lapita villages consisted of houses built on stilts, over lagoons teeming with marine life. They fished these lagoons and the ocean around their islands, planted the usual Polynesian plants and trees:, including coconut palms, candle nuts, iron wood, taro, yams, bananas, hibiscus trees, pandanus, and breadfruit. They weren't only fishermen and gardeners, however; above all, they were traders. It has been possible to trace their trade routes over distances of up to 2600 km in Melanesia. Their most popular goods were the highly decorated pottery, which archeologists now regard as the visiting card of the Lapita sailors. Obsidian and flint were also very highly prized trade goods. There is no doubt that these wide-ranging traders also possessed domesticated animals, including pigs, dogs, and chickens. Rats and lizards appear to have stowed away on their canoes as well.

Following their first archeological appearance in about 2000–1900 BC in eastern Indonesia and Melanesia, the Lapita peoples did not tarry long. They moved out rapidly to the east, using large outriggers or double-hulled sailing canoes, probably with carved bow and stern figures. Trade goods and supplies were stored on large platforms between the hulls or on the outrigger booms. Driven by the desire to find commodities to trade, and additional trading partners, they populated the Bismarck archipelago, the Solomons, Santa Cruz, Vanuatu, New Caledonia, and Fiji in two or three centuries.

They reached Western Polynesia, Tonga and Samoa, by about 1600 BC, and again stayed a short while, adapting to their somewhat altered environment, before exploring further into the vast emptiness of the eastern Pacific. By 500 BC they had already reached the southern Cook Islands. Then it was only a few generations until the late Lapita seafarers reached the Marquesas. These Lapita explorers and their descendants were the first Polynesians.

he nearly dislikes
Heyerdahl

The potsherds that Bob found at Ha'atuatua were pieces of pots of the undecorated "Polynesian Plain Ware" type, brought by the first Polynesian settlers. A careful geochemical analysis of sherds showed that some of the Ha'atuatua pottery had actually been made in the Rewa River delta on the far-off Fijian island of Viti Levu. Other potsherds, however, appear to have been made in the Marquesas, of Marquesan clay.

As we noted above, three additional pre-Christian era sites have been found in the Marquesas since the excavations at Ha'atuatua. Additional pottery has been also been found on Ua Huka and Hiva Oa, and it's now pretty certain that the discovery and settlement of the Marquesas took place between 300 and 500 BC.

The general outlines of the settlement of Polynesia have been gradually revealed, and the greatest migration of all times can be attributed to the Lapita merchant sailors in their great canoes. These migrations deserve to be ranked among the greatest wonders of the ancient world, wonders of the spirit, of courage, seamanship, knowledge of the environment, and mastery of Neolithic technology. While the ancient Egyptians and Phoenicians were timidly exploring the Mediterranean and venturing into the Atlantic, always hugging the shorelines, the ancestral Polynesians were jumping off thousands of kilometers, on deep-water voyages of trade and exploration, and settling the islands they discovered. The so-called "theory" that the Pacific islands were settled from Peru remains, today as always, a totally devoid of any basis in fact. Not a single South American artifact has ever been found in the almost 50 years of intensive archeology in Polynesia. Most readers don't realize that Heyerdahl's Kon-tiki raft voyage was no test of ancient Peruvian voyaging abilities. That trip was made with a large supply of canned foods, solar stills for fresh water, a radio, and a lot of luck! It only proved that with the same 20th century hi-tech equipment and the indispensable luck, voyages from Peru are possible today, but it proved nothing about prehistoric Peruvian voyaging. There's absolutely no proof that any Peruvian exploration of the Pacific ever actually took place in the past. There is, however, fascinating archeological and linguistic evidence of long standing, indicating that Polynesians landed on the north coast of Chile, *among the tribe known today as the Mapuché, and that they may have stayed. But this evidence is ignored: it isn't exciting and doesn't sell books.*

Back in Ha'atuatua, our path brings us on the dune to the hill known as Te 'oho 'au ("the canoe shed"), the current name for the old temple site. The remains of the temple pavement are still to be seen on the hilltop. Some of the basalt pebbles poking through the surface remain in place. Others are sliding down the face of the dune. Beneath the temple platform, Bob came upon an ancient firepit among the graves, and from this pit removed charcoal and ashes which were dated to 125 BC.

On the north end of the beach is the area called Mouaka, a house-cluster site in ancient times. In addition to the treasure trove of artifacts recovered here, the researchers found rather unusual burials under the house floors, including two young women buried in fetal positions. Their bodies were interred with skulls intact, which was not a common custom in the Marquesas. Normally, the corpses were allowed to decay and the bones were cleaned. Then the skulls, considered the seat of the individual's supernatural power, were separated from the rest of the body and placed on the temple platform, after which the other bones were disposed of in a variety of ways. We can only guess why things were different for these two young girls, who were buried intact, but there are many possibilities. Were they captives from another tribe? Had they broken some strict *tapu*? We'll never know, but they speak to us, across time and space, from Hawaiki.

The hill on the southern end of the beach is called Matahuetea. Here excavations are forbidden. According to still-current Marquesas beliefs, this is the place where the souls of departed Nuku Hivans meet before they set off for Cape Kiukiu on Hiva Oa, where they begin their last voyage to Hawaiki, the Polynesian afterlife.

168

The Marquesans claim that on Matahuetea at night, they can hear the souls of the dead laughing and singing. They say that if you know how, you can go there, grab the soul of a loved one and bring that person back to life. The woodcarver, Teikivahiani, told Bob a lot about this place and the strange happenings there. Teiki once had some frightening experiences on Matahuetea and always avoided the place thereafter.

Instead of returning with the group, we remain behind on the beach where two Marquesans are trying to launch themselves with a parasail. We watch for a time, but all their efforts to take off into the stiff trade winds seem to be in vain. We wander off to an erosion gully, the site of a workshop where the ancients carved their stone fish-line sinkers and net weights. We're actually successful and return to the temple area with an example as a souvenir!

In spite of the stories of spirits, and the often tragic dramas which had occurred here, we feel strangely secure in this magnificent valley. Is it the unusual peacefulness, the desolate beauty of the beach, or the eternal song of the surf which awoke in us this feeling of absolute well being?

The departure from Ha'atuatua is quite difficult. Over and over, we stop along the way to look back, until the hibiscus forest finally swallows us up. I know that the fascination of this place will never let me go: someday, I'll be coming back here.

The picnic is almost at an end when we finally return to Anaho beach, but what remains of the feast is more than enough to satisfy us both.

Wherever we look on this afternoon, we see scenes of total relaxation and happy, carefree living. Some people loll sleepily on the beach, listening to the sailors' guitars; others, like us, wander along the beach or cluster in small groups, laughing and talking. The tide is going out and the water seems to draw us back toward the *Aranui*. The distance is quite deceptive, it almost looks as if you might actually be able to walk back to the ship.

Such a walk is definitely inadvisable, however, because there's no limit to what the coral can do to bare feet. Many of our diver friends swear that they'll never again partake of this pleasure without reefshoes. For those of us who sit on the sand, the on-going "Coral Ballet" provides some wry laughs. Best of all the *"danseurs"* was "The Gov'" a slightly over-the-hill American Adonis on the 1997 trip who, wincing and grimacing, picked, faltered, and flopped his way through the coral like the proverbial "octopus on a hot griddle." After many detours, he finally regained the soft sand in sadly battered condition, holding up his bleeding fingers like a battleflag. His deflated appearance bore no resemblance to the self-possessed "Sportsman" who had so confidently disappeared into the waves with a brave splash only a few hours previously.

Margitta and I revel in our memories of these events the rest of the afternoon, without paying the slightest attention to the tiny flies which are wandering about, here and there, on our exposed skins. When we finally realize that these are blood-sucking *nono* flies, we regret our carelessness, but by then it's already far, far, too late.

These little beasts may be small, virtually unnoticeable, but a surprisingly large and tangled mythology has woven itself around them, as is always the case with anything that torments mankind.

There are two types of *nono*: the black-winged and the white-winged varieties. The latter are known as *"nono purutia,"* i.e., "German *nono*," and are the worst of the two. My German heart begins to protest, because I don't want us to have to take responsibility for this plague, too.

With insatiable appetites for human blood, the *nono* are always on the look-out for a meal. Who can blame them for passionately concentrating on the pale, and often broad, exposed expanses of tourist skin? The tourists, despite being well-warned about the "wee beasties" are often so enchanted by the magic of the South Seas that they pay no heed to the warnings. And so, over the course of several hours, an uncontrolled giving and taking goes on, just as it did with us! These transactions finally bring us, the donors, to the painfully itching realization that this South Seas Paradise also has its dark side.

A lot of nonsense has been put out about these tiny poisonous flies, and this nonsense has been accepted and further elaborated by the Marquesans themselves, to the extent that they often can no longer differentiate between pure fantasy and fact. The latest published versions state confidently that the "Germans" were responsible for sneaking this insect plague into Polynesia, in some kind of sinister pre-World War I plot.

Should we seriously accept as a bitter truth that Germany's already tortured soul must also bear the burden of the *nono* of the Pacific? Why must this be so? Well, as the story goes, it was Germans trading ships which off-loaded their ballast of New Guinea earth in the Marquesas. That earth contained *nono* eggs, and so the *nono* were smuggled in! We have a really malicious temptation to see this story as a Gallic idea calculated to further enhance Franco-German friendship.

But what *is* the truth about these little nuisances? To begin with, a neutral scholar must affirm in strongest terms that the Germans had nothing to do with the *nono*. Thanks, Bob! The bug is not only known in the Marquesas, you see. To this very day, in some languages of West Polynesia and the remote "Polynesian Outlyers" in Melanesia, separated from the Marquesas by 3500 years or more, the word for the same type of bug is the same as the Marquesan word: i.e., *nono!* The little beasts were brought to the Marquesas by the first settlers, the late Lapita peoples. These mariners were representatives of groups which had originated in other islands in the Indo-Pacific where the white-winged *nono* are found. The Lapita sailors had helped to spread the little bugs by inadvertently carrying the insect eggs in their food supplies as they spread out over the Pacific. Only a few years ago, such a transfer almost took place between the Marquesas and Hawai'i. The crew of the Polynesian Voyaging Society's double-hulled voyaging canoe, *Hawaiki Loa,* had visited the Marquesas and upon their departure had been given popoi and other foods, packed in traditional fashion. A few days out of Hawai'i, the crew was attacked by clouds of *nono* emanating from these food containers. The Hawaiian Chamber of Commerce was quite concerned, foreseeing dire consequences for tourism if the bugs were to get established ashore. The offending food was "deep-sixed," insecticide was air-dropped to the crew, and both crew and canoe were once more thoroughly disinfected before coming ashore.

The *nono* are mentioned frequently in ancient Marquesan legends, as well as by European visitors. They assaulted the indomitable Capt. David Porter and his crew in 1813, long before any German trading ships appeared, and in 1896 they warmly greeted Arthur Baessler, who didn't fail to mention his well-bitten posterior in his already-cited book, *New Pictures of the South Seas (Neue Suedseebilder)*

And the story about the dirt brought from New Guinea? The tale is merely a fantasy based on the fact that some German trading ships setting out for the South Seas normally carried dirt as ballast, but the dirt was from Germany! Before the return trip, the ballast was off-loaded to make room for cargoes of copra, pearl shell, etc. This happened, for example, in the Marshall Islands, which are situated far to the west of the Marquesas, but there are no *nono* in the Marshalls! The only foreign earth scattered around the Pacific is therefore German earth; and in the Marshalls this earth proved very good for the environment. Further, there was never any trade between New Guinea and the Marquesas, and we can confidently affirm that the tale of the German-introduced *nono* is just another myth in the rich fantasy-history of the Marquesas. But what about the adjective "German" applied to the *nono*? This is a 20th century appellation, tacked on to the little bugs, reflecting the Marquesans' admiration of the white-clad, dauntingly agressive and well-disciplined sailors of Admiral von Spee's Asiatic Fleet who called in at Nuku Hiva in September, 1914. These men, on their way to death at the Falklands, apparently took no guff from anyone, and the Marquesans were quite impressed by their agressive manner of dealing with the French gendarmes and administrators.

A final note needs to be appended here: the *nono* are found all over the world. We've both encountered them personally in New Zealand, Brazil, Iceland, North America, elsewhere in Polynesia, and even Indonesia and Borneo, as our own skins can attest. Must Germany always remain a handy scapegoat?

Well, that's enough of archeology, ethnology, history, and biology! Unfortunately, that's also enough of Anaho's beautiful beach. It's time to go! With the greatest regret, we watch this fascinating day draw irrevocably to a close. Loaded down with swimming gear, cameras, rucksacks, baskets, and handbags, we wade through the knee-deep water to climb into the whale boat, handled by a boat crew which has spent the entire day aboard the *Aranui*. They're stone cold sober; there's been no partying for them. The sailors who provided the music ashore have obviously enjoyed prolonged and intimate contacts with Hinano, Heinekens, and Budweiser, and seem to be in a rather "elevated" state. Don't worry, the other watch has "the duty!"

The clear evening sunshine bathes the landscape in warm gold. We go up on deck for one more look at Tukemata, now honey-colored in the slanting sun rays. In this failing light, the cliff walls of Ha'atuatua seem even more mysterious and once more forcibly evoke the uncanny feeling that we experienced there earlier, a feeling that will never be forgotten.

At 1700 we weigh anchor, and with a touch of melancholy settling over the entire group, we gather below in the foyer by the dining room entrance. Near us sits the young Hawaiian cowgirl. Even in the tropical heat, she and her partner never shed their brown cowboy hats, long-sleeved shirts, Manchester trousers, and cowboy boots.

They're real Hawaiian cowboys, *paniolo*, representatives of an unappreciated stratum of that island culture, and they are every bit as good as the cowpunchers on the mainland. Many Hawaiians might be said to have been "born in the saddle," on the large ranches of Hawai'i and Mau'i.

It isn't our interest in Hawaiian cowboys that kicks off the conversation, however, but the young woman's naked swollen foot, which is covered with tiny blue-black spots. She tells us that she stepped on a sea urchin.

"You using any medicine? What kind?"

"Yeah, I put some ointment on it, but piss helps too, for anything like that. So I got some of the sailors to help me out."

Speechless, I look at Bob, but his inscrutable expression looks as though this kind of medication were completely normal. He wants to hear a bit more about the treatment, but the cowgirl is not forthcoming with details. We wonder what her guy was doing while the sailors were being "tapped"? We finally decide to simply let the delicate subject lie in peace, and head off, half-starved, for dinner.

Nuku Hiva: Hatiheu Valley

The coastal landscape that we pass on our course to Hatiheu invokes strange fantasies. Mighty lava flows, looking like huge greedy black tongues, slide down the slopes and sink into the iridescent sea, while the sun conjures up a wondrous multiplicity of shades of green in the folds of the mountain ridges.

Suddenly I'm torn out of my reverie by an unusual uproar breaking out onboard. Everybody runs to the starboard side, shrieking and hooting. "What's up?" I ask one of the Seniors who trips over me as she tries to load a film into the camera. "Dolphins, dolphins!!" she pants, disappearing around the corner. Soon the railing is jammed with photo enthusiasts, camcorders humming, cameras snapping madly away. With this light they won't get much, but don't fault them for trying: these "spinners" are wonderful!

Hatiheu is a jewel nestled in a bowl formed of three steep volcanic ridges. On one of these ridges, we note the white figure of the Madonna of Hatiheu which already occupied that peak in 1888, when Stevenson visited Hatiheu. Her story is not lacking in irony, an irony arising out of the collision of the radically dissimilar cultures of the ancient Marquesas and that of the European missionaries of the late 19th century.

The missionaries wanted to erect a statue to honor the Virgin Mary, and they wanted this statue to be carved from a single tree. In keeping with traditional Marquesan ways, a seemingly endless palaver had to take place before everyone agreed on a specific breadfruit tree. This particular tree was greatly venerated, not only for its abundant fruit but for it's sap, considered to be the most effective of any of the local breadfruit trees for healing the circumcision wounds of adolescent Marquesan males. This tree was a noble specimen, clearly endowed with miraculous powers, all of which seemed in the end to be admirably suited for a representation of the Mother of God. The tree was felled, the carvers began their work. When the statue was finished, it was wrapped in layers of bark cloth and hoisted up the vertical face of the Te Heu volcanic dike to its present-day position, overlooking the valley. It stands on a wide pedestal ringed with branches of elkhorn coral, the same kind of coral which decorated heathen altars in the old days. The coral is probably no accident, only further proof that some things change every slowly, if at all.

Arthur Baessler describes his experiences in Hatiheu:

"... in a gradually sloping, heavily wooded valley, the road to Hatiheu can be seen, snaking downward toward the village, which lies on a beautiful bay of the same name. At the same time, from this point you can look out eastward, over somewhat lower ridges into the valleys of Anaho and Ha'atuatua. It takes more than an hour to arrive at the village, which has already totally lost its Polynesian character. You can understand that as soon as you visit the mission compound, containing a replica of the Grotto at Lourdes, where the statue of Mary and the miracle-working spring are not lacking. You then look up to the tip of one of the highest, almost insurmountable peaks above the village, from which a statue of the Virgin, several meters high, looks down on the faithful. Many hundreds of Marquesans were invited to the consecration of the Grotto and brought to Hatiheu at the expense of the mission. Things in the valley were just like the good old days, except that the men wore black jackets instead of just tattoos, and the women sinned with them covertly, which they certainly would have done earlier, but in a completely natural and innocent fashion. That the assembled multitude did not seize one of their own number and devour him had nothing to do with the miraculous spring, but with the fear of punishment from on high. Without this fear, they would certainly have done it, despite the formal dress and the presence of the Virgin Mary."

176

Back to today! We arrive on the main street, running parallel to the sea. This road is lined with palms, blooming oleander, and hibiscus bushes. Flowering shrubs surround a replica of a *me'ae*, a temple platform, crowned with a modern frog-mouthed *tiki*. The beautifully cared-for houses and front yards impart the feeling that a highly engaged mayor is at work in this valley, a mayor who wants to transform this place into an oasis of harmony and beauty. And such is the case: the mayor's name is Yvonne Katupa, a gentle, soft-spoken but dynamic person, respected throughout the entire archipelago and holder of several decorations from the government of France. Following the death of her husband around 15 years ago, she took over the position of mayor. Her charm, understanding, and ability to get things accomplished have ensured that when her term comes to an end, she will always be re-elected, mainly because no one will run against her! She is the owner of a store and of the Chez Yvonne Restaurant, whose fame also extends far beyond the rocky rim of Hatiheu valley, even as far as Switzerland where it has been favorably mentioned in the *Neue Zuericher Zeitung*. Europeans as well as Marquesans put up with the rutted, rocky trails from Taioha'e and Taipi just in order to treat themselves to Yvonne's cherished cuisine. Her menu features lobster, fish, and traditionally roasted pork, fresh out of the earth-oven, all enhanced by a variety of other Marquesan delicacies. *Aranui* passengers are also regular guests at this establishment, which is yet another epicurean highpoint on the cruise.

Before we turn in at Chez Yvonne, we hike to three archeological sites. Hatiheu Valley is filled with ruins of large stone structures, the works of the two main Hatiheu tribes and some nine sub-tribes, all of which were related to the Taipi tribes from over the ridge to the south. One of the larger sub-tribes was known as Ati He'u'u. Early European visitors didn't hear the name correctly and, introducing an "h" which wasn't there, erroneously transcribed the place name as "Hatiheu." The name, however inaccurate, has stuck, and now there's even a legend, "explaining" the "real meaning" of the name.

A wide, smooth dirt road leads up the valley to the first site, the ceremonial plaza or *tohua* known as Hiko Ku'a, ("Wonderful Banyan"), site of one of Bob's excavations. The ridiculously wide street, cutting a deep wound through the enchanting forest, is the work of the French Army engineers. After about 10 minutes we reach the ceremonial plaza, once the pride of the Ati Papua tribe. This sprawling site was restored under Yvonne's direction and the name was taken by the inhabitants of the valley as a symbol of the renaissance of Hatiheu and its people.

Hiko Ku'a, like all tribal ceremonial centers or *tohua*, is a large rectangular dance floor surrounded on all the long sides by low stadium-like platforms for spectators, upon which more massive *paepae* house platforms are interspersed. In the old days, sheds thatched with pandanus and palm leaves stood on the platforms flanking the dance floor, shielding the ritual attendees from the sun rays, but these shelters are long gone. The seaward end of the dance floor is filled by a broad and impressive low platform made of huge dressed slabs of red tuff, the sacred *ke'etu* stone of the Marquesans. Platform of this type, known as *tu'u*, were used for the display of human sacrifices. The legends tell of a warrior named Tu'ehu from Ha'apa'a, who was sacrificed on this platform. Three *tiki* have been set into the facade of the *tu'u*; two of these are small and badly damaged, but a third larger figure represents the goddess Tevana'uau'a. Like Taua Pepe from Puama'u, Tevana'uau'a was a prominent woman who died in childbirth, and was elevated to the status of chief goddess of the Ati Papua, as well as the goddess of the Anaho tribes. Behind the *tu'u*, at the extreme end of the plaza, stands a temple platform on which a sacred banyan once grew. Shortly before Bob's arrival, in 1956, this banyan was burned by the owner of the land because it supposedly sheltered evil junglecock spirits, which disturbed the owner by incessant crowing.

178

The passengers assemble on the site, and Bob describes his 1957 excavations in amusing detail. He employed a workcrew which would have won Olympic Gold if drinking and carousing had been accepted Olympic sports. He describes how he had uncovered a huge earth oven in the northeast corner of the plaza where four distinct strata were visible. This discovery raised his heart rate considerably because the charcoal-crammed oven gave good promise of a reliable series of radiocarbon dates. It was a bitter disappointment, however, when he encountered in the very lowest layer a fragment of a brandy bottle with the French word *vieux* ("old") written thereon. In this case, "old" acquired the contradictory meaning of "young" in archeological terms, and left no reason for doubting that the Marquesans had made this deep, seemingly ancient oven, and much of the rest of the site, around the time of the arrival of the French in 1843. After much digging, he concluded that the earliest occupation at Hiko Ku'a was about 1300 AD, while the platforms visible today and the three figures were all erected between 1750 and 1850 AD.

In the meantime, all the spectators find shady spots under the trees along the west side of the plaza and await the beginning of the famous Marquesan "pig dance" (*maha'u*) with great curiosity. The muscular tattooed men of the Hiko Ku'a dance troupe, their heads and hips encircled with garlands of once-sacred *ti* leaves, evoke sighs of longing from the ladies. My neighbor, a woman somewhat advanced in years, murmurs speculatively: "You'd have to be young again, for this ... !" (I'm not sure however, what she meant by "this!").

The dance begins with the invocation of the souls of the ancestors of the old Taipi Nui Ava'angu tribe. Then stamping, crouching low, the dancers begin the *maha'u*, accompanying their movements with loud throaty grunts in a distinctive rhythm: "Huhrrrrrh, huhrrrrrh, mmmm-haaaah-huhrrrrrh." The strange gutturals send cold chills up your spine. The explicit, graphic movements (representing pigs mating) leave some of our less

179

worldly companions in astonished perplexity. Then comes the unavoidable conclusion: the spectators are invited to dance with the group! Some ladies willingly indulge in the requisite hip-swinging and bravely give themselves to practicing with a partner. The pig dance becomes a kind of multi-cultural event which, although certainly not charming, never fails to amaze.

From Hiko Ku'a, we hike further up the valley to the temple of Te I'i Poka, where a huge stone temple platform is crowned by a giant banyan tree. All banyans were sacred in the Marquesas. Until the mid-1800s, human sacrifices were brought to this temple. The tangled roots and aerials of the massive banyan were also formerly filled with human skulls and long bones; the remains of the ancestors of the Ati Papua tribe.

The restoration of this temple and its surroundings, including the small but beautiful ceremonial plaza of Kamuihei and many surrounding house clusters, has been carried out in an impressive fashion. This long careful effort was conducted by the delightful and supremely competent French couple, Drs. Pierre and Marie-Noëlle Ottino, working as a team under the sponsorship of ORSTOM, the French overseas scientific research organization. Pierre is an archeologist and Marie-Noëlle an ethnologist, their specialties complement each other perfectly since both talents are needed to restore a complex such as Te I'i Poka and Kamuihei. The Ottinos have worked for over 5 years in the Marquesas with very decisive results. Among one of the most impressive accomplishments in their inventory is the 150 BC date from the cave at Anapua on the island of Ua Pou. They have also found and recorded a host of interesting and unusual petroglyphs including a unique three-meter long canoe design in Hiko'ei valley in Taioha'e. On Nuku Hiva alone, the Ottinos have restored 5 ceremonial plazas. In addition, they have produced the extremely attractive volume: *Te Patu Tiki: Le Tattouage aux îles Marquises*, (Inscribing images: tattooing in the Marquesas Islands), an exhaustive, spendidly illustrated treatment of

Marquesan tattooing, containing invaluable information reveal-ing the complex meanings of various motifs. Bob was pleased to have this book along with him and he used it to very good ad-vantage in his talk on tattooing.

The area surrounding the temple Te I'i Poka was cleared by French army engineers under Pierre's direction. The cluster of structures formed a neatly definable community, with house clus-ters ranged around a chief's house and a ceremonial center. Many pits were found for storing *ma,* the all-important fermented breadfruit paste, used in flavoring the beloved *popoi,* the staple of the Marquesan diet. In the middle of the complex stands the mighty Te I'i Poka temple dedicated to the ancestors. Further up the steep slope, above this temple, we see more temple plat-forms and arrive at massive moss-covered boulders where a "gal-lery" of petroglyphs have been deeply incised. These petroglyphs include human "stick figures," turtles, fish, bug-eyed *tiki* faces, female fertility symbols and tattoo motifs. Bob explains to the surprised hikers that while petroglyphs are often found in the vicinity of ceremonial centers, the significance of these figures is very murky indeed. Perhaps they commemorate offerings, or special events; on the other hand, they may relate to invoca-tions of tribal gods or protective spirits. Whatever they repre-sent, it was very sacred indeed, because virtually no information has ever been recovered from anywhere in Polynesia to indicate why these designs were made. We can be certain, however, that they are not "doodles," as one of the Omniscient Ones long maintained.

Returning to the big temple, we meet Pierre Ottino, who is quite happy to give a short talk about his research. His modesty awakens great admiration in the audience. He never mentions how little support he has received for his work, nor does he tell the listeners how often he and Marie-Noëlle had to fight the highly politicized and imperceptive archeological establishment in Tahiti, just in order to successfully finish their work. Bob translates his talk into English and is happy to see the great interest Pierre's work arouses. As usual, the Seniors ask the most questions at the end of the talk, which is a very welcome contribution.

Pierre Ottino has revolutionized Marquesan archeology; thanks to him and his broad spectrum "community" approach, we know more about the tribal life and settlement patterns of the old Marquesans. This dynamic couple has more publications to their names than all the archeologists of Tahiti combined, and they've cleared the way to a far better understanding of the mysterious Marquesan culture.

My decision to head back to the beach ahead of the rest of the group was quite well founded. There's a spring in my step as I walk alone through the lovely but alien vegetation, reveling in the peace and quiet, and listening to the melodious bird songs. We meet up again on the beach near the newly constructed *tiki* temple. Beneath a cloudless sky and the kindly eye of the Madonna, we drink in the peaceful beach scene. A small droplet of bitterness taints my cup of happiness during this magical afternoon. The incessant itching on my back is driving me literally crazy. A companion stares, awestruck: "Good God, your back is covered with *nono* bites!" This is the result of leaving *pani* (coconut oil), and insect repellent in my rucksack in Anaho when I took the Ha'atuatua hike.

In the meantime, at "Chez Yvonne," a series of long tables have been set beneath the high arched palm-thatched roof. We find a place with a friendly group, and sit down. This is paradise! Lillies and flaming bougainvillea trees combine with the creamy white *tiare* blooms, reaching upwards into the clear blue sky. Multi-colored oleander bushes intertwine with large white, lemon-yellow, or dark red hibiscus flowers, as though all were striving for supremacy in this brilliant panoply of color. Soulfully rendered songs of Tahitian and hawaiianesque "Pan-Pacific" origin lend a touch of romanticism to our dreamy mood,

182

but the real delights of the moment are the cans and bottles of cool beer which are passed around, finally quieting the long endured thirst brought on by the morning's exercise.

Before the meal is served, everybody has to participate in the special ritual of the opening of the earth oven. A well-seasoned pig has been roasting deep within for hours, before enriching our noontime meal. Rua, a huge Marquesan (and a good archeologist who worked with Bob in 1993) lifts the hot stones out of the oven with his bare hands and frees the pig from its banana leaf wrappings. The pig, a bit pale but quite clearly well-cooked, sees the light of day once more.

Back in the kitchen, we again encounter the Ottinos. We congratulate them once more on their striking book on Marquesan tattooing and discuss the idea of further meetings. Bob once worked with Pierre on a series of intriguing sites in deserted Ha'apa'a valley, enjoying the association very much. Pierre and Marie-Noëlle hope to set up an archeological field school in Hatiheu, a school where interested students could work with them on their excavations and receive a certificate for academic credit at the end of their stays. This idea is fascinating, especially when combined with accommodations at Yvonne's bungalows in Hatiheu, and meals Chez Yvonne. The more we talk about it, the more it seems to be workable. It would be a new kind of vacation for me, to be involved in real archeology for once. And not only students, but interested tourists could profit greatly from this kind of an offering. Bob is going to stay in contact with the Ottinos on this matter. They are returning to France in the relatively near future for a well-deserved vacation. This makes me wonder a bit, because I've got to admit that consciously swapping the gray wetness of Paris for this paradise is an incomprehensible decision!

The meal is delicious, the menu consisting of assorted salads, fried fish, raw fish in a delicate sauce of coco cream, roast pork from the earth oven, rice, breadfruit "French fries," *popoi* breadfruit paste, and for desert, a traditional Marquesan pudding, *poke,* made of baked pureed banana in sweet coco cream. The mood at the table becomes increasingly relaxed and undergoes an additional lift when I recount my experience with a tourist on the last trip.

She seemed to us to have come from another world, clothed like a direct import from a Parisian *couturier,* she captivated us by her striking simplicity and the following non-stop monologue, to no one in particular:

"Ja, I'm from Switzerland, and you? ... I'm on a world tour with my husband ... we came to Hatiheu on a helicopter ... Oh yes, certainly, it 's really very pleasant here ... there are so many flowers; so beautiful ... no, my husband is sleeping, he's seen lots of islands ... we've already been to Las Vegas three times ... we're traveling on from here ... we want to go to Hong Kong; it's pretty there too, just like it is here."

My Swiss neighbor kept whispering in my ear: "Say nothing, nothing at all; there are foreigners here at the table with us; when they hear her, they'll think the whole damn Swiss nation is like that!" Margitta's mildly questioning glance and the pointed commentary of my neighbor on the left make it very hard to hold back the laughter. Thank God, the woman was distracted by something else, and the monologue ceased.

In 1956–58, Bob and his wife spent several months in Hatiheu and the valley is full of memories for him. Several friends from this period are still living, although the majority have already made their voyages to Hawaiki, the Polynesian eternity, located far away in the sunset. Among these was Tini Te 'Oho ("thousands of powers"). She was a slender woman, with a piercing glance. Because of her greatly advanced elephantiasis, she covered her swollen legs under a long, tent-like "Mother Hubbard."

You didn't often see Tini without her pipe. She was known as a sorceress because she worked spells known as *nani kaha* ("tie the bait"). That's an ancient type of black magic spell found under various names throughout the Pacific. The sorcerer needs a lock of the intended victim's hair, a fingernail clipping, or some left-over food. These items would be wrapped up with a lizard tail, in various kinds of leaves, and the packet would be placed under a fire pit, with appropriate chants. The end results of this procedure were determined by the choices of leaves and chants.

Tini was not only good at *nani kaha*; she was also a clairvoyant, and had engaged in another more or less occult field of activity. Using the old methods for handling corpses, Tini had also mummified her only child. When it became known, this caused quite a stir among the population of Hatiheu and brought her to the very unfavorable attention of the French administration and the mission.

She was already old and lived with her near-centenarian mother when Bob and his wife, Rae, met her. She taught him about the world of Marquesan medicine and its associated beliefs. She gave Marquesan names to him and his wife, and later to all his children. In the Marquesas, this is an unusual honor. As we've remarked earlier, when the Marquesans exchange names, it means that they also exchange the rights, privileges, and responsibilities that go with those names. Such people refer to each other as "names" (*ikoa.*). Bob later learned that Tini had given him the name of her son, a handsome, happy young fellow who died in his late teens. Bob was therefore a son to her and she became his mother. Her son and Bob became identical because both held the same name. Bob finally had all this explained by the sculptor Teikivahiani, who knew Tini's son well. When Teiki recounted the story, it seemed to Bob as though a hand had reached out to him across the boundary of Hawaiki and he heard a voice saying: "So at last we've met, *e te ikoa e!* (Oh, my name!)"

Another friend in Hatiheu was Karoro Te Va'a, a clairvoyant, who was also not lacking in sorcery skills himself, and was an enemy of Tini. Te Va'a worked directly against her with his own powers and a regular exchange of blows had taken place in one well-known case. That Bob was friendly with both these people didn't bother them in the least, and in keeping with good professional ethics, they never mentioned each other to Bob. In addition to his esoteric talents, Te Va'a was also an outstanding archeological field worker. His detailed knowledge of the ancient culture permitted him to identify at once many otherwise inexplicable artifacts and interpret much of what was found. Ever popular, he had many close friends who all respected his powers as much as his enemies feared them. As an attractive, quiet, and extremely courteous fellow, he also enjoyed enormous popularity among women of all ages, but never bragged of these relationships, in sharp contrast to the rest of the male population.

Often, when the excavation team had to stay overnight in the field, Bob was awoken in the predawn darkness by Te Va'a's soft chanting, as he invoked the old gods. He told Bob about the source of his powers, explaining that for him, all of nature was an immense and complex book of arcane signs, intended to be read by the initiates. A bird flying, sun rays streaming through a gap in the clouds, the sounds of certain insects, dreams, all these and more were highly significant, and he interpreted these signs in formulating his prophecies. Speaking with great modesty, he emphasized that although these signs held the ultimate truth, his capacity to read them was limited by his own human fallibility. He said that Bob should never blame the signs themselves, or the forces behind them, for any erroneous predictions, because the blame belonged to Te Va'a alone. You meet so many self-styled omniscient scientists, who actually only possess a small part of the knowledge and powers of observation that Te Va'a had. It was a shame that this highly intelligent man was never able to attend a university. Or maybe it was better that he didn't!

We'll end the stories of Bob's friends with that of Te Hono, the tiny smiling "titanium butterfly" who was Bob's cook in 1993.

186

When the team came back to the base camp hungry, thirsty, and dirty after a long day on the site at Ha'atuatua, snacks were always ready and the evening meal was already cooking merrily on the stove. But when Bob arrived, Te Hono's wink signaled him to come into the cook house. There, she always had something very tasty, especially prepared, for him alone.

"Sit down! Eat! Drink!"

"Thanks Te Hono! And now tell me: who came to the camp today? Who asked for some of our food? And what did Te Hono do?"

Then and there, Te Hono would provide Bob with a detailed "core dump" of the day's events. The tough little lady, who by her own admission had an extremely colorful past, understood very well that she had to protect the camp against all interlopers. With her on watch, no one could indulge in the Marquesan (truly pan-Polynesian) custom of "borrowing" food or utensils. Te Hono's powerful dark side confronted anyone attempting to turn the camp into a lending institution. Rushing out of the kitchen, with chin high in the air and eyes narrowed to angry slits, her redoubtable mien kept even the biggest Marquesans at a distance.

I'm getting a bit sleepy, and everyone is longing to enjoy this beautiful day in the fresh air, in the shade of the coconut palms. A lyrical quote from a tourist brochure comes to mind: "The air is like balm, with a hint of the delicate scent of flowers. You hold your breath; the beauty of the scene is so perfect, almost painful." On this spectacular afternoon, the inconsequential and the serious, the laughter and the tears, have drawn so close to each other that they can no longer be separated. Is it the melody of the surf that pours out onto the black sand beneath us which engulfs and bewitches us? Is it the fast-approaching and unavoidable departure? The feelings follow their own courses. They leave us lost for words, but they also open the heart.

It's difficult to take leave of this place. The music accompanies us a long way down the path to the waiting whale boat. The last look goes across the bay to the sharp saw-tooth valley walls, coated in glowing emerald vegetation. We wrap ourselves in a kind of cocoon, in which the wonderful memories of this valley represent a myriad of silken threads. In this cocoon, this day will remain forever unchanged.

Back on the *Aranui*, we're back into the daily routine. A shower, a change of clothes, a cup of tea or coffee in the salon. There, I get some very affectionate care from Frances, the Floridian who has taken such a motherly interest in me. When she hears of my discomfort from the *nono* bites, she treats me immediately with capsules of some kind of oil that is supposedly effective against insect bites. I take everything and anything that seems to hold out a promise of help, and thank her from the heart.

Up on deck, a most unusual evening mood envelopes us. Who could free oneself from the spell of a spectacular sunset, especially South Seas sunsets of such unparalleled beauty? As we pass along the northeast tip of Nuku Hiva, Ha'atuatua and the coastal terrain become indistinct in a mysterious veil of sea haze. Golden sun rays peek through the low hovering, gray clouds, constantly transforming them into ever-new fantasy-evoking impressions of light and shadow and making futuristic creations of the sharp, dentated mountain ridges, creations which no human hand could ever fashion. From behind darkly shadowed ridge lines, the last garlands of sun rays glow in the twilight, ending on remote cloud banks above an amethyst sea. Finally, there remains only a strange tiny red-orange spot, sinkling slowly behind the mountains into the boundless ocean, from which the night with its starry heavens rises swiftly up.

It takes great effort to tear myself away from such scenes and return to what passes for the reality of the moment. The bell calls us to a fine dinner, followed by a meeting of the German passengers. Since the lectures are normally in French and English only, the German minority is generally a bit short-changed on information. This evening there's an opportunity for them to get answers to their many questions. We meet on the pool deck and a lively question-and-answer period begins with inquiries on such topics as the nature of the Austronesian language family, the position of the Polynesian languages within that widespread family, the Lapita culture, and the finds at Ha'atuatua.

They also want to learn more about the lives of present day Marquesans. How do they make a living? With whom do they engage in commerce? How can they buy these very expensive trucks that we see everywhere if their income is next to nothing? What kind of education is available to them? What future awaits the young people and children?

The Marquesan economy has undergone constant changes since the 1950s. The most important export of that era was copra, sun-dried coconut meat, which is used to make soap and cosmetics. This was very hard manual labor and hardly worth the effort, but it was the only cash crop. Occasionally, there were also woodcarving and such specialties as coffee, dried bananas (*pieri*) and other fruits, but these were produced in very small quantities and had no monetary significance for the overall economy, since they benefitted a very small number of individuals. Tourists hardly ever appeared, and when they did come on the copra schooners, they had to stay with private families because there were no hotels or pensions in existence at that time.

Today things have changed greatly in the "Land of Men." The Marquesans still make copra, but far less than before. The biggest export item at this moment is the fruit of the *noni* tree (*Morinda citrifolia*). This fruit is collected by the Marquesans and sold to a commercial patent medicine company which seems to be a front for a missionary sect. The fruit is then shipped via the *Aranui* to Tahiti, where the vile-tasting and malodorous *noni* juice is extracted and mixed with other fruit juices to make a "health drink" or dietary supplement which is sold in the USA and other countries. The unknown "active ingredient" in this fruit is an enzyme, supposedly only detectable through a secret process.

The *noni* health drink has acquired a certain reputation. In the USA, you'll pay plenty for a bottle of this "medicine of the ancient Polynesians." It's only available in a pyramid scheme; you have to buy four bottles per month; use one, and sell the other three bottles to your friends, at a profit of course! This "Tahitian wonder drug" has in the past been hawked with labels and publicity which would lead the user to believe that the juice had medicinal value as an effective treatment for just about every disease from hang-nails to cancer, but fortunately such claims have been stopped by Federal intervention, or so the *noni* sellers on the Internet complain.

The truth about the *noni* drink is quite different than it's strident publicity. In the past, *noni* fruits and leaves had supernatural significance and were often used in black magic spells and rituals. The juice was also sometimes used to dye *tapa*, but relatively little use was made of the fruit as medicine, and it was certainly never used as a daily health drink, either mixed or "straight up". In the old Marquesas, *noni* was an ingredient in only a few minor medicinal preparations ; e. g., mixed with other plant materials in a topical remedy for venereal disease, and for caked breasts. The fruits were also eaten raw or baked (but not ripe) during famines. It's importrant to note that the *noni* drink craze of today is a very recent phenomenon. Forty years ago, no one was drinking the wonder juice. The credulous inhabitants of French Polynesia have only recently been taken in by a publicity campaign which convinced them that *noni* medicine was a major part of their heritage. One of the unfortunate side effects of this campaign has been a rise in emergency admissions to Tahitian hospitals of cases of *noni* poisoning, because the stuff is definitely toxic, even to believers!

If this medicine is so beneficial, it's strange that so much secrecy surrounds it's contents. Just try and get hard scientific data about it from any of the official sources. Suddenly, no one knows anything! One might also ask why the pious missionaries don't make it freely available to mankind. After all, Fleming didn't sit on his discovery of penicillin, neither did Jonas Salk try to capitalize on his polio vaccine. The Nobel Prize would certainly go to anyone who could prove that this concoction was even half as efficacious as claimed.

And the *noni* isn't the only thing being sold. Through other "fronts," missionary organizations are peddling oil extracted from the fruit of another Polynesian tree, as well promoting the culture and use of *kava*, the befuddling and addictive Polynesian intoxicant. But then, what does the welfare of unsuspecting consumers matter when weighed against cash in mission coffers? For such people, prosperity and sanctity are directly linked, if not identical.

We hope that a neutral scientific body will investigate *noni* and all such "miracle drugs" and disseminate the truth about their value, or lack thereof. In the meantime, we also hope that the Marquesans don't become overly dependent on the income derived from this fruit, because some day the bottom may very suddenly drop out of the market. That day will likely be the first time a fatality can be linked to *noni* consumption.

In addition to working in copra and *noni* production, a large portion of the Marquesan population works for the state in one capacity or another, e. g., building and maintaining roads, harbor facilities and airfields, or installing electrical power and water systems. In addition, there are positions in schools, on hospital staffs, in agricultural projects, forestry and livestock breeding, all of which are supported by the state. There's also an extremely liberal program of social support so that everyone is cared for. And this information may answer the question as to why you encounter so many luxury recreation vehicles, trucks, and jeeps on the streets and roads of the archipelago. The Marquesans can buy them, although with the freight and import taxes they are much more expensive than they are in the USA. The desire for these powerful machines arises at least partially from a concern for prestige, a very important consideration in the Marquesan culture. Why ride a horse when you can jolt more rapidly over the bumpy roads and trails in something like a Toyota Landcruiser? Wait until they see the "Hummer!" In many areas of the archipelago, you'd think you were in Idaho because of the often barren basalt cliffs which so closely resemble those of the Gem State, and the many recreation vehicles and trucks standing around. There's a standing joke in Idaho that foreplay begins with the command: "Get in the truck!" Here, things have not yet gone quite that far, but one recent accident on Nuku Hiva appeared to have been the result of a driving instructor being unable to contain himself with a pretty young student, on a narrow mountain road.

The schools on the islands are good, the opportunities for education having dramatically improved in the past 40 years. The prospective student has a choice between the state school system and the Catholic Mission schools. Many state schools, like Ioteve Kaiha's on Ua Pou, try to maintain the native culture and give instruction in Marquesan, but French is emphasized in the main valleys such as Taioha'e and Atuona. After the completion of primary education, the student can go to a boarding college (high school) in the Marquesas, or travel to Tahiti to attend the lycées or boarding schools there. After college, there are university opportunities for qualified students in Tahiti, at the French University of the South Pacific, or at universities in metropolitan France.

After our meeting ends, we climb up to the bridge to study the map of the heavens which Théodor had so kindly sketched for us. The starry heavens unfold before us in all their glory, sparkling in incomparable clarity. We find Saturn, Jupiter with a few of its very faint satellites, Mars, and the Pleiades. The Southern Cross and the Hook of Maui, known to Europeans as Scorpio, are invisible at this time.

Is it the Russian "Mir" whose orbit carries it directly over our ship, or is it another of the innumerable satellites which clutter near-Earth space? We look at this object as it hurtles overhead and Bob recalls 1957, when the first Sputniks went up. The Marquesans were very much interested in what they called *hetu ui'a,* or "electric stars." Many of them were able to glimpse the Sputnik on its orbital path, but there were also a few who claimed that they'd seen the Sputnik stop and circle their island or valley, or radically change course. A bit too much palm toddy can do wonders for a man's perception!

The marvelous heavens can't make up for the wind, which is growing much cooler. It's time to seek the warmth and comfort of the salon. The 45 *nono* bites on my back, ears, legs and arms do not augur well for a comfortable night, so I ask Bob to tell the tale of the origin of the coco palm with the hope that it will calm me down and make me sleepy.

In the salon over a cup of hot tea, Bob begins. He knows many Polynesian legends, but to tell them as did the master story tellers whom he knew, would obviously be impossible for him, and he begs my indulgence. He remembers well the chief Taniha Taupotini, the adopted son of the last queen Vaekehu. Taniha was a portly fellow, weighing well over 125 kg., whose noble head was framed with a mane of snow-white hair, contrasting beautifully with his walnut skin. His stories were full of life; he imitated the voices of each character, grunted like the pigs, and sang the chants which were part of these tales. When Taniha recited for Bob, Bob knew that he was listening to a master performance, experiencing a great moment in Marquesan oral literature.

Bob's favorite legend is the legend of the origin of the coco palm. It was especially dear to him because the heroine in the story was named Hina, the Marquesan name which Bob's daughter had received from Tini Te Oho. Bob's Hina (her English name was Jennifer) was taken from this life very prematurely in 1997. She had never been able to visit the Marquesas, although she wanted very much to accompany her father. Bob felt that she was especially close to him on this trip, as on all the trips he's made since her death.

In the legend, Hina was an exquisitely beautiful girl who lived in the remote prehistoric times of Polynesian gods and heroes. Her story begins on an island far to the west, in the Samoa group. One day this island was visited by Te Tui Fiti, the king of Great Fiji. When Tui Fiti saw the lovely Hina, he immediately fell desparately in love. But Hina wanted nothing to do with him. Deeply hurt, he returned to Fiji to consult with his high priest. He wanted to remain with Hina for eternity, and asked the priest how he might achieve his desire.

The priest listened to him intently, with growing dismay. He told Tui Fiti that there was only one way to achieve his goal: he must be transformed into an eel! In eel form, he would be able to swim across the sea to Hina's island and remain there forever, in the river or in the bathing pool near her house. Perhaps the beautiful Hina would adopt him as her pet! There was a big catch, however, because once transformed into an eel, he could never take on human form again. Tui Fiti listened carefully to the priest; and without hesitation gave the fateful order: "Change me into an eel, I cannot live without Hina!" With a heavy heart, the priest granted Tui Fiti's wish and the transformation was accomplished on the spot. Tui Fiti swam off at top speed to Hina's island. He found her village, and when he saw her his joy was complete. At first, he kept a respectable distance, but each day dared to approach her a bit more closely. Hina was initially somewhat fearful, but with time she gradually got used to this big homely creature, brought him things to eat, and came to feel quite comfortable with him. And the eel followed her everywhere.

But others, including some chiefs, were greatly displeased by the sight of the eel. They feared that this ugly creature, who constantly accompanied Hina would cast a bad light on the daughter of a chief. They decided to kill the eel and would not give Hina any peace until she allowed them to do so. With a heavy heart, Hina finally agreed, but with one provision: she wanted to talk with the eel before he was beheaded. She was overcome with sorrow when she told the eel the decision that had been made.

The eel who had been Tui Fiti understood her, and he in turn had only one request: she must promise him that she'd bury his head near her house. If she would do this, he told her: "From my head a great gift will rise up for you, a tall noble tree which will be of great use to mankind. It's leaves will cover the roofs of their houses, the trunks will provide houseposts, and from the husks of the nuts you will be able to make cord for fishing and lashing canoes. When you husk the nut, you will see my face, with two eyes and a black mouth in the middle. When you break through the spot representing the mouth and press your lips against it, just like I have always wanted to kiss you, the sweetest water will assuage your thirst. The white flesh inside the nut will also guard you and your people against hunger."

Hina wept bitterly when she heard these words. The parting was unspeakably difficult. But her lover didn't fear death, because he knew that they would always belong to each other. The eel was beheaded and as promised, Hina buried the head near her house. Soon, a small tree sprouted up from the grave, and from this tree grew a mighty coco palm; the gift that Tui Fiti had promised to Hina! And to this day, the coco palm is the constant companion of the Polynesians, fulfilling a wider variety of needs than any plant of the Polynesian arboretum.

With this moving tale of a love that always gives and never takes, a love which does not fear death, we end this eventful day and go to our respective cabins lost in thought.

Last calls at Nuku Hiva and Ua Pou

We enter Taioha'e bay at about 0500, and I'm wide awake. *Nono* bites and engine noise are not the best combination for sound sleeping. It's therefore a welcome change to be on deck watching the sailors as they off-load freight onto the broad dusty pier.

There's plenty of free time after breakfast for everyone's own preferred leisure activities. I remain aboard, others head for Taioha'e on foot or hop onto the school bus which is always pressed into service for the *Aranui* passengers. The main road runs along the sea side and makes a nice walk. There are shops, the mayor's office, a number of recent (i.e., non-archeological) *tiki*, and as always, a monument to fallen French military personnel flanked by antique cannon and an anchor.

Bob is finally able to deliver the war clubs and bowls from Ua Huka to Rose Corser who is waiting on the dock with great anticipation. He wants to visit her museum and then pay a visit to Teikivahiani, the woodcarver, who lies in the hospital, seriously ill.

Rose Corser is an enthusiastic collector of Marquesan artifacts and artwork, which she exhibits in a museum in her house near the Hotel Keikahanui. She plans to have a two-story building in the near future to hold the ever-growing collection. The plans are already complete, but as with everything else in the Marquesas, it will take time. Nevertheless, I feel certain that the neat, attractive "Iron Lady" will be able to get the construction project moving at the Marquesan version of top speed. She can certainly count on the help of the Catholic bishop in this regard; he's already loaned her extremely valuable unique pieces from the mission collection for her museum. Many Marquesans have followed his example, loaning Rose their own prized family heirlooms. The clubs and bowls from Ua Huka will further

197

enrich her collection. One day in the near future, Taioha'e will have the best museum in the archipelago and this museum will be Rose's own personal monument.

Those who have remained aboard, like me, find it quite pleasant to spend the time on beauty care, an area of concern that has not received much attention in the last several hectic days ashore. But what can you do when the water in the shower suddenly dries up and the most energetic pounding on the pipes will not conjure up a drop more? Wiping off the shampoo as well as I can, I search with burning eyes for the water bottle in the cabin, carry it below one deck to the drinking fountain which is still working, fill the bottle up and then disappear once more back to the shower with the water-filled bottle. This procedure is repeated five times, and it takes five liters of ice cold water to wash away the shampoo and bring my head and what it contains to the point of freezing. I ignore a bystander's snide remark that I must be terribly thirsty that morning; in my high state of irritation, I can't think of even a remotely pleasant reply.

A much-needed, positive state of mind finally overwhelms my heightened frustration with the ship's plumbing. My return to peaceful normalcy is considerably aided by Herbert Rosendorfer's hilarious book "Unplanned Exits." Rosendorfer offers a series of short stories about the unforeseeable consequences of otherwise innocent actions; the title and text are not without irony in the present situation! By the time Bob returns with the latest news, everything has returned to the usual *Aranui* coziness.

It isn't going well with Bob's friend, Teikivahiani. He's breathing from an oxygen bottle, and can only rise with difficulty to greet Bob, his friend and teaching colleague. Teiki has been ill for years, suffering from a severe heart ailment and chronic lung inflammation. Still, he has always delayed in seeing his doctor or in reporting to the hospital when necessary. He usually waited until it was nearly too late. Bob tells me with great emotion about their parting. It's painfully obvious how hard it was for both of them, because both he and Teiki knew that they were embracing for the last time, on this earth at least. "*Na Te Etua te tiaki, Teiki!*" (God watch over you, Teiki) The two *tiki* in my cabin are his last works, and I'm very proud that they belong to me.

A month later the sad news arrives. Teiki is gone; he had stubbornly refused to be transferred to Tahiti for medical treatment. He wanted to begin his journey to Hawaiki, the Paradise of his ancestors, from his own island, Nuku Hiva. "*Na 'oe te mo'u, e hoa pi'i.*" (Peace be with you, my dear friend).

At about 1030, we stand out of Taioha'e bay, on course for the bay of Hakahau, Ua Pou. Deeply moved, we look back on the peaceful harbor, ringed by its jagged basalt battlements, as it becomes smaller and smaller, its features ultimately blending into the dark mass of the island of Nuku Hiva, which itself recedes below the northern horizon.

A *pae*, beautiful island of beaches, of history, and unfathomable riddles which will never be totally revealed to us. We must always return to you, just to be captured once again by the magic of your spell!

The bell for lunch rings, breaking the melancholy mood. As an enrichment to the routine dessert of melon sections, we friends enjoy the last bar of Swiss chocolate, the lamentable remains of a large supply that many have enjoyed during the course of the trip. Frankly we plunged unabashed into the enjoyment of this delicacy, which simply melts in your mouth, as one especially addicted chocolate lover puts it.

All the lounge chairs have been occupied during the voyage to Ua Pou. The sun is enjoyed in all conceivable positions and costumes, from the totally covered to those whose only cover is a tiny bit of tanga "dental floss" between the buttocks. My "tribal ceremonial center" is in the pool because the only things that soothe the *nono* bites on my back and legs are the salt water, and the cool and gently stroking wind, acting in concert to banish the itching. Our conversation today takes us to Munich, to crispy roasted pigs knuckles, big white radishes, Munich Weizenbier (wheat beer), shady beer-gardens and all the other amenities which this city has to offer. Regrettably, Hinano conjures up much less enjoyment on the tongue than that which the mere dream of a cool, effervescent wheat beer can produce.

Among the sun worshipers, some movement commences, as the striking volcanic "needles" of Ua Pou greet us again, and we maneuver into Hakahau. As before, a majority of the population greets the *Aranui*. Containers and goods stand on the pier, ready to be loaded.

Most of our fellow passengers leave the ship, to enjoy for the last time the majestic landscape of this lovely valley. At the same time, an unusual display of bamboo flutes, the traditional Marquesan musical instruments, takes place in the salon. There are several types, including the nose flute (*pu ihu*) and the mouth flute (*pu hakahau*). All are decorated with tattoo motifs, burned into the polished yellow surface of the bamboo tubes. In the old days, the tattoo masters often engraved their designs on flutes which they then used as models for their work. And once again, we must thank Karl von den Steinen that the forms and designs of these instruments were preserved for posterity. The flutes which are being sold in Hakahau today are not, however, Marquesan-made, but produced by a French gentleman man on Ua Pou. They are certainly beautiful, but they have little to do with the original flutes of long ago.

We also disembark, to check out the "open-air *Aranui* office," which is now a scene of bustling commercial activity, operating under the pavilion near the dock. The majority of the valley population seems to have gravitated there, all talking and gesticulating at once, while dogs skulk around the fringes of the crowd. And there in the midst of the indescribable din sits Hu'uveu, quite unperturbed, with a faint patient smile. He's watchful as a lynx, however, and has everything under control, especially his black attaché case which is the miracle coffer of the *Aranui*. What kinds of stories might be told by the hundreds of slips of paper in that briefcase? These are certainly some of the best-kept secrets of the *Aranui*, they will never be brought to light as long as the immensely discreet Hu'uveu is the ship's supercargo.

The tempo of work in the local canoe construction hangar is moving in the familiar leisurely fashion, slowly bringing a beautiful double canoe to completion. The Marquesans are enthusiastic canoe racers and have built a reputation in competitions outside of the archipelago. This canoe, however, is not a racer but a double hull vessel, built in modern Hawaiian style. The hulls are made of many narrow pieces of wood, placed longitudinally and glued. Dugout hulls are apparently becoming *passé*! Cockpits, another new feature, are built into the decks. We ask the shipwrights, a bit hypocritically, whether this is a genuine Marquesan design. "Of course it's real Marquesan!" comes the speedy answer. Bob smiles: "So, the people from Hawai'i haven't helped you?" An almost angry laugh is the answer, followed by an emphatic: "'A'e!" (No!). This is of course not the case, since it's no secret that Hawai'ian canoes have visited the Marquesas many times recently with great fanfare. There's been much exchanging of information on the topic of canoe design and sailing, so it's no surprise that the Marquesans are orienting themselves on Hawai'ian technology. But whatever design it may reflect, we are really impressed by the lovely lines of this craft and we wish the builders and the crew all the luck in the world.

With this new canoe, Ua Pou will send it's delegation to Nuku Hiva to take part in the ceremonies welcoming the new Millennium. In Hokatu on Ua Huka we already saw the Ua Huka craft. Among the honored personages aboard the Hakahau canoe will be Toti, the chief of the Motu Haka Society, an institution which has as its goal the preservation of Marquesan language and culture. The voyage across the open sea from Ua Pou to Nuku Hiva is not long, but the sea in this passage can be quite dangerous. In the collapse of their culture, the Marquesans lost virtually all their traditional long-range navigation knowledge and skills. They do not use sails any more, and build most of their boats and canoes out of plywood and planks instead of making them out of *temanu* trunks. More than a hundred years ago, the Marquesans had a variety of different types of canoes. There were one-hulled canoes with outriggers, double-hulled war canoes about 18 m long, and large double-canoes with hulls 2 m wide and deep, and 30 m long, used for long sea voyages.

On the first trip, I was strongly motivated to wander out to the end of the Hakahau pier, which is built of undressed volcanic stones. It's an enchanting, sunny afternoon, and just as I suspected, you get a sweeping view of the bay from this point. The surrounding mountains and "needles," all beneath a steel-blue heaven, stand out in an especially splendid fashion. Beneath us, swarms of aquamarine fish play among the rocks by the pier. A bit further out, the fins of predatory sharks flash from time to time, telling us that the harbor surface conceals more than pretty little fishes. In even, sleep-inducing rhythm, the waves break against the pier. It's the ideal mood in which to once again savor the magic of Ua Pou.

We sit on the stones and time seems to stand still. We talk about the past two weeks and recall the first trip. Although we followed much the same route, things were much different this time. On the first trip, I did not often participate in Bob's groups because my English was simply insufficient to follow his explanations. For this reason, I seized the initiative and asked him to hold a separate question period for the German delegation. Happily, he fulfilled my wishes in this regard. Since then, we've remained in contact, planned the trip, corresponded about it, and gave much thought to writing a book in which we would record our impressions. Now we've done it!

In front of us lies the *Aranui*, with people swarming all over her like ants. The cranes are working furiously, as cargo is unloaded and loaded. Kids are doing gymnastics on the bow and stern lines, falling into the water with loud shrieks, while young girls are trying to attract the eye of one or another of the handsome sailors. We know that the days of this *Aranui* are numbered; the wonderful old girl already belongs to the past. Everything must end, sometime, somewhere, and who knows what will come from the new *Aranui*? We turn and head slowly back to the ship. Théodor is leaning on the railing, taking everything in, watchful as usual. His familiar friendly laugh snaps us back into the present and I head straight away for the pool, because the *nono* legacy will give me no peace.

About 1600 we weigh anchor. The departure from the Marquesas is unavoidably underway. We sail along the rugged coastline of Ua Pou with its high cliffs and deep valleys, and then the *Aranui* slowly swings its bows toward the southwest, on course for Rangiroa.

Wrapped in the soft light of evening, the peaks, battlements, and towers of Ua Pou are irrevocably disappearing from view. The cameras are clicking fast and furious; everyone is on deck to enjoy for the last time the fairy-tale castle outline of this island, as it slowly slips below the horizon.

I know the thoughts which are running though Bob's mind right now. He looks at the island and his mind is filled with memories. Faces appear before him, faces which have long since departed, but remain bright and alive in memories of shared experiences. Feelings from the old days are recalled, experiences both good and bad, successes and failures, laughter and tears. He's visited other islands and other countries and has met many people, but these islands, lost in the vastness of the Pacific, have touched him most deeply from the very beginning. As long as it's possible, he'll be coming back, because there are always new plans to carry through. He says that this trip was the most interesting he's ever made. Now in the autumn of his life, he understands fully the happiness which the islands have given to him, and he wants to experience this happiness many more times before he sets out himself for Hawaiki.

Sylvie joins Bob at the rail; she's the friendly, pretty, and extremely professional French hostess. With her charm and her concern for the safety of all the passengers, she has led us on our trip in a delightful fashion, slipping quite naturally and imperceptibly into every heart aboard, including Bob's. He prefers to work with her since they understand each other quite well, in all three languages. She is successful in dragging him back from his reverie into the present. One of Yoyo's Piña coladas also helps break the spell.

The communal nature of shipboard life permits many good friendships to arise during the course of the cruise. Addresses are exchanged, invitations made, and it seems in this moment that we'll all remain firmly in contact, because we all want to preserve this mood of international camaraderie as long as we can. But the night springs upon us, called up from the glistening obsidian sheet of the eastern sea, and the first stars appear. The Marquesas have finally, irrevocably, returned to their own mysterious world, and have left us once more with longing and the pain of separation. We promise to return because it's impossible to break the spell: it will always bring us back.

At dinner the melancholy has already dispersed, to be replaced by a mood of exuberance. The repartee is brisk and hilarious; not infrequently tears of laughter appear on many cheeks, but I'm not really sure whether they might not be mixed with tears of the other kind.

On Course for Rangiroa

With the exception of the notorious early risers and the breakfast buffet assault group, the rest of the passengers straggle in to breakfast with little enthusiasm. Many of them seem to be in such a bad mood that they can't even mouth a "good morning." Somebody mentions an atmosphere of anticlimax, an observation which seems to have come very close to the mark.

Of course, the weather isn't showing its very best side either, with towers of dark gray cloud all around the horizon and strong gusting winds. It's nevertheless pleasant on deck, and when you find a spot that's sheltered from the wind, as did Eveleyn and I, you feel pretty well even with the doubtful meteorological conditions. There is a definite charm in watching the white caps and spray of the agitated sea.

During the voyage, I came to treasure Evelyn and her uncomplicated, straightforward manner. Her position as a museum docent interests me and leads to a very exciting conversation which included a discussion of the book: *"Death and I, the Two of Us"*, by the critic and satirist Arnold Stadtler. We've both read this book, and amuse ourselves delightfully, discussing Stadtler's enchanting humor and his use of bold satire in dissecting the life of a worthless member of the German upper-class counterculture, who spends his time hunting up legacies and losing them. During our conversation we often get the feeling that rain is gradually coming to accompany the wind. But only when a gray cascade falls straight down upon us do we seeks refuge in the bar. In the meantime, lunch time has arrived. The gray unpleasant morning ends in a boisterous, harmonious mood.

Usually Bob gives a lecture on Capt.Cook at the end of the voyage, and most of the passengers attend. Today it seems that Cook has not lost his attraction because the salon is full.

Cook, with his "gentlemen," as he called his international staff of scientists and artists, discovered many islands in the Pacific, explored the east coast of Australia, and ranged the length and breadth of the Pacific from Alaska to the Antarctic on three epoch-making voyages. He and his staff made astronomical, meteorological, and oceanographic observations that were quite useful to later seafarers, but they did far more than that. They intensively studied and recorded information about the customs and languages of the native groups which they encountered, and collected a large number of highly interesting artifacts. Representative collections were also made of the pristine flora and fauna of all the islands visited, while Cook's artists busily set down their impressions of people, places, and events in numerous detailed drawings.

The scientific results of these expeditions created a great sensation in Europe, although Cook was certainly not the first European in these waters. It's well known that the Portuguese and Spaniards were there more than 200 years before him, but these earlier explorers had other intentions than did Cook and his men, for whom the wonderful South Seas environment, its brilliant native cultures and peoples were far more important and interesting than the dreams of gold, spices, gems, and slaves that drove Spanish efforts. The results of Cook's voyages were also regularly published, in contrast to those of the Spaniards and Portuguese, who often kept the results of their explorations under tight security.

It is worth noting in this connection that Cook had Mendaña's journal with him when he want to the Marquesas. This journal was held in the archives in Seville and was not made public until the mid-1800s. How did Cook get access to this document? One can only surmise that a British agent was snooping around in those dusty archives. Cook's discovery of Hawai'i also appears to have had the benefit of Spanish maps, at least one of which shows an island group in the vicinity of the Hawaiian chain.

Seville, with all it's security precautions, may have been "penetrated." There may be a great 18th-century spy story lurking here, a forerunner of "007!"

Cook only stayed four days in the Marquesas, in Mendaña's old anchorage at Vaitahu on the island of Tahuata. The Marquesans gave him a very cool welcome. As we pointed out above, this is undoubtedly traceable to the oral traditions of Mendaña's bloody depredations of 200 years earlier, as well as the shooting of one of the first Marquesans to approach Cook's ship. The population seems to have been largely in hiding. This was especially true of the women, as the scientific staff had to travel quite a distance overland to find any of the fair sex (to sketch, of course!). Due to these circumstances, Cook's staff was only able to collect a few artifacts, including a war sling, one of the deadliest weapons in the Marquesan arsenal. Bob shows slides of the sling as well as of an unfinished necklace of coco fiber. It's likely that the Marquesans gave Cook these "souvenirs" with the hope that he'd be satisfied, and leave as soon as possible. Bob says he can imagine a Marquesan chief exclaiming: "Who cares if the damned necklace isn't finished? Give it to the white skin anyway; give him anything he wants, but just get him out of here! *Now*!"

The drawings completed at Vaitahu are most informative. One shows Marquesan men with jungle cock headdresses in graceful bird head-prowed canoes. There's also a portrait of a beautiful Marquesan girl, wearing a white *tapa* robe, with her right shoulder and breast exposed, in the normal style of the period. On her head she wears a voluminous turban, also of white *tapa*, a headdress which Hollywood has never associated with Polynesia!

Yet another sketch shows a Marquesan male in full regalia, with a headdress of mother of pearl and tortoise shell, and strange pointed "ears" made of bone or wood. He's also wearing a collar of flat wooden segments upon which red berries had been glued, and a *tapa* mantel. Clearly Cook's artist was in a hurry and didn't have enough time to precisely reproduce the tattoo designs on the subject's face; instead, he simply threw in an odd network of lines. As a result of his unfortunate haste, we'll never know a thing about the tattooing of the 18th century Marquesans. Even one sketch would have provided some basis for comparison.

There are also some types of artifacts in the Cook collection which the passengers have seen still in use on the islands. These include drums, *poi* pounders and *tiki*. But there are many tools which have totally disappeared, such as great wooden shark-hooks, bone chisels, and basalt adze blades. The latter one only finds in excavations, or occasionally on the surface, where they were dropped long ago.

The wood carvings in Cook's collection were made with knives of basalt or shell, and teeth of sharks or rats. Today metal tools are used, but the modern carvings are not any better than Cook's examples; in fact, the exuberance of the older pieces has been lost with the introduction of modern tools.

There are also drastic changes in the Polynesian *tapa* cloth, produced from the bark of paper mulberry, breadfruit, and banyan trees. Cook collected many of these cloths in Hawai'i, Tonga, and elsewhere, but not in the Marquesas. Marquesan *tapa* was not painted and possibly therefore not terribly interesting, at least to him.

The fine texture of these old fabrics, the complex designs, and the manifold pigments used in the decorations, all stand in sharp contrast to modern bark cloth. A Hawaiian *tapa* expert, Pua van Dorp, produces bark cloth in the old way (in Hawaiian the word is *kapa*). It takes her a very long time to produce one work, and depending on the size, a bark cloth may cost thousands of dollars. Pua's *tapa* are thin and finely textured, almost like facial tissues, resembling very closely those worn as clothing in the past. Pua was recently honored to be asked to produce the *tapa* used to envelope the remains of the Blessed Father Damien, the leper priest of Molokai, at his beatification ceremony in Rome. Her work has thus acquired a definite international reputation.

The most beautiful pieces in Cook's collections are without doubt the magnificent feathered mantels and cloaks given to the captain by the Hawaiian chief, Kalaniopu'u. The red cloaks with wide yellow stripes were produced from the feathers of thousands of birds: the red and yellow from the *'i'iwi* bird (the scarlet Hawaiian honey creeper), yellow also from the *'o'o* bird (black honey eater) Small amounts of frigate bird and jungle cock feathers were also used. While the *'i'iwi* still exists in small numbers, the *'o'o* is extinct, a victim of the Hawaiian chiefs' love of these garments.

According to a latter-day "green urban legend," the ancient Hawaiians possessed the miraculous skill of stripping these birds of their feathers without killing them. This myth is another of the many that purport to show that native peoples had more respect for their environment than so-called civilized man. Only the uneducated or intellectually blind can believe such tales. The truth is that the Polynesians, like all native peoples everywhere, did not worry much about their environment. They exploited nature to the full extent in order to survive. They really had no choice! On every island in Polynesia where archeological excavations have been made (and this includes the Cooks, Samoa, Tonga, Easter Island, Hawai'i, New Zealand, and the Marquesas) about 10–15 species of birds completely vanished soon after the arrival of the Polynesians. The worst example is New Zealand, where several species of the ostrich-like giant *moa* were totally exterminated by the early Polynesian settlers.

The surviving feather capes, the most beautiful examples of Cook's bequest to the modern world, are to be found in the Bishop Museum of Hawai'i, and in the museums of Wellington, Vienna and Sydney, although other interesting material also ended up in St. Petersburg, by most circuitous routes.

We are sailing in Cook's wake at the moment, on course for Tahiti, but we're sailing under much more comfortable conditions than those endured by Cook and his men. The HMS "Resolution" was only 33 m. long, and with a compliment of around 90, living space was at a minimum. Tensions between the sailors and Cook's officers and gentlemen could have easily arisen. For this reason, a squad of 12 marines was quartered in a miserable crawl space, 140 cm high, between the sailors in the fo'c'sle and the officer's quarters. This was to ensure the maintenance of general good discipline and order, and most importantly to minimize chances of a successful mutiny. The poor accommodations provided for these "soldiers of the sea" seem to have been intended with malice aforethought to produce a certain shortness of temper if forced to deal with the sailors, whose quarters, although also cramped, were much more roomy by comparison. It's no wonder that these precautions had to be taken, because in addition to the variegated nature of the sailors themselves and the physical stresses of shipboard life, there were also health problems and other psychological problems to be dealt with. Most of the time the sailors lived on porridge, salt-pork, and hardtack, eaked out by the occasional fish. There was naturally no contact of any kind with home, not only for weeks and months, but for years at a time. In spite of all this, there was the unending fascination that came with the search for new and exciting adventures among exotic lands and peoples, which were always lurking, just over the horizon. These expeditions were not joy-rides: many lost their lives, including Cook himself.

On the island of Hawai'i, Cook established initially good relations with the chief, Kalaniopu'u, who generously presented him with ample supplies of pigs, breadfruit and bananas for the crew, as well as the strikingly beautiful cloaks and other artifacts. This good relationship came to an abrupt end when Cook refused to provide military assistance to Kalaniopu'u in the latter's projected conquest of the neighboring island of Maui.

The Hawai'ians turned suddenly hostile, and began to pilfer items from the ship, including tools, and a small boat. These acts exasperated Cook, who had been ill for many weeks and had reached the limit of his patience. He humiliated Kalaniopu'u by briefly holding him as a hostage. Later, when he went ashore with a few Marines to personally retrieve the lost items, Cook was surrounded and attacked by a group of Hawai'ians. He retreated to the waters edge, where he was stabbed or clubbed from behind and killed. He was then eaten in a ceremonial feast. His hands and a few other small portions of his body were later returned to the ship. A bitter end for the most famous navigator of the Age of Discovery, who has bequeathed so much to the world.

During Bob's lecture, the clouds have cleared away, the air seems wonderfully clean and mild, and the decks are once more well-populated. As I've done so often on these trips, I climb up to the weather bridge with Margitta. To be sure, the smoke stack spits it's soot on us, but we have the feeling that we're a bit closer to heaven. It is, and will always it main, a fascinating feeling to pitch and roll through the waves of the seemingly infinite Pacific, all alone, without another ship in sight, watching the play of the sun's rays on the waves and looking for rarely-seen fish and sea mammals.

On the bridge, Brutus has the helm and seems to be doing a masterful job of it. All the sailors must stand watch, even on days like this, when there's nothing else to do. Iakopo, his "co-pilot," is engrossed in a science fiction comic. On the other side of the bridge, Lieutenant Steve sits on the rail, absentmindedly plucking at a ukulele and singing a song which almost certainly has to do with love, homesickness, and pretty women. I timidly ask: "Can I touch the helm?" "Sure you can!" responds Brutus, but for some reason the *Aranui* doesn't react to my touch at all. Brutus laughs; he tells me that the autopilot is engaged and nothing changes the ship's course. Rangiroa is dead ahead, far over the horizon, as we reenter the Tuamotus with its secret ancient religion, its warriors, pirates and buried treasure, and its U-boats.

The closely situated islands of this archipelago are influenced by currents and winds from both the east and west. They lie, like a fish net flung across the endless eastern Pacific, catching everything that winds and waves bring from either direction; animals, sailors and their ships, wreckage, and all sorts of flotsam and jetsam.

In the minds of most visitors, these charming atoll paradises and their lagoons invoke only images of black pearls, copra, and diving excursions, but the lagoons and their surrounding coral strands hide many alluring secrets, dating from the earliest human presence here right up the most recent times.

Since the beginning of the 20th century, it's been known that an esoteric cult devoted to the god Kiho existed on the Tuamotu islands for many centuries, possibly even more than a thousand years. This cult was apparently introduced by a group of unknown seafarers and thereafter spread over a large part of the archipelago.

The legends tell of shady temple groves, far from villages settlements, where priests and well-chosen, sexually adept beauties participated in fertility ceremonies involving the most exquisitely elaborated orgies. These ceremonies were not for their own pleasure, but were designed to sexually arouse the god Kiho, whose aroused libido supposedly would in turn increase the fertility of sea, lagoon, and garden.

The Kiho cult had been a very well kept secret, protected by the most stringent *tapu*. The merciless punishment of Kiho awaited anyone who revealed anything about it to the uninitiated. It was only in the 1920s that J. Frank Stimson, an American linguist and expatriate, was able to win the trust of several elderly men who were willing to risk breaking the *tapu* and passed on their knowledge to him. There was no written documenta-

212

tion, as was of course the case throughout Polynesia, since all traditions were always orally transmitted from generation to generation. Stimson remedied that by arranging with his informants, who were all literate, to record their knowledge for the first time in written form. These informants initiated him into their philosophy and unusual world-view, revealing to him that even at the beginning of the 20th century, cult ceremonies were sporadically held, but were naturally strongly denounced by the missionaries as "satanic paganism."

But whence came these mysterious seafaring priests of the Kiho cult? No one knows! They were certainly Polynesians, since Kiho is a Polynesian deity, worshipped in New Zealand and Hawai'i, but they didn't come from the Tuamotus. The answer to this question remains hidden in the darkness of the past; Stimson is long dead, as are the old men who revealed their secrets to him; and the Tuamotu dialects of Polynesian are almost extinct. All that remains are Stimson's publications and his invaluable dictionary of Tuamotu dialects, all of which provide a tantalizing glimpse into this dark corner of Polynesian prehistory. Also remaining are the vicious diatribes unleashed against this uniquely talented linguist by the illuminati of Polynesian anthropology. Stimson's main problems seem to have been that he spoke several Polynesian languages far better than certain of his colleagues, and that he had the temerity to discover something that everyone else had missed.

Following the Spanish conquest of South America, the Tuamotus were also visited from the east. When Mendaña left the Marquesas in 1595, for example, he sailed past a few of the Tuamotu atolls. Landing on the atoll of Ana'a, not far from Rangiroa, he met an otherwise completely ordinary woman who was wearing a golden ring set with an emerald. The Spaniard, always turned on by gems, shrewdly tried to induce the woman to swap the ring for one made of brass, but were unsuccessful. During the same visit, the Spaniards also discovered a ship's yard arm of cedar, which they said had clearly been made on the coast of South America and represented further evidence of contact with Europeans from South America. Ten years later, the Dutchmen Le Maire and Schouten arrived in the archipelago. They found that the Tuamotu islanders were already quite familiar with iron, happily pulling much sought-after nails from European ships.

Whence came the gold ring with the emeralds? Who introduced iron to these people? Might it have been the same shadowy navigators who introduced iron to the Marquesas from the west? It might also be that many wrecks, or possibly even intact ships, were blown by the trade winds from South America to be stranded in that sprawling archipelago. This seems to have happened in Hawai'i, where some of the supposedly-lost Manila galleons came to grief. But when one speaks of Spanish ships, isn't there also a chance that some of them may have been carrying a bit of the plundered wealth of the Inca empire?

Because of their isolation and the dangerous waters surrounding them, the islands presented a welcome hiding place, where pirates and other such rabble could hide their loot. In fact, at present, there's an expedition fitting out to search for and recover a legendary gold horde that has been stashed somewhere in the Tuamotus. Up until around 1840, this horde had been held in a church in Peru. A group of pirates, posing as concerned gentlemen, convinced the priestly guardians of this treasure that the gold had to be moved and temporarily placed board a ship "for security." With full confidence in the pseudo-gentlemen, the priests helped them to move the treasure and load it aboard. As soon as the gold was loaded, the priests were slaughtered and the rogues headed for the open sea with their glittering cargo. While sailing through the Tuamotus, they decided for some reason to hide the treasure on one of the islands. The choice fell on a small, plain-looking atoll, where they cached the gold and moved on, eventually going their separate ways.

Time passed, until only one of the original crew remained alive, retaining in his possession a crude sketch showing the location of the treasure. After he too died, the sketch changed hands many times, providing the impetus for several unsuccessful expeditions which were mounted before World War II intervened. Will the up-coming expedition be successful? It seems questionable, when one considers the way the islands change their topography and shoreline features in response to winds and waves, but one can only wish the searchers the best of luck in their efforts.

Some of the legendary Nazi gold might also be stashed in the Tuamotus, and to be sure, such is a vague rumor. In this connection, there's also some talk about the Marquesas being a hiding place for this loot. The story goes that a German U-boat was cruising in the waters of Polynesia at war's end. It's well known that German subs occasionally operated in the western Pacific, transiting to and from Japan (in fact, four U-boats were sunk in the western Pacific during the war), but why this boat might have been hiding gold in Eastern Polynesia (if, in fact, a sub were actually there!) is completely unclear, and defies logic. It's also important to note that the fates of all U-boats have been officially established, but who knows what secrets may be covered by "official" statements?

We won't talk about the missions of the other subs of several nations which crowded into the waters of the Tuamotus to spy on the repeated French nuclear weapons tests of the last 40 years. Their missions are much more obvious, and there might be some very exciting stories to tell, but these will remain forever hidden, indelibly stamped with the legend: "Top Secret."

We're once more on the *Aranui*, returned from our flight into the world of pirates, U-boats, shipwrecks, and buried treasure. It's now evening and we spend the last hours of the day over coffee and tea, hoping that the coming day will bring this sensational voyage to a worthy up-beat end.

Rangiroa

In sharp contrast to yesterday morning, a radiant blue sky awaits us as the *Aranui* steams inerrantly toward Rangiroa. The majority of the passengers are on deck, their cameras at the ready, hoping to catch the first signs of land rising above the horizon. At 0700 the island is there; appearing first when the tops of palm trees pierce the straight line of the blue horizon, looking like an expanse of dark green saw-teeth.

Located 500 km northeast of Pape'ete, Rangiroa is the most important of all the Tuamotu atolls. With a diameter of 80 km, it's the biggest atoll of the archipelago, and the second largest atoll in the world. Only Kwajalein in the Marshalls is bigger, with a length of 125 km and a width of 110 km. Rangiroa's lagoon is famed for its crystal aquamarine waters which sometimes change into a greenish turquoise under certain conditions of sunlight and cloud.

The name Rangiroa means "Long Sky." According to local navigational lore, long before the tips of its palm trees peep above the horizon, the lagoon is visible in the form of a reflection on the bases of the clouds above it. This reflection, the "long sky," referred to in the island's name, is a navigation aid, pointing mariners to the atoll. Experienced Polynesian sailors vouch for the existence of these reflections and so does Bob. He's seen them orient themselves with reference to the reflections of this and other atolls, although try as he might, he's never been able to distinguish the reflections himself.

The *Aranui* has slowly eased off on her speed, and we head for the bow in order to more directly experience the passage into the atoll. Our passage through the eddies and whirlpools of the narrow pass, escorted by frolicking dolphins, is a unique experience. The Senior ladies emit frantic, almost orgasmic,

216

shrieks; jostling each other at the rail. They look like they're about to tumble overboard!

There are six dolphins; five females and one Alpha-male. While the "boss" circles his beauties very watchfully, the little wives hang in the bow wave, close to the ship, swimming with their tummies turned upwards as if they want to retain eye contact with the curious throngs hanging over the rail above them. Have they become totally conditioned to respond this way to the *Aranui*? Possibly; they seem to know quite well what they should do for the tourists and exploit this opportunity to the fullest.

After we enter the pass, our escort disappears. The *Aranui* veers to starboard and soon drops anchor; not long after, we're heading ashore in the whaleboats.

There are many suggestions for today: we can venture into the coral gardens of the lagoon with glassbottom boats; if qualified, we also can go scuba-diving near the pass; or we can take a stroll and discover the island on our own.

Two years ago we decided on the glassbottom boats; these offer a fascinating view into the underwater world of the lagoon, at a spot quite near the pass. Clown fish, parrot fish, Moorish idols; giant wrasse, squirrel fish, and trigger fish romp about in a lively, colorful swirl. Rays skim through the water, briefly casting their bat-like shadows on the lagoon floor. Sluggish turtles paddle by, occasionally engaging in a little casual loveplay, while the lords of the reef, the sharks, lurk very sedately, waiting for the bait which the diver throws to them. They're so well fed and complacent that they really aren't interested in the snorklers kicking idly about, 15 feet or so above over their heads.

When we arrive at the observation station, the rather eccentric Marie-Claire involuntarily provides us with a good laugh. During the entire trip no one saw her dressed in any other costume than long beige trousers and an off-color green shirt. Clad in this outfit, she decided to go snorkeling, and when fully decked out in snorkel and mask she was an admittedly arresting sight. When the boatsman spied her, his eyes seemed to pop out, and his jaw dropped wide open. Then a rather sly grin spread over his broad, normally impassive Polynesian face. What did his crafty wink mean, what was he up to, anyway? The good woman swam slowly off away from the boat. Her trousers, filled with air, inflated like sails in the wind. But the peaceful atmosphere was deceptive, for suddenly the sea around her erupted in a storm of activity, with gleaming silver fish catapulting themselves out of the water, skipping and twisting into the air, colliding with each other and tumbling back again beneath the surface to rejoin their schools. It seemed as though the sea, placid a few seconds ago, had suddenly gone out of control. In the middle of this turmoil floundered Marie Claire, wildly gesticulating, and shouting: "What's happening? What's happening?" Helpful hands reached out to her, dragging her into the boat. Happily, she didn't give the fellow at the helm a glance, because tears were still rolling down his cheeks as he tried vainly to suppress the laughter that was only betrayed by his plump vibrating tummy. His empty food sack was also not noticed; a few minutes earlier it had been emptied into the lagoon, for the enjoyment of men and fish alike.

Today's walk leads us to the outside of the atoll, out where the surf pounds furiously, incessantly, against the almost vertical coral ramparts of Rangiroa. We lean into the strong wind, grab hold of everything that isn't firmly attached to us and struggle to catch our breath. In the palm grove, below the wind, we stop for a few moments breathing spell and then head off on the path leading through the grove to the wind-sheltered lagoon beach.

With all the other passengers, we spend a bit of time thereafter on the edge of the Hotel Kia Ora Village, the preferred playground for a spoiled clientele, as we learn from the travel guide. We also feel a bit spoiled, however, spoiled by the glass-clear air, the white beach beneath the fan-like leaves of pandanus and palms, and the subtle colors of the lagoon, changing from turquoise to sapphire blue. Once more, it's great to enjoy the South Seas and the "lightness of being," a very appropriate phrase to describe the charm of moments spent in such magnificent surroundings. Lost in thought, I play with the sand, which runs through my fingers, but somehow I can't allow myself to make a comparison or analogy between these sand grains and anything else that's going on.

Sailors and passengers have mixed well, happy groups are scattered about under the palms; talking, laughing, and working away at Hinano beer or soft drinks. The flirtation between Dagmar, the beautiful Berliner and Friedrich, the Tahitian-German with the long dark hair, seems to be still going strong. Off shore, a couple of people are trying to master the intricacies of Polynesian outrigger canoes: every time they capsize, and that's quite often, there are gales of laughter from the many onlookers.

The tasty picnic allows us to once more appreciate the culinary mastery of the *Aranui* galley staff. The odd sand grain caught between the teeth is accepted in the bargain, and without a murmur: you can't stop the wind from blowing!

For the last time, the whaleboats are underway: this is sad because it means one more good-bye, a good-bye to something that we have grown to love. Lost in melancholy, I head for the showers and begin to think with horror of the inevitable packing task looming before me. The way to the bar where we hope to cheer ourselves up with a piña colada and popcorn, leads by Hu'uveu's cramped office. His book-keeping is over and the earnings have disappeared into the battered safe. At last he can breathe easily because yet another trip is coming to a most satisfactory conclusion. How many hundreds of voyages has he made in his long career? The radiant grin on his normally concerned face shows how relieved and happy he is. Hu'uveu, a highly reliable and capable archeological field worker, experienced sailor, trusted guardian of the affairs of the Wong family and wonderful friend, has also become a dear friend to me. He's the embodiment of all the best and most noble traits of the ancient Marquesans, and for that reason he's irreplaceable aboard the *Aranui*.

Whether they want to thank me for the happy ending of the voyage, or whether they have other reasons for not appearing, my cockroach friends have disappeared. The suitcases will be traveling onward without a single one of them involved. But the bags will be heavier. With sadness, my archaeological finds are stowed away in the depths of the trunk. They were my cabin decorations, and without them the cabin seems empty.

In the final meetings, Bob receives hearty thanks from all passengers. I see how much it pleases him; he really deserves it. With his seemingly inexhaustible knowledge and experience here, his willingness to deal with all questions and to find the correct answers, he's contributed substantially to the "*Aranui* experience" for many of our fellow travelers.

At the evening meal, there's once more a fashion show of sorts, as everyone tries to give this last evening a special air. There's a lot of laughter and a lot of wine is consumed, but here and there shadows flit across the laughing faces, often lingering momentarily. Evelyn's slogan: "It's better to be painted by Picasso, than to be drawn from life!" contains an ironic element of bitter truth.

I stand on deck, staring up into the heavens, seeking a shooting star on which to make my wish. It's the same wish as it was two years ago: to come back one more time to this enchanting world which, in spite of shadows and "background noise," will always remain a paradise for me, a paradise for which I long on cold gray winter days as well as on those other days which for many other reasons may be hard to endure. Even as the *Aranui* band strikes up, Dr. Robert C. Suggs remains up on the bridge, also allowing himself to be carried away by the feelings of the moment, and he's joined by all the others on deck.

Return to Pape'ete

It's 0600, and I stumble drowsily around over suitcases and hand luggage. There's nothing that can keep me in this cabin any longer because I want to once more experience the way in which Tahiti rises out of the sheltering sea. The dark volcanic cone comes nearer and nearer; we pass Point Venus, and Mo'ore'a appears in the morning light.

The sailors rush about intently, cleaning up their last duties and getting everything ship-shape for our arrival. They have to be happy to have put one more problem-free trip behind them. For a few days, they'll be with their families or at least be able to spend the time in Tahiti in an entertaining fashion, before preparations for the next trip begin.

Our trip, however, is over. The reception looks like an overturned anthill, with waves of frantic activity spreading out from the tiny desk by the dining room door to all parts of the ship. This morning, the normally breakfast driven Seniors hardly give breakfast a passing glance.

The starboard railing is mobbed. *Aranui* enters the harbor, slides effortlessly into her berth, ties up, and the ladder goes down for the last time on this voyage. Below on the quay, the first taxis are arriving. Transfer vans get in the way, curiosity seekers and private autos render the chaos complete. As always, several members of the Wong family stand on the quay observing how punctually and well kept-up their *Aranui* has been returned.

The farewells begin, and not infrequently they're accompanied by tears. Adieu Trudy, with that wonderful Vienna charm that we've grown so fond of, and your faint scent of alcohol from last night's farewell drinks, when you were celebrating the cruise's end with several of our shipmates. And there's Helmut from

Munich: "Here we go again! Take it slow and easy, Burgl!" Helmut with his beautiful Sybille have made this trip really entertaining. Evelyn and Ed promise to write, quiet Nancy looks even more sad than usual and Francis plants a kiss on my lips repeating her invitation to Florida. "A safe trip back home, Uschi and Karl! It was wonderful to meet you both!" From a distance our Captain Cook shouts his farewell greeting: "We really enjoyed it, professor; 'twas a real pleasure to meet you!" No, he wasn't an Australian, but from Geneva. And so it goes, on and on. Bob is distributing visiting cards right and left, like a regular professional, and giving out last-minute tourist information in response to questions, while greeting members of the Wong family as they come aboard.

I'll meet Margitta and Dagmar again, when the Easter Island trip begins. In the meantime, they'll be relaxing on Mo'ore'a. Are we still agreed to meet at Fa'a'a at 2200 on the night of departure?

In the middle of the confusion, there is a sudden resounding crash of broken glass! There on the dock stands a young and very unhappy sailor, surrounded by a mess of broken brown glass and a spreading pool of white foam. Trying to load a palette of 20 cases of beer onto a truck with his fork lift, he missed the target completely, and most of the palette ended up on the dock. He's ashamed, especially because a member of the elite *Aranui* crew should never let something like this happen. I hear a sigh of resignation from one of the spectators who is preparing to help the crew pick up the broken glass: "What a waste! I could have drunk the whole load myself!"

In the meantime, the transfer van of Marama Tours has arrived, and the luggage is loaded aboard. I cast a last melancholy glance at the *Aranui*; I may never see her again, and I've got to thank her for so many happy hours. Wherever she spends the twilight of her long and busy career, I can only hope that she doesn't wind up on some ignominious ship-breakers scrap heap.

As the noisy quay and the ship finally disappear from view, we shift our attention to concentrate on the coming days in Tahiti and how we're going to enjoy the most beautiful parts of Tahiti. One of the most beautiful sides of this island is the exclusive Outrigger Hotel south of Pape'ete, located directly above the reef pass and only about 15 minutes from the Fa'a'a airfield, where Bob and several of us are headed.

Sweaty and garbed in typically informal *Aranui* outfits, we're all out-of-place mildly exotic figures in the reception hall, with its local beauties clad in bright *pareu* cloth, and handsome young fellows in wrinkle-free aloha shirts. It doesn't seem to trouble my companion. In quick time the formalities are attended to, and we're ushered into the presence of the hotel manager. I tag along behind. One of the cooks standing in the manager's office area mistakes Bob for some kind of intruder, but Bob quite forcefully sets him straight about that. Sitting down with the conscientious director, Wayne Sterling, Bob finds out that he has to give a lecture, that very afternoon, for tourists debarking from the Renaissance III, a multi-decked luxury cruise ship. Looks like I'm going to be his assistant!

"What's my job?"

"Handle the projector for me, will you? It doesn't have a remote!"

"OK, I'll do my best, you can be sure! Which talk are you going to give, anyway?"

"It doesn't make any difference, the people just want to hear something about the South Seas!"

"Cook?"

"Right. Cook's always a big hit!"

There's another version of Bob's Cook lecture which focuses on Tahiti. Thank God, Cook was everywhere!

The elegance of my hotel room, the luxurious furnishings of the bath, and the clean soft coolness of the bathroom and the running water all combine to produce an unending joy! In the

Aranui community shower, there was always a hard rubber grill work, beneath which odd things sometimes seemed to be splashing about.

I flop on the bed, close my eyes for a moment and can't believe that the bed seems to sway slightly, but that's only horizontal version of "land legs." After two weeks at sea, my inner ear can't instantly adjust to the solid surface under me. What seems at first to be the faint sound of motors turns out to be only the air conditioning. Under a comfortable hot shower, the last traces of the *Aranui*, the quay, and the Pape'ete streets are washed away. Like Aphrodite (clearly an exaggeration for a variety of reasons), I emerge from the torrents feeling like I was reborn. The indescribable feeling of a new quality of life gets a further boost from a fresh salad and a cool beer in the shady hotel bar.

While Bob heads for his room to prepare his Cook lecture slides, I explore the hotel and the pool. The pool terrace offers an enchanting view of the pass through the reef, and the ships entering and departing the busy port of Pape'ete. Off to the south, you can make out Mo'ore'a, whose menacing fang-like crags jut high into the heavens and constantly change shape in a never-ending game of sunshine, shadow, and cloud.

The oddly-named island of Mo'ore'a ("Yellow Lizard") is the little sister of Tahiti. It possesses the same kind of beauty, but is at present much more peaceful than its big sister. In addition to a tumble of sharp volcanic peaks, the Mo'ore'a landscape is characterized by the deep bays of Opunohu and Cook, and many white sand beaches, all surrounded by a gleaming lagoon. Mo'ore'a is spectacular and seductive; with it's incomparable panorama, it's undoubtedly one of the most beautiful places in all Polynesia, and is said to have been the inspiration for James Mitchener's fabled island of Bali Hai.

The weather is not cooperating, however, for in the course of the early afternoon the clouds thicken over Mo'ore'a. Shortly thereafter it begins to pour rain. It's the best time to explore the fantastic interior decor of the hotel. Great lamps made of heavy clusters of seashells radiate a pleasant light. The widely divergent corridors are hung with original paintings of Tahitian artists, depicting scenes of South Seas life in styles reminiscent of the works of Max Ernst and Joan Miro'. The delicate, carefully executed still-lifes of flowers and animals lend a unique finishing touch to the collection, which also includes monumental woodcarvings from various islands of Polynesia and Melanesia. In order to find the way out of this labyrinth of stairs and spacious rooms, you've got to have the sense of orientation of a trained pathfinder. Before the French doors, a huge plastic-swathed structure extends through two floors from the reception area to the bar and pool level. Curious, I dare to take a look behind the plastic shrouds and discover in disbelief that it's a monumental Christmas tree which is just about finished. I can't think of anything more absurd at the moment, but in fact, it's only 5 weeks to Christmas.

Outside beneath the arches of arcade, a small handicraft market has been set up. People from Fa'a'a, the poorest district of the entire island, have been invited by the hotel to sell their wares here. When things are so handy, it's hard to withstand the attraction of the *pareu* and the little *tiki,* and so the load of souvenirs to be carried home becomes a bit heavier.

It's time for the Cook lecture; I follow the passengers of Renaissance III into a large conference room in which an incredibly rich cold buffet has been set out. How can I resist these delicacies? My plate is already filled to overflowing when Bob suddenly reappears and reminds me of my duty at the projector. What else is there to do but take my place behind the apparatus and wait for the lecture to start? The room fills up rapidly and soon is crowded; I wait for Bob's hand signal and begin to flip the slides. Now and then I cast a longing glance upon the tempting roast beef and trimmings beckoning me from the plate reposing on the floor beside my chair. But I always come back to the task at hand to avoid interfering with the lecture which is arousing great interest in the audience.

At the end the more than 100 attendees thank Bob with prolonged applause. The following question period is very well utilized and is even more satisfying to Bob than the applause: "They really listened; the questions were great!" he tells me later.

The same applause earns a basket of fruit which, in the meantime, finds it's way to Bob's room. The tasteful arrangement includes mangos, oranges, kiwi fruit, apples, and a big coconut. The coconut forcibly reminds us of the legend of Hina and the handsome but unfortunate chief from Fiji, who in death gave Hina and the Polynesians the most important gift they would ever receive, the cocoa palm! We drink the coco water in memory of Bob's daughter.

This evening, the Outrigger offers seafood lovers a culinary flight of utter fantasy, and the exquisite food does not fail to attract a large crowd. From a nearby table we are greeted by Frau Helvetia from the Seniors group. There's something genuinely friendly in her "Hi there!" and now that she's separated from the very stiff and formal behavior code of that gaggle, we engage in a relaxed and unusually interesting conversation with her.

In the meantime, young Tahitians have gathered in the garden outside the bar; with laughter that sometimes threatens to drown the orchestra, they're putting away the Hinano and Heinekens with great gusto, and packing the dance floor. The local forms of "dancing" are markedly differentiated from the dancing school norms known to us. It often seems that you couldn't insert a feather between the tightly-pressed bodies swaying in arousing rhythm to the music.

How would an archeologist perform in this thrusting, rubbing crowd?

"May I request the pleasure of this dance, sir?" Astounded eyes stare back at me.

"Who, me?"

"Yes, you!"

"Oh my God, I haven't danced in years!"

"Then it's high time to start again ... !"

The years of non-dancing are quite noticeable at first, but then he's caught up by the rhythm too, and I'm led out into the midst of the jammed dance floor. When the orchestra begins to play the melodies of the '50s such as: "*Ua taetae roa te ava'e*" (The moon is shining brightly), *Mauiui to'u mafatu* "(My heart aches), *Te vahine anami*" (The Annamite girl), memories of the early Polynesian years seem to return. In his surprisingly melodious voice, the Tahitian songs are truly quite moving. A long and eventful day comes to an end, and we part, but I treasure the thought that I've got two more days to spend here, a thought which unites the day's experiences to my dreams in a very pleasing fashion.

A trip around Tahiti

Heading south, we pass the markets of Fa'a'a, with their offerings of fish, fruits, vegetables, and their banks of brilliant flowers destined to adorn heads and shoulders of Tahitian beauties and their lovers. The road leads to Puna'auia and the Musée des Îles, where the natural history, cultures, and history of French Polynesia are displayed in several neatly arranged wings. The anchor before the museum door belonged to Captain Cook's ship and was lost at Tautira Point. Among many worthwhile archeological and ethnological attractions, we meet old friends from the Marquesas Islands, including beautiful carved wooden clubs, stilts and paddles, and the biggest wooden *tiki* to survive the breakdown of the culture. It's about the same size as old Taka'i'i in Puama'u. The most impressive part of this figure is the rendering of the classical body and its contours, which are masterfully emphasized by a pattern of highly controlled adze strokes, attesting to the skill of the carver. This figure is definitive proof of the level of artistry attained by the early Marquesan carvers. With their simple tools of shell and stone, they created absolute masterworks such as this *tiki*, which ranks among the leading examples of their enormous creativity.

Behind the museum extends a long beach, offering a good view of Mo'ore'a. It's pouring rain, however, and the glorious view is drowned amidst a succession of fast-moving showers.

We proceed south to Pa'ea, where we turn suddenly to the left, to head up a narrow road into a deep green valley. After a short bumpy ride, with rain drops beating a *concerto grosso* on the roof of the car, we reach ancient Marae Arahurahu. It's a Polynesian religious site with a restored temple of the classic late Tahitian style. The temple itself consists of a wide rectangular forecourt surrounded by a stone wall of neatly dressed basalt stones. On the inland end of the court rises an impressive three-story altar made of dressed basalt blocks. A horizontal row of white coral blocks decorates the second step of the altar. With restored wooden figures in the forecourt, this is a very good example of the best of Tahitian ceremonial construction. The rain has ceased and we're alone on the temple, enjoying the peace and quiet, and taking the time to examine this unique cultural monument. It's not only Marae Arahurahu itself that had a special meaning for the ancient Tahitians. Bob points out that the entire valley inland of the temple was once sacred territory. There were many burial places in the cliffs on both sides of the valley behind the temple. It was here that Bob began his research in Tahiti in 1956, while awaiting the copra schooner to the Marquesas. At that remote time, Marae Arahurahu had already been restored, but Bob was recently surprised to learn that one of the publicity hogs of Polynesian archeology claimed to have first restored the temple in the 60s. Amazing, these archeologists and their dates!

Along the coast, where the well-to-do Tahitians and *popa'a* (Europeans), hide their fine houses in splendid gardens, we repeatedly discover fascinating views of the reef with its roaring surf, and the stretches of black volcanic sand for which the island is noted. Other villas cling to steep slopes and crests inland of the coastal highway, and I can imagine that the views from these eyries is breathtaking. Bob tells me of a friend of his whose triangular living room features floor-to-ceiling walls of glass. From one side you look out toward Mo'ore'a; from the other side toward the pass at Pa'ea, both awe-inspiring spectacles at any time of the day, in any season.

In the district of Pape'ari it was possible for the American botanist Harrison Smith to realize his dream of founding a botanical garden and assembling rare plants from the tropics of America, Asia, Africa and the Pacific. Later Smith's heirs sold the garden to the American millionaire Cornelius Crane, a well-known patron of scientific explorations in the South Seas, including Bob's work in the Marquesas. Crane, with the help of Prince Karl von Schoenberg von Hohenzollern, himself an expert on tropical flora, built up the garden to the point where it is presently one of the major attractions of the island. Bob got along famously with the Prince and after his first expedition, on which Prince Karl took part, they carried on a fascinating correspondence long after the Prince returned to Europe.

Near the Botanical Garden, stands the Gauguin Museum, in which placards, photos, and reproductions are used to trace Gauguin's life and keep alive his memory. There's even a huge menhir from his beloved Brittany, standing strangely misplaced in a corner of the Museum. Sending a menhir to Polynesia seems to us like sending oil to Saudi Arabia. The museum poses an interesting problem, however, for among the exhibited works, you've got to search diligently for an original. There are a couple of his earlier paintings and one or two questionable woodcarvings, but the paintings which made Gauguin famous, and for which no one would pay a *sou* during most of his lifetime, are today distributed among the world's great art collections, zealously protected, and sold at astronomical prices. No one would expose any of Gauguin's important works to the mildew, termites, and other tropical threats that abound in this museum.

The landscape is becoming more primitive as we head south. We drive through little villages, clusters of cottages with corrugated iron or palm-thatched roofs, as the peaks of Aorai and Orohena cast their long shadows on us. Here and there, valleys open to us offering magnificent views into the interior, with its almost vertical cliffs and knife-edge ridge lines.

We reach the isthmus of Taravao linking Tahiti Nui to Tahiti Iti, and head for the district of Fa'a'one, toward a hotel which is regarded as "Tahiti's best -kept secret," at least for those who savor the extraordinary.

This unique hotel, Fare Nana'o, consists of seven huts or "bungalows," which were built out of local woods by Jean-Claude Michel, a talented wood-carver. The huts, each different from the other, lie on a wooded beach. Some are tastefully integrated into the jungle-like background, one is built on a tiny offshore island, and there are a couple of lofty tree houses. The construction is airy, with wide-open windows, and the furnishings are deliberately original. Nothing stands in the way of enjoying a real Robinson Crusoe adventure here. The homey relaxed atmosphere of Fare Nana'o is directly linked to its harmony with nature; Monique Mériaux and her family see to that. The Mériaux daughters are readying the tree house and island house for the next guests, and we're grateful to them for permitting us a look into the refreshingly individualistic ambiance of each these bungalows.

With a loud "hallo" Bob greets a young couple with a little boy, and it's my pleasure to learn that this handsome couple is Danee Hazama, and his beautiful wife Alice. Danee is a good friend of Bob's, they worked together during Bob's last excavations at Ha'atuatua. The little fellow with his dad's face and the Polynesian touch of his mom, is an enchanting child. His sunny laugh steals your heart away. He's Tama'evanui, the delight of his proud parents.

This meeting was planned as a surprise, and it turned out to be just that. Because Monique already has a full complement of guests for lunch, we head off to a near-by restaurant, *Le Rouge et Noir* (The Red and Black), where we enjoy a tasty and leisurely meal together. Danee and Alice tell me about themselves: he's of Japanese ancestry from Pasadena, California. A former paratrooper, with a paratrooper's "can-do" drive, he's now a much sought-after photographer who's worked on assignment for many well-known magazines as well as on many scientific expeditions. He lost his heart in Tahiti, lost it irretrievably to his charming wife, Alice. She is a dancer, a fact which is quite evident in her naturally graceful movements. In her artfully tied *pareu,* she is the embodiment of everyone's dream of a Tahitian beauty. Both of them dance with a leading dance troupe, while Danee also participates in the incredibly strenuous sport of canoe racing. The lively conversation, the refreshing relaxation, and the total peace which we experience allows us to totally forget the Tahiti of the tourist brochures.

Danee and Alice invite us to accompany them on a visit to a piece of property which they have just purchased on the slopes of Tahiti Iti, facing the isthmus. They want to put a bit of distance between themselves and their "Tahitian family." This rather extended group not infrequently places heavy demands on the couple. As we drive up a steep slope, the entire environment changes around us, it's noticeably cooler, the coco palms become increasingly rare, and are replaced by mangos and ironwood trees. We reach Danee's land in Pu'u Nui, and the view is literally breathtaking. To the north, our gaze is riveted on the cloud-covered volcanic cone of Tahiti Nui, while both coasts are delineated by sinuous white ranks of surf striking the encircling reef. There's almost no noise, only the wind and occasional bird songs break the stillness. We enjoy discussing future hopes and plans with this attractive young couple, and we encourage them to build their own little oasis of happiness here. Tama'evanui listens attentively. His beguiling little-boy face already betrays the strong confident personality which lies hidden in him. It's difficult to tear ourselves away from this warm family, but hopefully we'll be able to keep the promise to see them again.

Fortunately today is not a work day; we encounter none of the usual 20 km traffic jams, and the trip back to Pape'ete goes quite quickly. Following the sign posts, we make a sudden detour to the left and head inland up another narrow road into a trench-like valley which leads to the waterfalls of Fa'aruma'i. At the end of this valley, heavily overgrown with tall hardwood trees (Tahitian chestnut trees and flowering Barringtonia, used in the

232

past for fish poison) the surprisingly cold cascade drops vertically over 30 meters into a deep wide pool. This basin feeds a narrow stream which winds through a small Tahitian settlement, emptying into the nearby lagoon. Whoever wants to can bathe in these near-frigid waters but that's not for me!

Back again on the main road, it's only a short distance to the Arahoho Blowhole. Under certain sea states, incoming waves send great fountains of water shooting up through holes in the coastal bedrock, drenching the road, and spectators, and presenting a very exciting spectacle. There's a bit of action today, but nothing really special and we move on.

It's been a long day; I'm becoming a bit tired and so the lighthouse at Cook's Point Venus gets only a brief glance. We're back in Pape'ete again and manage to successfully negotiate its complex system of one-way streets and traffic circles without a problem, arriving back in the Outrigger by late afternoon.

A dip in the pool is pleasant and entertaining, the entertainment being provided by a little Tahitian girl who splashes around us with great curiosity and wants to know everything about us. She interrogates us with such an intensity that we answer her in all seriousness. When she begins to ask about ages, however, Bob tells her that he's 37 and I'm 24. Deep folds crease her little forehead; she spins around two or three times on her heel, and then announces that we've lied to her, for the first time. Bitterly chagrined, little Vai'a runs to her mother, who until then had been unsuccessfully trying to entice her out of the water to take her home. We head for the whirlpool, which crowns the top of a huge artificial boulder, like an eagle's nest. Bob calls it a California party whirlpool, built to hold about 30 people in very chummy proximity.

The mountains of Mo'ore'a were already draped in cloud on our arrival, but they have now shed their covering and stretch into a delicately pink-tinted heaven. It's an evening sky that explodes into a fireworks of color as the sun sets. From a soft light pink to the deepest fiery red, the clouds and light are constantly changing, until in the end the light fades into a dark violet. In this light, the rustling palms in the garden appear to be artificial cut-outs. It's very hard to capture in words this magical experience, which only comes into being here, and I'm tempted to fall back on Rainer Maria Rilke's words of surrender: "... the entire gift of speech is exhausted ..." It's not the sight alone, but the feelings aroused by the sight that make words falter on the tongue.

Still under the influence of this great sunset experience, we head for dinner and meet other *Aranui* friends who came here with us. There's an American couple that we've spoken to on the ship several times and we pick up the conversation where we left it off a few days earlier, discussing Marquesan psychology and various interpretations thereof. This is a subject which is interesting although a bit sensitive with Bob, a staunch defender of his "people." We enjoy with them the rest of the evening, in happy camaraderie, reflecting on the friendships which have become deeper and stronger through the experiences of the voyage, and of this fine day.

The last day in Tahiti

It's very hard to open my eyes on this Sunday, because it's the last day of the trip, an experience that began, and will end, in Tahiti. It seems as though the sun is concerned to soften the impact of the departure and keep up my spirits for the last few hours here, as it beams brightly down on us from a cloudless sky.

The breakfast buffet may have been hardly touched in the previous mornings, but today a long line has already formed when I arrive. The dining room is fully occupied by Tahitian extended families. It seems like everyone in Fa'a'a is there! The older women are all wearing the traditional Sunday costume of long Mother Hubbard dresses made of colorful *pareu* cloth, and hats made of gleaming white pandanus leaves. The Polynesians love these buffets and return over and over again, either filling their plates or the plates of other family members while someone is always tending to the kiddies.

It's an extremely pleasant surprise to run into an *Aranui* sailor in the midst of this feeding frenzy. It's Tima'u, the coxswain of one of the two whaleboats, a hulking bear of a man with strength to match. Today his bulging biceps are encased in a very smart shirt, his Calvin Kleins sit perfectly on his hips and his glorious bushy locks are well hidden beneath an expensive cowboy hat. It's hard to believe that this is the same laconic fellow who uses hand signals, grunts, and body language to give directions to his boat crew. He's happy to see us too and introduces his little daughter who is clutching his huge hand. She only has eyes for her proud papa! It seems to me that this meeting is a favorable omen; once more the *Aranui* is greeting us with one of its most impressive personalities.

The rest of the day we spend by the pool, reading, or as in Bob's case, writing up a résumé of the trip for our journal. I ask him whether the expectations, hopes, and fantasies have been fulfilled for him. He says that he'll be going home quite happy and satisfied on all scores. But he's also unhappy because a period of harmony, of lively discussions, and plenty of hilarity, with many fascinating people is also coming to an end for him. His eyes fill with tears as he thinks of Pélagie and Teiki the wood carver. Two of his fellow- travelers from the old days will no longer be on the islands when the next cruise brings him back. Since the first Polynesian settlers set foot on these islands, there have always been comings and goings, separations and reunions. The people here have learned to place their hopes in the hands of those powers which determine their fates: "Let's do the same as they have done. If it's the will of Providence, our paths will cross again. We'll write our journal, and many people will follow us here!"

The afternoon drags slowly on. The safe in my room gets stuck and has to be opened by a hotel service man. This problem arises from the same inner turmoil which makes me search for things that seem to be irretrievably lost in packing, but which finally turn up in the most inconceivable places; namely, exactly where I left them!

Once more, time seems to stand still at dinner. We laugh and enjoy the exquisite meal and swap memories of the trips we've made on the *Aranui*. We recall little Marie-Antoinette, the wife of Teiki the woodcarver, Pélagie with her fascinating powers, taciturn Théodor of the quiet confident smile; our model first mate/astronomer/chessmaster, Hu'uveu, the ever-watchful supercargo; and Josephine the resolute chief of the female housekeeping staff who has Bob's interests so deeply at heart. These images are joined by the faces of Nancy, Frances, Frau Helvetia, Trudy, Sybillle, Helmut, Lancelot and the Lift Princess, and the whole Senior gaggle! They're all there, parading before our eyes once more. We realise how much pleasure this cruise has brought and I must admit that it's going to be difficult for me to get used to the gray late fall of Switzerland.

It's time to go; the taxi waits for me at the reception. My bag is stowed and there's nothing to hold me back. It's only a few minutes to the airport. Everywhere in the long crowded and noisy waiting room separations are taking place. There are tears; despairing, sad embraces, but at the same time, there are happy reunions; laughter and shouts of joy. And it's always been that way on these islands. I think about what Bob told me to cheer me up: "A man once described a ship departure in this way: he said that when the ship lets go from the quay and sinks below the horizon, the onlookers say: 'It's gone!' but then people on the other shore will soon be saying: 'See, it's coming!' And you've got to think like this: the ship is coming."

But my heart is hammering in my chest, and the feelings that catch in my throat, the understanding that it's finally all over, these are the things that hurt, that make me quake within. I'm still feeling tropical warmth, I'm breathing the scent of the flowers, I'm longing for the rolling of the ship, the sight of the islands as they slowly rise out of the sea. I yearn to hear again the "Ka'oha nui" of the "Men," and to enjoy the comforting quietude of Ha'atuatua.

I stumble through customs, showing my passport. Beyond, there's only emptiness. As the aircraft climbs, I see the lights of the hotel beneath me and know that the trip is finally at an end. But the pain of separation gives way to a small spark of hope that I'll someday return to these islands where my heart remains.

Acknowledgments

This book is not only the result of our joint writing but of the help which we've received from many people throughout many years.

We're only two of the happy passengers who have enjoyed the "*Aranui* Experience" during the last 20 years. Without the *Aranui* we would have never met to discover our common interests, and would have never written this book. Everything revolves around the *Aranui*. It's therefore our most pleasant duty to honor the Wong family of the Compagnie Polynésienne de Transport Maritime (CPTM) of Pape'ete and San Mateo California, the owners of the *Aranui*, and to thank them for their support and cooperation throughout this entire project. M. Jules Wong and Mlle. Romina Wong have provided us with unfailing assistance at every step of the way, and we are deeply grateful to them.

Skillfully, tenaciously, and not infrequently against the opposition of the French government itself, CPTM has built up steady and reliable shipping connections between Tahiti and the Marquesas over many decades. In the 1980s, the *Aranui*, once only a freighter, was renovated to carry tourists to offer for the first time the spectacular possibility of a trip to these mystery-swathed islands, accompanied by experienced guides. This was a risky and expensive gamble, but it succeeded admirably. Thousands of visitors have availed themselves of this possibility and returned filled with enthusiasm. We must also thank the wise decision of the Wong family for having so significantly raised the standard of living in these isolated islands with a prudent and "soft" tourism which did not produce abrupt changes in the living conditions of the Marquesans.

The friendship with Hu'uveu Teikitekahioho, known on the ship by his baptismal name of Casimir, is as rock-solid as the *tiki* which silently guard his islands. A man of few words but most impressive actions, he has preserved in himself all the best character traits which have always distinguished the Marquesans, and which so impressed Capt. David Porter nearly 200 years ago. We, and the Wong family, have many reasons to thank him for his amazing dependability and reliability. He is for them, and for us, the standard against which fidelity is to be measured. Bob has known him since 1956, and shares many fond memories of moss-covered ruins in Taipei, mysterious caves crammed with artifacts, canoe trips in shark-infested waters, and many dangerous landings. We also both remember him for his benevolent presence on *Aranui* trips. When Bob goes to Tahiti he's always at home with Hu'uveu, who's like the brother that Bob lost years ago, and Bob is as welcome at his home as if he were a blood relative.

But what would the *Aranui* be without it's crew, it's sailors? They're responsible for the peace and security with which we sail aboard this ship, and they have every right to claim that they're members of a truly elite unit. We salute them with a well-known US Navy signal: "BZ" or "Bravo Zulu" which means "Well Done!" the finest tribute a ship and its crew can receive. We're in their debt.

We were able to turn to Danee Hazama, another highly reliable long time friend, any time we needed help in Tahiti, and we thank him for his hospitality and invaluable assistance.

We also want to thank:

Mme. Rose Corser of Hotel Keikahanui Pearl Village, Taioha'e, Nuku Hiva. It's a pleasure to stand in the debt of this charming and strong-willed lady, for her help with our photos as well as for her hospitality and friendship. Thanks so much, Rose!

Mme. Monique Mériaux, owner of Fare Nana'o for her fine hospitality and her photos.

The administration of the Hotel Outrigger Corporation, principally Ms. Mary Lou Foley, for arranging Bob's lectures in the

240

Hotel Tahiti Outrigger, and Wayne Sterling, the highly creative former director, and his staff for their hospitality in their wonderful hotel.

Dr. Horst Cain and Frau Annette Bierbach, who helped us greatly with their friendly suggestions and led us to Frau Franziska Land in Berlin who spontaneously declared herself ready to publish our book. We thank them all from the bottom of our hearts.

Dr. Ulrike Zophoniasson who with her great fund of experience, remained by our sides throughout the whole book and gave us many valuable suggestions.

In the FESPO in Zuerich I got to know Frau Dagmar Levi of Tahiti Tourisme, in Frankfurt. We were immediately drawn to each other by our shared experiences in the Marquesas. She provided additional motivation to write this book and helped with many details concerning the travel agencies.

And last but by no means least, our spouses, Hans Ulrich Zueblin, and Rae Suggs, both of whom must be thanked for their endless patience through all of the "overtime," the sky-high phone bills, proof-reading the drafts, and other technical assistance, wherever our own abilities failed us completely. And we must also include our thanks to Bob's sons, Donald and Wayne, for their technical computer advice. In the final analysis, our families deserve the greatest thanks of all.

Suggestions for further reading

Since the Marquesas were discovered, over 4 centuries ago, many books, in many languages, have been devoted to these fascinating islands. The majority are either rather superficial picture-books, however, with a minimum of banal text, or they present half-baked theories advanced by self-styled experts. These books, like those dealing with UFOs, etc., are easy to find anywhere, but if one knows what to look for, there also is a large, reliable literature on the Marquesas. Readers who wish to venture deeper into that literature may find the following suggestions helpful.

The Best!

The single best academic source on the Marquesas is the 3-volume master work of the German ethnologist, Dr. Karl von den Steinen, who conducted field research in the islands in 1896. This work contains an excellent description of the native culture as well as an interesting analysis and evaluation of the historical sources, such as Porter, Cook, etc., and a long bibliography.

Unfortunately, von den Steinen's work is not available in English translation! Furthermore, his ponderous 19th-century academic German causes problems even for native Germans. The pictures of these volumes are well worth seeing, however, even if the text cannot be read. These volumes are most often found in library rare book collections today, although an offset reproduction was produced by Hacker Art Books in New York.

For those with the fortitude to search out this gem of 19th-century ethnography, and work with the German text, the following reference is provided:

Karl von den Steinen: "*Die Marquesaner und ihre Kunst*", *Band I: Tattauierung*; Berlin, 1925; *Band II, Die Plastik* ; *Band III, Die Sammlungen*. Berlin, 1928. (The Marquesans and Their Art, Vol. I, Tattooing; Vol. II, Sculpture; and Vol. III, The Collections.

Dr. von den Steinen also published an interesting collection of Marquesan legends in the German journal, *Zeitschrift für Ethnologie* (1933–34). These were translated into English and published as: *Von den Steinen's Marquesan Myths*, M. Langridge, trans; J. Terrell Ed. Canberra, Target Oceania and Journal of Pacific History, 1988.

English Sources

Historical accounts

Perhaps the best and most widely known book on the Marquesas is Herman Melville's: *Typee; a South Seas Romance*, first published in 1846, New York, and reprinted in various formats many times since. *Typee* is Melville's first novel, the product of a six-week sojourn on Nuku Hiva in 1843. It's explicitly a novel (a "romance"), and must not be considered as either an ethnography or an historical report, as many Melville fans seek to do. Melville combined information from many primary sources with a substantial amount of pure fantasy in creating this book. *Typee,* the first of the voluminous "South Sea romance" genre, nevertheless provides an entertaining if not precise overview of Marquesan culture.

The single best English-language source on early 19th-century Marquesan culture is the eye-witness account of the under-appreciated US Navy hero, Capt. David Porter. While refitting his ships at Nuku Hiva during the War of 1812, Porter developed a keen and highly positive appreciation for the Marquesans, despite having to go to war against them. His journal, with his own excellent illustrations, has been recently reissued:

Porter, David. *Journal of a cruise made to the Pacific Ocean by Captain David Porter in the United States Frigate Essex in the years 1812,1813,1814.* Annapolis, US Naval Institute 1986.

Another interesting but brief look at the native Marquesan culture can be found in the accounts of the Russian expedition of 1803, which touched at Nuku Hiva, under the command of Capt.-Lt. (later Vice Admiral) Ivan Fedorovich Kruzenstern. These include Kruzenstern's own journal: *Voyage around the world in the years 1803–1806, on the ships Nadezhda and Neva.* London. This expediton also produced the journal of G. H. Langsdorf, a natural scientist who accompanied Kruzenstern. Langsdorf's book: *Voyages and travels in various parts of the world, during the years 1803–1807.* London; discusses everything from Marquesan politics to tattooing.

Edward Robarts, an English sailor who jumped ship in the Marquesas in 1797, has also left an interesting first-person account of his long stay, published under the title of: *The Marquesan Journal of Edward Robarts; 1797–1824.* G. Dening Ed. Honolulu, 1974, University of Hawai'i Press. The text is fascinating, but the editorial notes in this work betray a lack of acquaintance with both Marquesan language and geography and must be used with caution.

Narratives

Willowdean Chatterson Handy, a member of the 1920 Bayard Dominick Expedition to the Marquesas, wrote two interesting popular works based on her experiences. *Forever the Land of Men: an account of a visit to the Marquesas Islands,* 1965, New York; Dodd, Mead, and Co., is a narrative of Mrs. Handy's experiences collecting ethnographic information containing many rare insights into the Marquesan culture and the minds of the Marquesan people.

Mrs. Handy's posthumously published last work, *Thunder from the Sea*, 1973; Canberra, Australian National University; is a novel, explicitly written in the narrative style of the ancient Marquesan legends. It tells the exciting story of one of the Marquesan hero- martyrs of the French occupation, the chief Pakoko.

Robert C. Suggs presents an account of the trials, triumphs, and pleasures of digging and living among the modern Marquesans in: *Hidden Worlds Of Polynesia: the chronical of an archeological expedition to Nuku Hiva in the Marquesas Islands*, New York, Harcourt, Brace and World. 1962

Scientific reports

Ethnography

For those who wish to get into detail in various aspects of Marquesan culture, the following principal sources of ethnographic literature are suggested:

— A series of reports by the American ethnologists, Dr. E. S. C. Handy and W. C. Handy of the Bayard Dominick Expedition to the Marquesas appearing in the Bulletin Series of the Bernice P. Bishop Museum in Hawai'i, including:

— E. S. C. Handy: *The Native Culture of the Marquesas*, Bulletin 9, 1923; *Marquesan Legends*, Bulletin 69, 1930; *Music in the Marquesas Islands*, Bulletin 17, 1923.

— W. C. Handy: *Tattooing in the Marquesas*, Bulletin 1, 1922; *String Figures from the Marquesas and Society Islands*, Bulletin 18, 1925.

— An investigation of Marquesan sexuality and its influence on the depopulation of the Marquesas Islands, by Dr. Robert C. Suggs: *Marquesan Sexual Behavior: an anthropological study of Polynesian practices*. New York; Harcourt, Brace and World,1966.

— A superb study of Marquesan music, which does for Marquesan music what Karl von den Steinen did for Marquesan art, by Prof. Dr. Jane Freeman -Moulin: *He Koina: Music, Dance, and Poetry in the Marquesas Islands*. 1991. Ann Arbor, Michigan; U. M. I.

Archeology

In the field of archeology, there are papers in scientific journals, but the most significant literature includes the works of:

— Robert C. Suggs: *The Island Civilizations of Polynesia*. New York. Mentor Books, 1960.

— Robert C. Suggs: *The Archeology of Nuku Hiva, Marquesas Islands, French Polynesia Vol 49, Part 1*; Anthropological Papers of the American Museum of Natural History, New York, 1961.

— Rolett, Barry: *Hanamiai: prehistoric culture change in the Marquesas Islands, (East Polynesia)*. Yale University Publications in Anthropology No. 81, The Peabody Museum, Yale University, 1998

French Sources

There is naturally a wide range of French literature on the Marquesas. For those who are fluent, two very impressive and sympathetic works describing the colonial period are:

— Gracia, Père Mathias. *Lettres sur les îles Marquises*. (Letters about the Marquesas Islands), Paris, 1843. Fr. Gracia was with the first Catholic missionary party to arrive in the Marquesas.

— Radiguet, Max. *Les derniers sauvages; les vies et les moeurs aux îles marquises (1843–1859)*. (The last savages; lives and morals in the Marquesas Islands) Paris, Duchartre et Van Buggenhoudt, 1929. Radiguet was the adjutant of French Admiral DuPetit-Thouars, who took the Marquesas for France in 1843.

The only sources on the Marquesan language are in French: Monsigneur R.-I. Dordillon: *Grammaire et dictionnaire de la langue des Iles Marquises*. Paris, 1904 (recently republished in Tahiti by the Société des Études océaniennes, 1999). Mgr. Dordillon, Apostolic Bishop of the Marquesas, and a leading figure in the early colonial period, combined the results of 60 years of study in producing this essential reference work.

Mgr. H.-M. Le Cléac'h: *Pona Tekao Tapapa'ia: Lexique Marquisien –*
Francais. (French–Marquesan Lexicon) Pape'ete, Tahiti, 1996.
This is a new dictionary produced by the energetic former Bishop
of the Marquesas, who has contributed so much to the renaissance of Marquesan culture. Contains many helpful summary
lists of names of plants, fish, birds, anatomical terms, kinship
terms, musical instruments, etc.

Finally one must note an outstanding in-depth study of
Marquesan tattooing by Pierre and Marie-Noëlle Ottino-
Garanger: *Te Patu Tiki: le Tatouage aux îles Marquises*. (Writing
Images: Tattooing in the Marquesas Islands) Ch. Gleizal Éditeur.
1998

The *Aranui* loading at Motu Uta docks, Pape'ete.

The *Aranui* off Takapoto, Tuamotu Islands.

A man of many names: Brutus, Te Kohu, Teikimahalonui,
King of the Nubians.

The first whale boat arrives at Takapoto.

A stilt-house boat landing in Takapoto lagoon

Hakahetau.

Ioteve Kaiha and his students in Haka he tau, Ua Pou.

Stone gate of the Cathedral of Sts. Peter and Paul;
Taioha'e, Nuku Hiva.

View of Taioha'e Bay from the road to Muake Pass.

The "David of Muake".

Bob and Burgl with the double-headed *tiki*, Te Puamama'u Etua
(God of the Shadow People); at Pa'eke, Taipivai, Nuku Hiva.

Cemetery in Atuona, Hiva Oa, where Jacques Brel and
Paul Gauguin are interred.

Pélagie; Atuona, Hiva Oa.

Overhanging cliffs – are they nuns, virgins, or what? Hanavave,
Fatu Iva.

On the way from O'omoa to Hanavave, Fatu Iva.

Sunset mood, departing from Hanavave.

The temple of Te I'i Pona; Puama'u , Hiva Oa; The *tiki* called Taka'i'i stands on the platform.

The face of Maki'i Tau'a Pepe, the Buttterfly Priestess; Puama'u, Hiva Oa.

Tiki on the temple site of Me'ae Meiaiaute; Hane, Ua Huka.

Palmgrove in Anaho Valley, Nuku Hiva.

The dune of Ha'atuatua, Nuku Hiva; looking toward the southern cliffs with the famous buttress-like ridges which gave the bay it's name.

Ha'atuatua Beach archeological site, looking north.

Hibiscus flower *(koute)*; Hatiheu, Nuku Hiva.

Aranui at anchor in Hatiheu, Nuku Hiva.

The black sand beach in Hatiheu, with Te Heu ridge.

A trusty whaleboat crew.

Hu'uveu (Casimir), the Aranui cargo master, and "Brutus," going ashore at Rangiroa.

Coral sand beach and blue lagoon on Rangiroa. Tuamotu Islands.

Iakopo, a sailor
from Hatiheu.

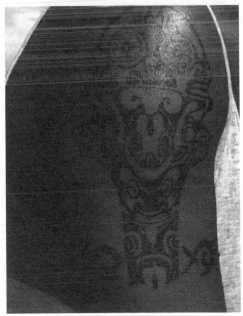

Typical Marquesan
tattooing on an Aranui
sailor.

Bungalows at idyllic Fare Nana'o; "Tahiti's best kept secret."

Sunset.